Robert Triffin

OXFORD STUDIES IN THE HISTORY OF ECONOMICS

Series Editor: Steven G. Medema, Duke University

This series publishes leading-edge scholarship by historians of economics and social science, drawing upon approaches from intellectual history, the history of ideas, and the history of the natural and social sciences. It embraces the history of economic thinking from ancient times to the present, the evolution of the discipline itself, the relationship of economics to other fields of inquiry, and the diffusion of economic ideas within the discipline and to the policy realm and broader publics. This enlarged scope affords the possibility of looking anew at the intellectual, social, and professional forces that have surrounded and conditioned economics' continued development.

Robert Triffin

A Life

Ivo Maes

With Ilaria Pasotti
Preface by Jacques de Larosière

OXFORD
UNIVERSITY PRESS

OXFORD
UNIVERSITY PRESS

Oxford University Press is a department of the University of Oxford. It furthers
the University's objective of excellence in research, scholarship, and education
by publishing worldwide. Oxford is a registered trade mark of Oxford University
Press in the UK and certain other countries.

Published in the United States of America by Oxford University Press
198 Madison Avenue, New York, NY 10016, United States of America.

Library of Congress Cataloging-in-Publication Data
Names: Maes, Ivo, 1956– author.
Title: Robert Triffin : A Life / Ivo Maes.
Description: New York : Oxford University Press, [2021] |
Series: Oxford studies in the history of economics |
Includes bibliographical references and index.
Identifiers: LCCN 2020027261 (print) | LCCN 2020027262 (ebook) |
ISBN 9780190081096 (hardback) | ISBN 9780190081102 (updf) |
ISBN 9780190081119 (epub) | ISBN 9780190081126 (online)
Subjects: LCSH: Triffin, Robert. | Economists—Belgium—Biography.
Classification: LCC HB112.T75 M34 2020 (print) |
LCC HB112.T75 (ebook) | DDC 330.092 [B]—dc23
LC record available at https://lccn.loc.gov/2020027261
LC ebook record available at https://lccn.loc.gov/2020027262

1 3 5 7 9 8 6 4 2

Printed by Integrated Books International, United States of America

Robert Triffin and his wife, Lois Brandt © Kerry Triffin

CONTENTS

FIGURES AND TABLES

FIGURES

TABLES

PREFACE BY JACQUES DE LAROSIÈRE

This biography of Robert Triffin presented by Ivo Maes has the merit of highlighting very clearly the intellectual path chosen by the great Belgian economist right from his early formative years.

To do so, Ivo Maes has methodically collected and analyzed archival records available not just in the universities, but also from the Fed, the International Monetary Fund (IMF), and the European Commission.

Some lines of force run through this narrative, which is both concise and captivating. First of all, it should be pointed out that Triffin was far from being doctrinaire. He would always look closely at the facts and the statistics before drawing any conclusions. His personal involvement in observing and helping to redress the balance of payments in some Latin American countries where he had been sent on mission by the Fed, just like the decisive role he played in the negotiations for a European payments system after the war, gave him the opportunity to work on empirical issues and not fall into the trap of ready-made solutions.

For instance, the balance of payments of a country relying heavily on exports of a few raw materials—whose prices depend largely on the cyclical position of the big purchasing economies—could not just be restored to health through a contraction of its domestic demand. Triffin tailored solutions to specific problems, hence the extreme care that he took to distinguish between the different sources—whether cyclical or structural—of imbalances, and to propose suitable remedies, even if they were only transitional. And he did that with an open mind. As it was, Robert Triffin had the foresight to point up that correcting balance-of-payments disequilibria through a contraction in domestic demand—a policy deriving from the mechanical application of the gold standard—was procyclical and, in many countries that didn't have a developed and diversified economic structure, could lead to even worse situations than the one needing to be redressed. In Triffin's view, it was better to neutralize such countries' exchange rate fluctuations by acting directly on domestic money creation as well as by controlling destabilizing movements of capital.

It was this contact with reality and the good fortune he had—and had been able to seize the opportunity of being involved in substantive high-level negotiations—that help explain, at least in part, Robert Triffin's originality.

It is worth adding that Triffin did not work in isolation, "in a closed circuit." He sought contact and friendship with other economists of his time. Keynes had a profound influence on him, as he did on all his contemporaries. Harvard University had given him the chance to get to know and recognize the eminence of men like Frank Taussig, Joseph Schumpeter, Wassily Leontief, Edward Chamberlin, Paul Samuelson, Lloyd Metzler, and Gottfried Haberler. Later on, at the Fed, the IMF, Yale, and the Bellagio Group, economists such as Alvin Hansen, Edward Bernstein, Jacques Polak, Fritz Machlup, and James Tobin made up a genuine "collective"—a kind of "republic"—of free spirits who borrowed ideas and research findings from each other. The importance of Jacques Rueff should also be mentioned.

* * *

But what characterizes Robert Triffin above all, in my view, was his gift of foresight. He saw—before all the others and often against their views—the weaknesses, the shortcomings, and the threats inherent in the international monetary system. The famous "Triffin dilemma" that he had come up with as early as 1957 threw new and stark light on the contradictions inherent in the situation that had developed 15 years after the Bretton Woods agreement. Triffin's implacable prediction of the inevitable destruction of the system turned out to be right and, even today, still provides the analysis grid necessary to "understand" and—if we were listening to him—avoid the dangers of the present-day world of finance.

* * *

The lessons—still relevant today—that Robert Triffin taught us can be summed up quite simply:

- Abandoning the Bretton Woods system for a floating exchange rate regime—and uncoordinated monetary policy interventions—not only failed to solve the problems but also actually made them worse.
- Exchange rate chaos encourages distortions in international trade and can trigger currency wars.

- A—more desirable—system of stable yet adjustable exchange rates assumes active cooperation between the main economic policy participants.
- Making international liquidity supply dependent on one sole country's balance-of-payments deficit is not a viable solution in the long run; it carries multiple disadvantages as well as serious threats.
- Adjustment of balance-of-payments disequilibria must be symmetrical and not just be applied to debtor countries.
- Excessive liquidity creation (notably through currency market interventions) inevitably leads to excessive indebtedness and inflation.
- If we are to avoid nationalist and disruptive (beggar-thy-neighbor-type) policies that undermine multilateral trade, we need to look for a "more international solution" for our global monetary strategy.

Every aspect of these preoccupations has withstood the test of time since Triffin's death in 1993. In reality, the relevance of this work has never been so acute as it is today.

* * *

The monetary authorities have just celebrated the 75th anniversary of Bretton Woods. This evocation was tainted with a dose of hypocrisy or, at the very least, ambiguity. We are celebrating, but are careful not to reform.

Yet, the message that the Bretton Woods agreement sent out to our world is simple and Robert Triffin did a great deal to clarify it. This message tells us that the dramatic developments that mark global finance today (e.g., overindebtedness, excessive and extended dependence on money creation and on low interest rates, exacerbation of financial cycles) have been favored by the collapse of the Bretton Woods system in 1971.

Looking back at this event, it becomes clear that the decision to abandon the system of fixed parities sowed the seeds of profound consequences that had not been well understood at the time and that are still largely underestimated today.

It is important to understand that the international monetary system set up in 1944 was much more than a set of technical rules about exchange rate management. The system was in fact, and above all, a way of maintaining a common framework for monetary stability thanks to effective coordination of economic policies between the main stakeholders. If a member state chose to pursue a policy that was incompatible with the common framework (e.g., by letting its budget deficit grow or speeding up credit issuance), pressure on its exchange rate would soon build up; with capital outflows and inflation weakening the balance of payments of the country in question, the exchange rate would be pushing up against the 1% margin of fluctuation allowed. This country would then have to ask the IMF for permission to devalue. The IMF made sure that the necessary "conditionality" accompanied the authorization to devalue. The system did not allow the very existence of "free riders" and prohibited competitive devaluations of the likes of the 1930s that had contributed to the origin of World War II.

It was precisely to evade the joint discipline that the United States decided, on August 15, 1971, to end the gold convertibility of the dollar. The Americans needed to fund the Vietnam War by deficit financing and regain the freedom of action that the Bretton Woods system had severely constrained. They had to get out of the "Triffin dilemma" by protecting the United States' gold reserves, reserves that had fallen too low to ensure the convertibility of the dollar.

At the time, the economists' profession had generally come out in favor of abandoning fixed exchange rates. The "consensus"—which Triffin did not support—can be summed up as follows: a country could not pursue the three objectives at the same time:

- autonomy of its domestic monetary policy to maximize its growth;
- maintaining free movement of capital; and
- exchange rate stability.

One of these elements had to go, and it was exchange rate stability. Advocates of exchange rate freedom also thought that floating currencies:

- would help deficit countries to regain competitiveness by allowing their currency to depreciate and
- would encourage surplus countries to adjust through an appreciation of their currencies.

But, in reality, the Jamaica Agreements (1976) were not conceived as a means of implementing a genuine floating exchange rate regime. The new texts incorporated into the IMF statutes led to serious abuse. Creditor countries that feared seeing their currencies appreciate to the detriment of their competitiveness embarked on a systematic and purely national policy of intervention by buying up dollars.

* * *

Four consequences emerged from this situation that Triffin fiercely denounced ("the scandal" of the new agreements):

- The creditor countries have built up massive dollar reserves, which has contributed to the expansion of international liquidity and the rise in global indebtedness.
- The United States was able to comfortably finance its structural deficits, without having to endure the consequences of a depreciation of the dollar (which would have resulted from a genuine system of floating exchange change rates).
- Coordination of economic policies—something that was at the heart of the Bretton Woods system—had disappeared. Expectations that had been anchored on exchange rate stability had been replaced by a "nonsystem" where each state managed its exchange rate as it wished.
- The structural reforms necessary for growth were put off until later because it had gotten so easy to borrow at low interest rates in the new environment.

Since the demise of Bretton Woods, there has been a profound change: the world has entered into the era of the credit-based economy. In other words, the expansion of credit has overtaken that of potential growth. Before the collapse of Bretton Woods, credit and economic growth moved at much the same pace. But since the end of the 1970s, credit expansion has been roughly twice as strong as the growth of the real economy. This has led to the "financialization"—and to the vulnerabilities—of the international economy.

* * *

What can be done?

There is no question of going back to the Bretton Woods system in exactly the same way. This effectively had many disadvantages (asymmetry of adjustments, excessively mechanical nature of the corrections, dependence on the dollar) about which Robert Triffin was very lucid and highly critical.

But it is imperative—and indeed feasible—to make the current nonsystem "more international." Under the auspices of the IMF, there is a need for monitoring balance of payments and exchange rates between major stakeholders. We see it every day with the currency wars, suspicions of exchange rate manipulations stemming from monetary policy changes. Never before have we been so close to the 1930s and "beggar-thy-neighbor" policies.

Under the benevolent hegemony exerted by the United States after the war, the international monetary system had worked properly for 20 years. But with the current abuse in terms of monetary creation and exchange rate variations being left wide open to market forces and state interventions, trade multilateralism is in danger. With China's rise in power, the monetary hegemony of the United States is becoming more difficult to unilaterally ensure.

It would be a nice way to celebrate the 75th anniversary of Bretton Woods by introducing, through negotiation, an element of international cohesion in the monetary strategy of the major powers and to draw inspiration, in this way, from the wisdom, common sense, and optimism of Robert Triffin.

It would be highly recommendable that the current policymakers read and draw inspiration from Ivo Maes's biography, which synthesizes a deep reflection urgently needed by today's distraught world.

INTRODUCTION: A MONK IN
ECONOMIST'S CLOTHING

In a little pizzeria in New Haven, in June 2019, I had a very pleasant dinner with Eric and Kerry Triffin, the sons of Robert Triffin and Lois Brandt. We talked about the deeper motivations of their parents and the values and experiences they transmitted. Recurring themes were "the ring of truth: that's where we need to go" and "if you buy your bread from me and I my butter from you, we won't go to war." Above all, Robert Triffin wanted to make the world a better place—more united, just, and peaceful. At home, Triffin was often working, doing calculations on little pieces of paper. However, they admitted that what they had initially seen as dry numbers was actually the currency of trust and peace; "he was in fact a monk in economist's clothing."

Robert Triffin was born in the small Belgian village of Flobecq in October 1911. During his university studies at Louvain, he was active in progressive Catholic circles and soon became a convinced pacifist. Like several of his friends, he was attracted to the emerging science of economics, as it offered real possibilities to improve the world. Crossing the Atlantic in June 1939 on the *Normandie*, he met Lois Brandt, his future wife. She was from New York, where her parents had a literary agency. After a passionate discussion of six hours, he proposed to marry her. They shared a common search for truth in all fields, a good sense of humor, and a "can do" and "why not?" spirit.

Talking with persons who have known Robert Triffin, they all tell about his dry and witty sense of humor. Eric and Kerry Triffin also very much remembered their father for his humor, sometimes deadpan. "He could tell a tall story with great seriousness only to lead you ever deeper into his silliness but only perhaps to create affinity and a shared laugh in the end." Triffin's sense of humor was also a method of negotiation, a way to convince other persons. "There was a method to his madness! He could describe the impossible in such an approachable, negotiable way that it was almost incontrovertible, or even funny."

As an economist, Triffin played a key role in the international monetary debates in the postwar period. His approach to economics was aptly summed up by Jacques de Larosière, a former managing director of the International Monetary Fund (IMF) and governor of the Banque de France. "The most remarkable thing about the work and personality of Professor Robert Triffin, in my view, is the combination of three aspects: his power of analysis, his institutional imagination, and his pragmatism as a practitioner" (de Larosière 1991: 135).

Triffin's power of analysis came to the fore in his trenchant analyses of the vulnerabilities of the Bretton Woods system. He earned fame with his book *Gold and the Dollar Crisis*, published in 1960, in which he predicted the end of the Bretton Woods system. In Triffin's view, there was a clear dilemma, as the increase in foreign dollar balances to meet international liquidity needs was only sustainable when there was no doubt about their convertibility into gold. But, with ever-increasing foreign dollar balances and diminishing US gold reserves, the credibility of this convertibility commitment was threatened. Triffin would stress time and time again the vulnerability of an international monetary system that was dependent on a national currency for its international liquidity. Moreover, for Triffin, the US balance-of-payments deficit was not only an economic issue but also a moral one. He was disgusted and outraged that the richest country in the world was financed by the poorer countries. Very much like Keynes, he was in favor of a true international reserve currency.

Isiah Berlin, the philosopher, wrote a famous essay on Tolstoy's view of history, entitled "The Hedgehog and the Fox." He quoted the Greek poet Archilochus: "The fox knows many things, but the hedgehog knows one big thing." Hedgehogs relate everything to a single central vision, a central principle around which they organize the world. According to Berlin (1953: 25), Plato, Dostoevsky, Nietzsche, and Proust were, in varying degrees, hedgehogs, while Aristotle, Erasmus, and Goethe were foxes. As argued by economic historian Barry Eichengreen (2011: 51), Triffin was a hedgehog. For Triffin, the inherent vulnerability of the Bretton Woods system was the starting point for his vision and way of analyzing the international monetary system. He focused nearly exclusively on it and he did this so single-mindedly that his name became synonymous with the issue. Triffin was indeed a man who was convinced of his ideas, willing to sacrifice also his career for them. He never tired of repeating his proposals.

But at the same time, Triffin also believed very much in a rational discussion of policy issues. A beautiful example was the discussions in the Bellagio Group, which played a prominent role in the debates on the reform of the international monetary system in the 1960s. Triffin (1967a) also proposed to delegate the official discussions on the reform of the international monetary system to an expert group to have a more rational discussion, driven primarily by "the *converging* interests of all countries in a sensible international monetary system." This might seem rather naïve as countries, especially big ones such as the United States, attached great importance to their national sovereignty. It was only much later that Triffin admitted that major international reforms were more the result of political than economic considerations.

Triffin's analysis has been the subject of major debates in the academic and policymaking world. Even today, the "Triffin dilemma" is still very much with us, as evidenced in a recent Bank for International Settlements working paper, "Triffin: Dilemma or Myth?" (Bordo and McCauley 2017). Farhi, Gourinchas, and Rey (2011) too have warned of a "new Triffin dilemma." In their view, the piling up of US debt might lead to a new confidence crisis and a run on the dollar.

Top policymakers often cite the Triffin dilemma, and not only "Atlantic" ones, as their ranks include the former Chinese central bank governor Zhou Xiaochuan (2009), who espoused Keynes's and Triffin's preference for a true international reserve currency. At a conference for the G7 presidency in July 2019 on the theme "Bretton Woods 75 Years Later—Thinking about the Next 75," several speakers referred to the Triffin dilemma. Among them was Jean-Claude Trichet, a former president of the European Central Bank, who argued for a "new multilateralism" to reinforce the resilience and the strength of the global financial system. He paid special attention to the broadening and strengthening of special drawing rights (SDRs)—an international reserve asset created by the IMF in 1969 to mitigate the adverse effects of the Triffin dilemma—and the idea that countries would have to accept some "tempered freedom" in the management of exchange rate relations (Trichet 2019).

In 2002, the Triffin International Foundation was established, with the late Alexandre Lamfalussy, former president of the European Monetary Institute (the precursor of the European Central Bank), as its first president. The aim was to preserve the intellectual heritage of Robert Triffin and to address the current problems of the global economy in light of his ideas. In September 2015, it was renamed Robert Triffin International (RTI). With the support of RTI, Michel Camdessus, Alexandre Lamfalussy, and Tommaso Padoa-Schioppa convened a group of 18 experts who met several times at the Palais Royal in Paris. In February 2011, the group submitted a report, the *Palais Royal Initiative—Reform of the International Monetary System: A Cooperative Approach for the 21st Century*, as a contribution to the G20 finance ministers' meeting (Boorman and Icard 2011). Since then, RTI has focused closely on how the SDR could be used as a lever to reform the international monetary system—a very controversial issue—paying attention to both a strengthening of the official SDR and the development of the private SDR market (Flor 2019).

With the Covid-19 pandemic, attention has also turned to potential liquidity shortages in the international monetary system and a new issue of IMF special drawing rights. Yi Gang, the governor of the Chinese central bank, compared SDRs to "liquid gold" and argued that they were the "missing piece" in the IMF's crisis response (Gang 2020). Gang further advocated to tailor the issue of SDRs to the needs of developing countries which are especially hit by the pandemic and are inadequately covered by current financial safety nets, an old idea of Triffin (see Section 4.5).

The late Padoa-Schioppa, in his 2010 Triffin lecture, argued that Triffin's analysis transcended the Bretton Woods system. He advanced Triffin's "general dilemma" that "the stability requirements of the system as a whole are inconsistent with the pursuit of economic and monetary policy forged solely on the basis of domestic rationales" (Padoa-Schioppa 2010). For Triffin (and Padoa-Schioppa himself), the so-called house-in-order approach (that every country would pursue domestic stability) was not sufficient for a sustainable and stable international monetary system. Triffin took a "systemic" view of the international monetary system, always looking for the "counterpart" in the international adjustment process.

There was a remarkable continuity in Triffin's Weltanschauung. From his earliest writings, Triffin, very much marked by the Great Depression, developed a vision that the international adjustment process was not functioning according to the classical mechanisms (Maes 2013a). This view was based on thorough empirical analyses of the Belgian economy during the Great Depression and shaped by a business cycle perspective with an emphasis on disequilibria and the transition period. His doctoral dissertation on imperfect competition theory and his Latin American experience further reinforced this basic view. So, as countries needed time for economic adjustment, Triffin argued that international liquidity should be at the core of the international monetary system, and he pleaded for better economic policy coordination as well.

Triffin was not only an eminent academic but also an influential policy adviser. Already in the late 1940s, Triffin played an important role in the creation of the European Payments Union (EPU). Eichengreen (1993: ix) described him as "the EPU's architect." Thereafter, he became the monetary expert of Jean Monnet's Action Committee for the United States of Europe and an official adviser at the European Commission. He was also involved with the Kennedy administration and in many academic settings, one of the most famous being the Bellagio Group.

Triffin put forward several proposals for reforming the international monetary system. But because he doubted that they would come to fruition, he also developed proposals for regional monetary integration, particularly in Europe. Triffin's advocacy of regional integration was consistent with his country-specific approach, which he had developed during his missions in Latin America in the 1940s. It is noteworthy that the new managing director of the IMF, Kristalina Georgieva (2020), in an article in the *Financial Times*, explained that the IMF was rethinking its advice to emerging markets. She emphasized very much the importance of a country-specific approach, as well as a better understanding of how various policies interact and close consultation with country authorities, all elements that were typical for Triffin's approach.

Triffin's plans for regional integration were very much based on his experience with the EPU and focused on the creation of a European Reserve Fund and a European currency unit. In his eyes, the regional and worldwide approaches were complementary, aiming at a new multipolar international monetary system, with the European Community as an essential pillar (Maes and Bussière 2016). Triffin thus became a great partisan of European monetary integration. As he observed in *Europe and the Money Muddle*, "Countries whose peace, progress and welfare are intimately interdependent must, in their own interest, learn to use or limit their national sovereignty in the light of their interdependence" (Triffin 1957: 30).

In a situation of threatening beggar-thy-neighbor policies, Triffin's analysis takes on particular relevance. As observed by Ghosh and Quresh (2017: 23) there are some "eerie similarities" between the Great Depression and the Great Recession: highly volatile capital flows, a scramble for reserves, asymmetry in the burden of adjustment between deficit and surplus countries, secular stagnation, and currency wars. Moreover, populist forces are gaining traction. Triffin had lived through the Great Depression of the 1930s with its disastrous trade and currency wars and the rise of fascism. This left a lasting mark on a man who would never tire of denouncing the dangers and deficiencies of bilateralism. Triffin was a genuine economist-statesman of interdependence and multilateralism.

Personally, I have some, admittedly relatively vague, memories of Robert Triffin's address at a conference held in his honor, in Brussels in December 1988. I was still a young economist then at the National Bank of Belgium's Economics and Research Department. Since then, Robert Triffin has taken an increasingly central place in the research programs I have been pursuing: the making of European monetary union, Belgian economic thought, and the reform of the international monetary system. I was very honored to be invited to take up the Robert Triffin Chair at the Institute of European Studies of the Université catholique de Louvain, Triffin's alma mater. I have become increasingly intrigued, not only by Triffin's contribution to European monetary union and the reform of the international monetary system, but also by his personality. Over the last decade, my research has increasingly focused on Triffin.

The objective of this book is to provide a comprehensive and balanced (intellectual) biography of Robert Triffin, focusing on the development of his (economic) ideas and his impact, both in the academic world and in policymaking. The heart of the book's analysis resides in six chapters. The first three of these cover the first half of Triffin's life, from 1911 to 1951, and follow a chronological pattern. They cover Triffin's studies, his time at the Federal Reserve System, and his involvement with the European Payments Union. From 1951 to 1977, he was at Yale University and focused his research on two main issues: the international monetary system and European monetary integration, which are the topics of the next two chapters. In the sixth chapter, his return to Louvain and his activities during his later years are discussed. The book concludes with a short epilogue.

The aim of a biography, including this one of Robert Triffin, is to place the person in the context of his times and to show how, in turn, he was shaping his world. In the first instance, it is then important to understand the world in which Triffin was living and working. An important issue is further the assessment of Triffin's influence. This is always a difficult, even tricky, issue for biographers, all the more so if it concerns persons who are not only public intellectuals but also behind-the-scenes operators, like Triffin (Howson 2011, Mata and Medema 2013). Like most biographies, this book is based on a combination of different sources of material, especially archival research, interviews, and study of the literature, both in Triffin's time and of today (an overview of the source material can be found at the end of the book).

* * *

This book comes at the end of my professional career at the National Bank of Belgium. I have to admit to my advancing years, and with a greater age comes greater intellectual indebtedness. This is even more so as, in this book, different strands of my research come together. Even if my expressions of gratitude may not be complete, I would like to mention a few people.

First, I would like to thank Jacques de Larosière. Not only has he written a thoughtful and elegant preface, but also he has been constant in his encouragement and support for this project from the first moment I told him about it. He read the manuscript thoroughly and I have fond memories of many discussions in Paris and Bovelles.

Life at the National Bank of Belgium has passed quickly. I would like to thank all my colleagues at the bank for their greatly appreciated cooperation over several decades. My thanks also for their interest in my historical studies. I have been privileged by a great openness by many people and stimulating discussions. In the first instance, I would like to thank Governor Pierre Wunsch as well as Hugues Famerée, the head of the Economics and Research Department. I would also like to express my gratitude to the former governors Guy Quaden, the late Luc Coene, and Jan Smets, with whom I had many insightful discussions. The bank has also provided excellent research support for this project. I would like to thank the secretariat of the Economics and Research Department, as well as the Archives Section and the Statistics Department for all their work. A special word of thanks to Philippe Van Lint for library support and Amanda Ellerton for the English revision.

I am also very grateful to Robert Triffin International (RTI), established in 2002 as the Triffin International Foundation, for preserving the intellectual heritage of Robert Triffin. In the first instance, my gratitude goes to some people who, regretfully, have passed away: Alexandre Lamfalussy (the first president), Tommaso Padoa-Schioppa, Philippe Maystadt, Fabrizio Saccomanni, and Jean-Claude Koeune. I still have fond memories of many fascinating discussions with them. I would further like to express my gratitude to some of the "pillars" of RTI: Bernard Snoy (the current president), Alfonso Iozzo, Christian Ghymers, Elena Flor, Flavio Brugnoli, and Michel Dumoulin (who introduced me to RTI).

Kerry and Eric Triffin, Robert's sons, provided me with many insights into the life of their parents as well as the photos that are reproduced in this book. Several people read the whole manuscript, offering comments and materials: Piet Clement, Jacques de Larosière, Servaas Deroose, Philippe Duvieusart, Hugues Famerée, Martin Fase, Bob Hetzel, Sue Howson, Steve Medema, Guido Montani, Bernard Snoy, Niels Thygesen, and two anonymous reviewers. To all of them my profound thanks for their comments and suggestions. Kenneth Dyson read several chapters and was a continuous source of support and advice. Thanks also to several others for discussions, comments, suggestions, and archival material: Francesco Asso, Emile Boelpaep, Eric Boyer, Eric Bussière, Erik Buyst, Helen Campbell, Lilia Costabile, Jacques de Groote, Eric De Keuleneer, Armand de Largentaye,

Hélène de Largentaye, Bob Dimand, Dennis Essers, Véronique Fillieux, Marie-Claude Hayoit, Alfonso Iozzo, Alfredo Gigliobianco, Bruno Kervyn, Véronique Kervyn, Olivier Lefebvre, Elisabetta Loche, Carlos Martinez Mongay, Rainer Masera, Voula Mega, Manuela Mosca, Theo Peeters, Sabine Péters, Paolo Santella, Sabine Seeger, Anthony Teasdale, Herman Van der Wee, Jacques van Ypersele, and Thierry Vissol.

Oxford University Press has been a congenial publisher. Thanks to Steve Medema, the series editor, who was always available for answering questions as well as for his comments and encouragements. My gratitude goes also to David Pervin, the commissioning editor who guided the project through its early stages; James Cook, who took care of the later phases; and Macey Fairchild, the associate editor.

Many thanks to several publishers who granted copyright permission to use publications of Triffin: University of Louvain for the *Bulletin de l'IRES*; *Banca Nazionale del Lavoro Quarterly Review*; Federal Reserve Board; P.I.E.-Peter Lang S.A. Éditions Scientifiques Internationales (through Copyright Clearance Center) for *Robert Triffin, Conseiller des Princes: Souvenirs et Documents*; Yale University Press (through PLSClear) for *Europe and the Money Muddle: From Bilateralism to Near-Convertibility 1947–1956* and *Gold and the Dollar Crisis: The Future of Convertibility*; and Princeton University for *Gold and the Dollar Crisis: Yesterday and Tomorrow*. Profound thanks also go to several archives that gave access to their collections and provided a rich series of documents for which I'm very grateful (a list of the archives consulted is in the sources). Naturally, I have also drawn from previously published articles, with, evidently, a significant reworking of the texts.

Last but not least, I would like to express my gratitude to Ilaria Pasotti. Since August 2006, when she considered devoting her PhD dissertation to Triffin, we have been in a more or less constant dialogue about Triffin, the international monetary system, and European monetary integration. I am very grateful for all her work on this volume. It was not only inspiring but also very enjoyable.

As in line with tradition, with these words of thanks come also the disclaimers. Neither the National Bank of Belgium nor the Eurosystem, nor any other institution, is responsible for any of the views expressed in this volume. The usual caveats apply.

Ivo Maes
Brussels, March 2020

ABBREVIATIONS

ADA	Americans for Democratic Action
BIS	Bank for International Settlements
CEEC	Commission of the European Economic Community
CEO	Chief Executive Officer
CEPIME	Centre Ecu et Prospective d'Intégration Monétaire Européenne
CEPS	Center for European Policy Studies
CIA	Central Intelligence Agency
CORE	Center for Operations Research and Econometrics
CRB	Commission for Relief in Belgium
DG II	Directorate General for Economic and Financial Affairs, European Commission
ECA	Economic Cooperation Administration
ECSC	European Coal and Steel Community
ECU	European Currency Unit
EDC	European Defense Community
EEC	European Economic Community
EFMC	European Fund for Monetary Cooperation
EMA	European Monetary Agreement
EMCF	European Monetary Cooperation Fund
EMF	European Monetary Fund
EMS	European Monetary System
EMU	Economic and Monetary Union
EPU	European Payments Union
ERF	European Reserve Fund
ERM	Exchange Rate Mechanism
ESM	European Stability Mechanism
FED	Federal Reserve System
FRB	Federal Reserve Board
G7	Group of Seven Countries

G20	Group of 20 Countries
GCA	Gold Conversion Account
IBRD	International Bank for Reconstruction and Development
ICHEC	Institut Catholique des Hautes Etudes Commerciales
ICU	International Clearing Union
IMF	International Monetary Fund
IMS	International Monetary System
ISE	Institute des Sciences Economiques
ITO	International Trade Organization
MIT	Massachusetts Institute of Technology
NATO	North Atlantic Treaty Organization
NBB	National Bank of Belgium
NDA	Net Domestic Assets
OECD	Organization for Economic Cooperation and Development
OEEC	Organization of European Economic Cooperation
OSR	Office of the Special Representative
PPP	Purchasing Power Parity theory
RTI	Robert Triffin International
SDR	Special Drawing Right
UK	United Kingdom
UNCTAD	United Nations Conference on Trade and Development
US	United States

CHAPTER 1
A Child of the Interwar Period

1.1 INTRODUCTION

Robert Triffin was born on October 5, 1911, in his family home in Flobecq, a beautiful and unspoiled village in the francophone part of Belgium. The area is known as "le pays des collines" (the land of the hills). Referring to Triffin's early years as a turbulent period in Belgian and European history would be something of an understatement. At the age of 24, the young Triffin had already lived through World War I, monetary and financial turmoil after the war, the Great Depression, the 1935 Belgian franc devaluation, and the rise of fascism. He became a pacifist: "My convictions . . . are avowedly those of an extreme *peace-monger*, and therefore of a *dissenter* from prevailing official and public opinion. I grew up in a world threatened by Hitler, and accepted the uncompromising pacifism of Albert Einstein" (Triffin 1987a: 28, original italics). He would remain a convinced pacifist for the rest of his life.

In this chapter, the early period of Triffin's life is discussed, covering the period from 1911 to 1942. It focuses on his youth, undergraduate studies at Louvain University, doctoral studies at Harvard, and early academic life at Louvain and Harvard. During these years, like many people of his generation, Triffin became a profound pacifist. Moreover, as an economist, he became convinced that the market economy was fundamentally unstable. Special attention will be paid to his two major publications during these years: an article on the 1935 devaluation of the Belgian franc (the young Triffin made the calculations) and his PhD on monopolistic competition and general equilibrium theory.

Robert Triffin. Ivo Maes, Oxford University Press (2021). © Oxford University Press.
DOI: 10.1093/oso/9780190081096.001.0001

1.2 EARLY YEARS

Triffin's birthplace, Flobecq (Dutch: Vloesberg), is a small commune in what is known as Wallonie Picarde, on the border with Flanders but also close to the French border. It boasts a hilly, bucolic landscape, which has served as décor for some paintings by René Magritte, the famous surrealist painter, who was born in the adjacent town of Lessines.

As Triffin said in his 1981 autobiographical article in the *Banca Nazionale del Lavoro Quarterly Review*, he came from a "very modest family." His father, François Triffin, was also born in Flobecq, on September 30, 1878. At the time of Robert's birth, his father was a butcher, living on Flobecq's Place Communale. Later, the family moved to France, where his father was a stockbreeder. He died in Lessines on July 16, 1958 (Lison (Triffin) et al. 1998: 3). His mother, Céline Van Hooland, was born in Nederbrakel, in Flanders, on March 20, 1880. She died at a young age, on May 29, 1935, from breast cancer, a few months before Robert's departure for the United States. Robert had one brother, Armand, who was 11 years older. Armand could not get along with his father, making for a harsh family atmosphere. He consequently quit the family for the Légion étrangère (the French Foreign Legion, an elite service branch of the French Army).

Even if Robert Triffin was only a young child during World War I, he still retained stark memories from this period. Some of his war reminiscences came up in his 1990 book, *Conseiller des Princes*. "One of the most vivid memories of my childhood was the arrival of the German Uhlans in 1914. But the 4 ½ years of German occupation also made me realize that the people we called the 'filthy Huns' were in fact themselves victims of their militarists. One of the Uhlans was the same age as my brother: 16 years old. He became his friend. We all cried when we learnt of his death a few months after he left for the front" (Triffin 1990: 10).

Robert Triffin was the first in his family to study at high school and university. Initially, at his primary school at Péruwelz, Triffin was not very much interested in his education. As Triffin himself said: "Students who do not succeed immediately in reaching satisfactory grades should be encouraged to hear that I was also far from successful at the start. I was, in my early years, a voracious reader of detective stories. Arsène Lupin—the 'Raffles' or 'Saint' of French novels—and Joseph Rouletabille—who anticipated Sir Henry Merrivale and Gideon Fell as solver of 'locked room' rather than 'whodunit' mysteries—interested me far more than my dreary teachers and their dull subjects. At the age of 12, I feigned sickness not to risk failure in my exams" (Triffin 1981a: 240). Triffin would remain a big fan of Arsène Lupin. He felt very much attracted to the fictional gentleman thief and master of disguise, who was a force of good on the wrong side of the law (somewhat like Robin Hood). The fantasy elements in the Lupin novels also appealed to Triffin's imagination, one of his great qualities.

Moreover, as Triffin revealed in *Conseiller des Princes*, wherein he told the story of his life to Catherine Ferrant and Jean Sloover, the local priest appreciated his work in catechism and urged his parents to let the young Robert pursue his studies. "During my junior secondary education at Péruwelz, a kind priest from the village, having seen me working on catechism where I excelled, God only knows why, advised my parents to open the gates to university for me by sending me to middle school" (Triffin 1990: 11). So, Triffin studied at a Catholic boarding school called Collège Notre-Dame de la Tombe (Our Lady of the Tomb) in Kain-les-Tournai. Triffin's experience in Tournai was rather mixed. As such, he did not really like the school. "I hardly have a single good memory of it, except perhaps for the friendship of people like Pierre Halloy, who became a priest in Tournai, or Pierre Piron, a future legal expert in the Congo. Like me, they preferred the long chatty walks to sport, much to the dismay of our teachers" (Triffin 1990: 11). However, Triffin knew the sacrifices his parents were making to enable him to study. It motivated him to work hard. He was rewarded by being uninterruptedly top of his class, with greatest distinction in every quarterly examination during his six years at Kain. This made it possible for him to continue his studies at the University of Louvain. Moreover, after earning greatest distinction in his first year at university, he received an educational grant from the Belgian Fondation Universitaire to continue his studies.

Going to the university in Louvain marked a dramatic break for Triffin, not only in practical terms, but also in terms of Weltanschauung, as he became an avowed pacifist. He was very much under the intellectual influence of Einstein, recipient of the 1921 Nobel Prize in Physics and a leading anti-militarist, even though he never met Einstein. Einstein was often in Belgium and even resided some months in De Haan in the spring of 1933, when Nazi Germany had barred Jews from teaching at universities. Einstein became a friend of the Belgian queen Elisabeth, widow of King Albert, a great patron of the arts and sciences. So, for Triffin, there was a strong contrast in atmosphere between his school years and university: "I was fed with official propaganda and militarism during my primary and secondary studies. But this 'brainwashing' rapidly wore off as soon as I arrived at the University of Louvain. This was in 1929 and I fully endorsed Einstein's anti-militarism and his refusal to be used as a tool to combat the rise of Hitlerism" (Triffin 1990: 10). Einstein also advocated that one should refuse military service. Later, in the 1960s with the Vietnam War, the "draft" would become a highly controversial issue in American society, with Triffin arguing strongly against the war and the draft (see Section 4.2).

The man who had the greatest influence on Triffin in Louvain was Canon René Draguet (1896–1980), a professor of the history of dogma at the Faculty of Theology. As a priest, he served as Triffin's "director of conscience" in his early days at the university. Triffin explained that, for Draguet, the real religion was exactly the opposite of established religions: "it is the sense of mystery, and an open mind to the most intelligent and reasonable attempts to build peace, mutual help and love between all men" (Triffin 1990: 14). Triffin often met Draguet for long discussions on religion, philosophy, and ethics. Draguet taught him the virtues of tolerance and independence. Triffin affirmed that these two features would also characterize his attitude throughout his career:

> I debated weekly with Draguet, late into the night, the multiple problems of the pre-Vatican II teachings of the Church, learning from him the need for an oecumenical tolerance for the attempt of men to answer questions which "logical positivists" considered as "nonsensical" since they are not susceptible to scientific reasoning and demonstrable, communicable solutions. Yet, these are questions which nobody can escape in his personal life, and which inevitably elicit more or less reassuring, comfortable answers (?) from men and organizations living from such an activity. Canon Draguet . . . remained to the end deeply scornful of any "orthodoxy," and our inclination either to follow supinely the views of the "establishment" or of mass opinion, or to pretend to impose our own on others. He taught me, at an early age, the virtues of both *tolerance* and *independence*. (Triffin 1981a: 255, original question mark and italics)

Although he never met him, Triffin became very strongly under the influence of the French theologian Teilhard de Chardin, even dedicating one of his books to Teilhard. Teilhard had a teleological vision of history: that humankind goes somewhere, that there is a finality that surpasses man (Cuénot 1963). The followers of Teilhard, including Triffin, participated in his enthusiasm. With "Dieu en soi" (God in oneself), and notwithstanding setbacks, the Good would prevail, as mankind was moving toward unification (interview Snoy). Suffering was also an element of Teilhard's vision as it contributed to a stronger resilience. Triffin completely adopted Teilhard and his teleological vision of human history. He would never be a cynic. In the spirit of Teilhard, he would never tire of repeating his arguments (pacifism, the International Monetary scandal, etc.). Even if one had to preach in the desert, one had to continue.

Triffin's years at Louvain were spent in an atmosphere of discussions and actions, centered around the place of Christians in the world (Dumoulin 2012: 24). The interwar period was a time of a Catholic revival, which was very marked in Belgium, a profoundly Catholic country. The revival was, to a great extent, a reaction against the communist revolution in Russia, as exemplified in the slogan "Rome or Moscow" (with Rome symbolizing the Holy See). It contrasted Catholicism with "materialist" Marxism. André Molitor, a contemporary of Triffin, who later became the Belgian king's head of Cabinet, discussed in his *Souvenirs* the vibrant atmosphere of his student days and the vitality of the Catholic movement in Belgium in the interwar period. "Our generation was particularly noted for the flourishing of discussion and study groups, and the large number of newsletters and periodicals at university. All in all, it showed the vitality of the Catholic Action movement" (Molitor 1984: 95).

At the University of Louvain, Triffin was very active in *L'Avant garde*, a progressive Catholic movement. Like many of his friends, he became a pacifist. Triffin condemned the 1919 Treaty of Versailles. Like all pacifist intellectuals and politicians of the time, he was convinced that a review of the Versailles "Diktat" was the only way to redress the blatant injustices of the treaty, "the complete antithesis of President Wilson's Fourteen Points," and to counter the rise of fascism (Triffin 1990: 18).

Triffin shared many of his friends' fascination with Henri De Man's new socialism. De Man, who had been a professor at the University of Frankfurt, was considered as one of the new theoreticians of socialism in the interwar period. One of his famous works was *Au-delà du marxisme* (Beyond Marxism, De Man 1927). Later, De Man became president of the Belgian Labour Party and launched the idea of "The Plan" to transform the Belgian economy and combat unemployment. It was a reaction against traditional Marxism, rejecting class warfare and collective appropriation of the means of production and exchange. But De Man wanted to give the state more leverage to steer the economy. One of his key proposals was the nationalization of the banks. Describing the meetings of *L'Avant garde*, Triffin observed: "During these meetings, I found growing enthusiasm for Henri De Man, his Labour Plan, his plan for nationalizing the banks, the partial assignment of military service to mandatory fulfilment of the most unpleasant civic duties that capitalism could only impose on the poorest members of our society, etc., etc." (Triffin 1990: 18).

De Man's influence was not limited to Belgium. Robert Marjolin, with whom Triffin would work so much in the postwar period (see especially Chapters 3 and 5), told in his memoirs, *Architect of European Unity*, how he and many of his socialist friends in the 1930s were under the spell of De

Man. The crisis years of the 1930s saw an enormous intellectual confusion. "As soon as a new explanation turned up it tended to become a fashion. . . . Such was the case in 1934 with *planisme*, a doctrine that Henri De Man had got the Belgian socialists to adopt in 1933. . . . In the months that followed their adoption by the Belgian socialist party the theories of Henri De Man won a number of adepts in France" (Marjolin 1989: 61, original italics). However, Marjolin quickly gave up the idea of planisme as he did not see how the plan "would help us over the crisis."

De Man became the topic of severe controversies as he accepted Hitler's expansionist policies. He was not alone with this attitude as many persons in Western Europe were more frightened by Bolshevik Russia than Hitler's Germany. During World War II, De Man stayed in Belgium and collaborated with the Nazis. Reflecting on this period, Triffin asked himself the question whether he would have followed De Man in his national socialism. However, Triffin observed that the German invasion of Poland marked a brutal awakening for him and most of his friends from *L'Avant garde*: "the invasion of Poland clearly showed that Hitler's racist arguments would not restrict his imperialist ambitions to dominate the whole of Europe, if not the whole world." The effect, Triffin went on to note, was that "September 1939 put a definite end to our flirtation with Henri De Man's national socialism" (Triffin 1990: 18).

Life at the University of Louvain had its more frivolous aspects too. In an article for the *Harvard Monthly* in 1937, written with Alan Geismer, Triffin painted a joyful, not to say anarchistic, picture of student life at Louvain. "Americans are prone to think of Louvain as the grim and tragic scene of the German atrocities connected with the destruction of the great library, but actually it is a gay and light-hearted college town. There are annual spring town-and-gown riots, and everyone has a wonderful time baiting gendarmes and stopping all the traffic by sit-down strikes in the middle of the road. The fun often overflows from the streets into the class rooms, and lectures are generally prefaced by five or ten minutes of moderate rough-house, mostly sailing paper beer coasters around the room" (Geismer and Triffin 1937: 14).

One of Triffin's classmates in Louvain was Léon Degrelle, who would become the leader of the fascist Rex movement in Belgium. However, Triffin was not impressed by him:

Degrelle, who already had all the brass and oratorical tricks to provide the basis for his future Fascist movement, found Louvain a splendid training ground for his publicity campaigns. He was nominally studying law, but that did not seriously interfere with his extracurricular frivolities. He was in no hurry to graduate and after four or five years he did not have his degree, and still does not, in spite of his ingenious methods of taking lecture notes in three or four colors of ink. Most of his time was spent haranguing his fellow-students and inventing practical jokes. (Geismer and Triffin 1937: 14)

In the article with Geismer, Triffin gave an overview of the political path and methods of "the Belgian *Fuehrer*." Following Paul-Henri Spaak, then a young foreign affairs minister, Triffin ascribed the following qualities to Degrelle: eloquence, with dynamism and sex appeal; a genius of publicity; no knowledge of politics or economics, but an astonishing flair; a formidable boldness. According to Spaak, these four ingredients constituted an "almost perfect recipe for a demagogue dictator." However, after his initial successes, Degrelle lost ground from 1935 onward, "for his excessive attacks, which are known to be false, have frightened his more moderate followers. His appeal, just as in the Louvain days, is again principally to high school and college students who get a certain amount of fun and excitement out of the various demonstrations" (Geismer and Triffin 1937: 18). Triffin's view of Degrelle was then very similar to Molitor's, who compared him to Mussolini. "He never had the demonic, obsessive streak of the Nazi dictator. He had a grotesque, bullying side more reminiscent of the bumbling Italian buffoon" (Molitor 1984: 155).

As regards his field of study at Louvain, Triffin reported that he had serious discussions with his parents, who favored a pragmatic approach, urging him to study pharmacy, which did not go down well with him as he preferred history and literature. The compromise was law and economics:

My parents were pressing me to prepare for the comfortable life of pharmacist, but I was adamantly opposed to it, being interested primarily in history and literature. Those interests could not be followed, however, since any professional career in the areas was clearly earmarked at that time in Belgium for the sons or relatives of the professors in charge. I thus registered in the Faculty of Law, where the first two years of study were devoted to history, philosophy and literature, and could be combined with complementary programs in Thomistic philosophy, politics, diplomacy and economics. The latter offered the most promising career for an impecunious youth, especially if the Louvain degree could be strengthened by a U.S. university degree. (Triffin 1981a: 240)

Robert Triffin enrolled at the Faculty of Law at the Catholic University of Louvain in 1929. He obtained the degrees of Bachelier en Philosophie in 1931 and Docteur en Droit in 1934. In 1934, Triffin started studying economics, obtaining a degree (Licencié en Économie) in 1935.

1.3 ECONOMICS AT LOUVAIN AND THE BELGIAN FRANC
DEVALUATION OF 1935

Until the early 20th century, most Belgian universities did not offer a separate course in economics (Maes, Buyst, and Bouchet 2000). As in several other continental European countries, economic sciences were often taught under the Faculty of Law, the so-called schools of political and social sciences. Consequently, most professors teaching economics had a law background, and considerable emphasis was put on institutional and descriptive elements. Research in economics remained limited in both scope and quantity.

The interwar period would constitute a fundamental break, with a strong "Americanization" of Belgian economics, in the sense of concrete and direct US influences on the Belgian economics profession. An important role was played by the Commission for Relief in Belgium (CRB). The CRB was established in 1914 in the United States to save Belgium from starvation during the German occupation. After the armistice, the remaining funds were used to set up several educational and scientific associations. One of them was the CRB Educational Foundation, which awarded grants to promising young Belgians to study at top US universities. After their return to Belgium, many of the CRB fellows would play a prominent role in the academic and policymaking world (like Paul van Zeeland and Gaston Eyskens, both of whom went on to be prime ministers, or Jacques Drèze, the founder of the Centre for Operations Research and Econometrics [CORE]). So, the CRB contributed to an early and strong "Americanization" of the economics profession in Belgium (Maes and Buyst 2005). Particularly important for this study is the fact that Robert Triffin would also go on to study in the United States with a CRB fellowship.

Moreover, in the aftermath of World War I, Belgium was confronted with severe economic imbalances, notably high levels of public deficit and debt as well as high inflation. So, more and better economic analysis was urgently needed to design appropriate policy responses. In the early 1920s, under the impulse of Director Albert-Edouard Janssen, the National Bank of Belgium (NBB) set up an Economic Service. The bank hired Paul van Zeeland, a brilliant young economist, as the first head of the service (Maes 2010). Like Janssen, Paul van Zeeland had studied law and political and diplomatic sciences at the University of Louvain (Dujardin and Dumoulin 1997). In 1920, with the first group of CRB fellows, he went to Princeton University to study monetary economics with Edwin W. Kemmerer, one of the leading specialists of central banking in the United States. In his (unpublished) *Mémoires*, van Zeeland described Kemmerer as "petit, mince, tout en nerf, ne vivant que pour et par sa science; le meilleur théoricien de la finance que j'aie rencontré" (small, thin, always on edge, living only for and through his science, the best finance theorist that I have ever met).[1] As a specialist in central banking issues, Kemmerer had been closely involved in setting up the Federal Reserve System in 1913 (Gomez Betancourt 2010). Kemmerer was a "money doctor," who established central banks in several Latin American countries in the 1920s (later, Triffin, when he was also a "money doctor" in Latin America, would become very critical of the Kemmerer reforms; see Chapter 2). During the winter break, van Zeeland did an internship at the New York Federal Reserve Bank. In his PhD thesis, van Zeeland (1922) provided an analysis of the establishment and early years of the US Federal Reserve System (Maes and Gomez Betancourt 2018). He also wrote a paper on "The Financial and Monetary Crisis in Belgium."[2] Back in Belgium, in the autumn of 1921, van Zeeland would develop stabilization plans for the Belgian economy drawing on the theoretical concepts he had learned from Kemmerer (Gomez Betancourt and Maes 2020).

However, the stabilization of the Belgian franc would be a long and painful process. Politicians, who counted on German reparation payments, were not willing to take significant measures in the immediate postwar period. In June 1925, a new government was formed, with Janssen as finance minister. The NBB, especially van Zeeland, played an important role in the preparations of Janssen's stabilization plan. However, it immediately ran into criticism, including from Belgian commercial bankers. In these circumstances, the government failed to obtain a loan on the international financial markets and the stabilization plan derailed. Only in October 1926 did a new government of national union succeed in stabilizing the Belgian franc, albeit at a very low parity of 175 francs to the pound sterling, a clear case of undershooting. This undervaluation of the Belgian franc led to an overheating of the economy and a significant increase in inflation in Belgium in the ensuing years. The long and difficult stabilization of the Belgian franc after World War I was a traumatic experience for Belgian policymakers that would haunt them in the following decades.

Janssen and van Zeeland were teaching courses on money and central banking at the University of Louvain, where Triffin was studying. Their approach was naturally also shaped by the Belgian experience of central banking. The NBB was founded in 1850, after banking crises in 1838 and 1848. The bank was, in essence, an issuing and discount bank (Buyst et al. 2005). It had three important missions: the issue of banknotes; the organization of short-term commercial credit, in particular the rediscounting of commercial paper (short-term debt obligations related to commercial transactions); and the function of state cashier. The US National Monetary Commission, which prepared the establishment of the Federal Reserve System, also produced a volume on the Belgian central bank in 1910, written by Charles Conant. It is noteworthy that the NBB was a model for the reform of the banking system in Japan in 1882. As argued by Count Matsukata, the then Japanese finance minister:

> In point of the perfectness of organization and the well-regulated condition of business management, the National Bank of Belgium stands highest. This fact is due doubtless to the lateness of its founding, which enabled it to consider fully the mistakes as well as the successes of older banks. Its regulations are for this reason more perfect than those of any others, winning highest praises from the financiers of the world. . . . In the case of a Japanese central bank, therefore, no better pattern can be found than the National Bank of Belgium. (as quoted in Conant 1910: 12)

Janssen and van Zeeland put strong emphasis on how the monetary system was evolving, with gold gradually being replaced by fiduciary money. Originally, banknotes represented claims on metal standard money and were intended mainly to facilitate large-value payments. At the end of the 19th century, banknotes became more widely established as payment instruments. This large-scale replacement of coins by notes in the monetary circulation led to a growing concentration of countries' stocks of precious metal at their banks of issue (the early central banks). So, the banks of issue became the custodians of their country's gold. As noted by Janssen, this contributed to the growing importance of the "monetary" function of the NBB, as compared to its traditional "credit" function (discount credit).[3] Later, Triffin would draw heavily on these ideas, arguing for "fiduciary" money in the international monetary system (see Chapter 4). These ideas were very similar to those of John Maynard Keynes, who also highlighted how gold was losing its role in the monetary system. Keynes, in *Auri Sacra Fames* (the accursed hunger for gold), emphasized the role of World War I in the withdrawal of gold from circulation but admitted that gold continued to exercise a strong psychological influence, "part of the apparatus of conservatism":

> War concentrated gold in the vaults of the Central Banks; and these Banks have not released it. Thus, almost throughout the world, gold has been withdrawn from circulation. It no longer passes from hand to hand, and the touch of the metal has been taken away from men's greedy palms. The little household gods, who dwelt in purses and stockings and tin boxes, have been swallowed

by a single golden image in each country, which lives underground and is not seen. Gold is out of sight—gone back again into the soil. But when gods are no longer seen in a yellow panoply walking the earth, we begin to rationalize them. (Keynes 1930: 183)

In the late 1920s, the backward condition of education and scientific research at Belgian universities was a matter of intense debate. To strengthen education and research in economics, the University of Louvain set up the Institut des Sciences Économiques (ISE) in October 1928. Janssen and van Zeeland played a key role in it. The new institute's research agenda was directly inspired by the activities of the Harvard Committee for Economic Research (van Zeeland 1929). For many years, business cycle analysis (the study of fluctuations in economic activity and prices) remained the cornerstone of the ISE's scientific work (Dupriez 1952). The institute also followed the Harvard model of combining scientific research with a short-term forecasting service for the business world. In the interwar period, the institute became the first modern economic research center in the Low Countries (Maes and Buyst 2005).

By setting up a specialized research institute and putting emphasis on statistical analysis of the business cycle, Louvain followed a more general trend of the 1920s. Business cycle theory was in fact the central topic in interwar economic research, and many modern research institutes were founded as institutes for business cycle analysis. Prime examples were the National Bureau of Economic Research in the United States, the London and Cambridge Economic Service in the United Kingdom, the Berliner Institut für Konjunkturforschung, the Österreichisches Institut für Wirtschaftsforschung (founded by Friedrich von Hayek and Ludwig von Mises), and the Institut de Recherches Economiques et Sociales of Charles Rist in Paris. Schumpeter (1954: 1155) described this tendency toward more quantitative and statistical analysis of the business cycle, like the Harvard barometer curves, as "Americanization."

The Louvain institute maintained close links with the United States in the 1930s. During that decade, some continental European economic research centers retreated from the international scene and became increasingly inward looking. Thus, for example, in Germany, the Institut für Konjunkturforschung became involved in Nazi economic policies (Krengel 1986; Tooze 1999). In Louvain, the CRB fellowships guaranteed exposure to American academia, as a result of which young researchers went more or less continuously to American universities. In 1933, the ISE received a grant from the Rockefeller Foundation, which further strengthened transatlantic ties (Craver 1986).

The dominant figure at the Louvain institute was Léon-H. Dupriez, who had studied at Harvard in 1918 and 1919. Dupriez became a leading scholar in business cycle analysis, considered in a broad sense (i.e., the interaction of growth and different types of cycles in economic life). The focus was on the different industrial sectors of the economy, which were then at the center of the economic growth process. Dupriez (1959: 468) described the industrial revolution as "une grande aventure *prométhéenne* de l'humanité" (a great *Promethean* adventure for humanity, original italics). Moreover, Dupriez, who also had a position at the NBB, felt that money and finance had a central place in economic life (Mandy 2005). He was a pioneer in introducing statistical methods of business cycle analysis in Europe. Two elements were typical for Dupriez. First, he based his analysis on extensive empirical investigations (with a lot of attention to descriptive statistical methods, as well as charts and tables). Dupriez himself described it as "une théorie conjoncturelle « collant aux faits »" (a business cycle theory "sticking to the facts," Dupriez 1959: VIII). Second, he was not in favor of new schools of economic thought, like Keynesian economics. He disliked the use of models, econometrics, and national income accounts. For Dupriez, it was crucial that economic theory should go back to individual economic decisions. From this perspective, Dupriez was very close to the Austrian approach. His theoretical framework resembled that of (the young) Hayek's general equilibrium-oriented business cycle theories of the late 1920s (Hayek 1928). Keynes was not very fashionable in Belgium. He was mainly known as the author of *The Economic Consequences of the Peace* (Keynes 1919), which criticized key elements of the Versailles Treaty, like the reparation payments. As Belgium had been invaded by Germany and had suffered badly from the war, it counted on reparation payments to finance its postwar reconstruction. This was an important factor in why Keynesian ideas only gained ground in Belgium in the postwar period, and very slowly (Maes 2008).

Molitor (1984) also tells about the attraction of the new School of Economics in Louvain. A clear factor was its innovative approach thanks to strong US influences. "This was something new because the School of Economics had only recently been set up and few people went to it. It was an innovative environment, greatly influenced by research in America, which at that time was way ahead of Europe in this field" (Molitor 1984: 94). Molitor further underlined the qualities of several young professors, like Dupriez, Eyskens, and van Zeeland, who had studied in the United States and were "destined for great things." He was very much impressed by van Zeeland, "about to become Prime Minister, . . . a rising star who taught the financial analysis course brilliantly, speaking in a low, persuasive voice and occasionally embellishing his explanations with theatrical flourishes like a magician or conjuror." Molitor further underlined the importance of the practical sessions, very much inspired by the US example, which contributed to the research of their professors: "we produced all kinds of statistical series which formed the basis of subsequent research by the School." This would also be a task for Triffin, who produced important statistical series for Dupriez and van Zeeland. While Dupriez and the French-speaking economists concentrated mainly on business cycle issues, the Flemish economists, under the leadership of Eyskens, focused much more closely on the structural problems of the Flemish economy, especially high unemployment (Abraham 1972).

Dupriez strongly dominated economics at Louvain and was not very pluralist. Alexandre Lamfalussy, a student of Dupriez in the postwar period, who later became the first president of the European Monetary Institute, the forerunner of the European Central Bank, was quite hard on Dupriez. While he admitted many positive aspects of Dupriez, he was very clear as to why he did not get a position at Louvain, after his PhD in Oxford: "Dupriez didn't want me. Because he thought I was intellectually dangerous. Dupriez was an arch-conservative. He hated or even looked down on English academic teaching. Anything to do with Keynes was diabolical. . . . When I came back from Oxford, the University of Louvain was not open to me" (Lamfalussy, Maes, and Péters 2013). This would also be Triffin's experience (see Section 1.7).

Triffin was one of Dupriez's pupils and became an assistant at the institute in 1934–1935. He undertook research in collaboration with Dupriez and under the supervision of van Zeeland[4] and Ferdinand Baudhuin,[5] who was professor of economic history and also an adviser to the Belgian minister of finance at the beginning of the 1930s.

During Triffin's time as a student, in the first half of the 1930s, the Great Depression was raging and Belgium too was badly affected. Yet, there was unanimous support for maintaining the existing gold parity, even after the devaluation of the British pound in September 1931. Indeed, the difficulty in stabilizing the Belgian franc after World War I in 1926 was still too fresh in everyone's memory. Nobody wanted to take the responsibility for another monetary adventure (very much like in France during these years; Mouré 2002). Socialist politicians argued that "le franc des riches est aussi celui des pauvres" (the rich man's franc is also the poor man's franc; Van der Wee and Tavernier 1975: 258). This implied there was no alternative to a deflationary policy, under which domestic prices had to be adjusted to the lower world market prices by cutting costs. However, the fall in nominal wages came up against stiff resistance. Moreover, company closures and restructuring led to a further rise in unemployment. The Belgian economy went into a downward spiral. The financial system was hard hit and some banks went bankrupt.

The deflation prompted major debates within the NBB as well (Van der Wee and Tavernier 1975). In the spring of 1934, Dupriez wrote a memorandum claiming that the deflation policy was not sustainable. In his view, a devaluation was the only solution. Vice Governor van Zeeland was close to Dupriez; both were also colleagues at the University of Louvain. With bank crises and rising unemployment, the deflationary policy was losing all credibility. In early 1935, capital flight accelerated, which put the Belgian banking sector under even more pressure.

In March 1935, the political cards in Belgium were radically reshuffled. Paul van Zeeland was appointed prime minister. According to Triffin, it was the best government Belgium had in the "last fifty years" (Geismer and Triffin 1937: 17). Van Zeeland was determined to "unchain" Belgium from its "golden fetters" (Eichengreen 1992). The new government immediately devalued the franc by 28%, and the young Robert Triffin was responsible for the concrete calculations of the devaluation percentage. In fact, Triffin elaborated the Louvain version of the purchasing power parity (PPP) theory, as well as the necessary statistical apparatus, continuously updating the statistical time series (Dupriez 1952: 314; Dupriez 1978: 107; see also Section 1.5). An important concern for van Zeeland and Dupriez was to avoid an undervaluation of the Belgian franc as in 1926 with the ensuing inflationary consequences.

John Maynard Keynes approved very much of the Belgian devaluation. In some rough notes for an international meeting of economists in Antwerp in July 1935, he observed: "Belgian example great impression on world. Calmness, moderation and skill of Belgian transition. . . . Currency changes much easier than usually supposed." Keynes further raged against the "Stupid and obstinate old gentleman at Banks of Netherlands and France crucifying their countries in a struggle which is certain to prove futile" (Keynes 1935: 356).

Triffin was actively involved in the ISE analyses. These showed how external shocks had hurt the Belgian economy. First, as a small and open economy, Belgium was heavily affected by the Great Depression in the early 1930s, especially by sharply contracting world trade and falling international prices. Second, the 1931 devaluation of the British pound had a major impact on the Belgian economy, as Great Britain was one of Belgium's leading export markets and British producers were the main international competitors of Belgian producers (Dupriez et al. 1931; Dupriez and Barboux 1933).

As mentioned, Dupriez had studied at Harvard and the Louvain institute was greatly inspired by the Harvard experience. Frank Taussig, the "grand old man" of the Department of Economics at Harvard, was prominent in the field of applied economics (Vademar 1968). Gottfried Haberler has noted that "His work was remarkable for its historical perspective and his intuitive sense both for orders of magnitude of economic variables and for the political feasibility of proposed economic, measures" (Haberler 1968). Taussig wrote a dissertation on the protection of young industries, and, throughout his career, tariff questions and international trade were at the core of his interests (Mason and Lamont 1982: 394). He was also interested in the sectoral structure of the economy. In a path-breaking article, Taussig (1917) developed the differential role of export, import, and domestic prices in the process of balance-of-payments adjustments. This distinction between domestic or "sheltered" sectors and "nonsheltered" sectors would also become a hallmark of Dupriez and the Louvain School of Economics. Jacob Viner, one of Taussig's most eminent students, argued that this was a seminal contribution:

> While the distinction between "domestic" commodities and those entering into international trade dates at least from Ricardo, and subsequent writers made clear that international uniformity in the prices of identical commodities after allowance for transportation costs was a necessary condition under equilibrium only for "international" commodities, Taussig was the first to lay emphasis on the significance for the mechanism of adjustment of international balances to disturbances of changes in level of domestic commodity prices as compared to the prices of international commodities. (Viner 1937: 323)

With this sophisticated theoretical framework, it should not be surprising that Taussig was critical of Gustav Cassel's PPP theory, which did not distinguish between these different types of prices (Sember 2013). Later, several students of Taussig, like Jacob Viner, Harry Dexter White, and John Williams, undertook empirical studies to test Taussig's theories of balance-of-payments adjustments, Viner (1924) for Canada, White (1933) for France, and Williams (1920) for Argentina. Later, during World War II, White and Viner also served at the Treasury, along with another student of Taussig, Edward Bernstein (see Chapter 2).

Some weeks after the Belgian franc devaluation of March 1935, Triffin published his first article in the *Bulletin de l'Institut des Sciences économiques*, entitled "Les mouvements différentiels des prix de gros en Belgique de 1927 à 1934. Calcul et interprétation d'indices de groupes comparables" (Triffin 1935). It was a largely statistical article, explaining the calculation and interpretation of differential group indices of wholesale prices in Belgium, very much in line with the analyses of Dupriez and Taussig. In the article, Triffin analyzed the movement of 25 agricultural product indices and 28 industrial product indices over the period from 1927 to 1934. One of the distinctions he made was between raw materials, semifinished products, and finished products, which had different patterns and affected the Belgian economy in contrasting ways. He also had separate indices for imported and exported industrial products and imported agricultural products.

Triffin's article argued that the differential movement of prices, with prices of manufactured products falling more than domestic costs, was causing serious losses in Belgian manufacturing, leading to closure of firms. "Far from conveying a stronger position in international trade, the relative stability of our sales prices solely reflected the rigidity of the internal components of our cost prices: wages and especially capital charges. And apparently favorable prices were for our industrialists actually famine prices, which, in 1934, pushed half the firms in the country into a loss" (Triffin 1935: 290). With such catastrophic losses, firms cut back production and investment, leading to growing unemployment in Belgium.

In his conclusions, Triffin argued that the deflationary policy pursued by the Belgian government for preserving the gold parity had contributed to "making things better in some areas, while aggravating them in others" (Triffin 1935: 290). He emphasized that there was a problem in the structure of relative prices in Belgium and that the deflation process was not solving this. In a later article, in 1937, also based on his studies at Harvard, he would delve deeper into the theoretical and empirical background of the Belgian devaluation (see Section 1.5).

It is further noteworthy that Triffin also concluded that agricultural prices were much more sensitive to the business cycle. "It is above all the sheer intensity of the farm crisis over the last few years, at least in plant products, which, by their very nature and the lower protection they are given, tend to follow the highly depressed world prices more closely" (Triffin 1935: 290). This would become an important theme in his later work, emphasizing that deflationary policies by countries at the center of the economic system would have even stronger deflationary effects in the periphery of the world economy. Here, he would be close to several ideas of Raúl Prebisch, the Argentinian economist, who would, in the postwar period, be heading the Economic Commission for Latin America (ECLA) and the United Nations Conference on Trade and Development (UNCTAD). Triffin developed a close relationship with him, both personally and professionally (see Chapter 2).

1.4 GRADUATE STUDIES AT HARVARD

In March 1935, Triffin applied for a fellowship from the CRB Educational Foundation to fund graduate studies in the United States. He not only was awarded the fellowship but also obtained two extensions, which enabled him to write a doctoral dissertation at Harvard. The reports that he wrote for the CRB, from January 1936 to August 1938, provide very valuable information about Triffin's studies and activities in the United States.

Initially, like most fellows at the time, Triffin intended to go to the United States for one year. After that, he planned to come back to Louvain for his PhD. With Dupriez's blessing, he planned to write his thesis on the theme of economic geography and location economics (Triffin 1981a: 240). Dupriez's suggestion was probably related to the introduction of industrial economics in the ISE research program in 1935 (Dupriez 1935: 50). In his CRB application, Triffin argued that Harvard was the best place to study economic geography. "I should find there namely Prof. F. Black, the best American writer on the subject of 'Production Economics,' who studies systematically, in his great treatise, the play of the different factors of production in this field." Moreover, Harvard was very strong in the area of international economics. As Triffin observed: "I should find myself in the scientific environment where worked Prof. Ohlin, the Swedish author whose recent treatise on 'Interregional and International Trade' has had such a great praise. . . . The guidance of Professors Taussig and Williams would appear useful, as well as contacts with Prof. Leontief."[6] Moreover, during the academic vacation, Triffin intended to visit some big manufacturing centers to get a first-hand view of useful applications of the theory to business life. "A visit in the region of Great Lakes appears especially instructive for this purpose," he wrote.

In his CRB application, Triffin also indicated that he wanted to take the opportunity to improve his knowledge of economic theory, especially by following Joseph Schumpeter's classes: "besides the special field of studies, it would be profitable to make the best of my opportunity at Harvard to follow the movement of ideas concerning economic doctrines; I could not miss e.g. the lectures of Prof. Schumpeter."[7]

Joseph Alois Schumpeter was the outstanding member of the Harvard Economics Department in the 1930s. Recruiting him was a major coup for Harvard. He was not only an outstanding scholar with major publications to his name but also had been a finance minister in Austria after the end of World War I. However, he had a "somewhat outré personality," sometimes regarded as "an exotic Austrian aristocrat" and a "somewhat cynical and certainly skeptical commentator on established values and thought" (Mason and Lamont 1982).

Although the opportunity to attend Schumpeter's courses was not Triffin's primary concern when applying, Schumpeter would have a profound influence on Triffin at Harvard. During the months that followed, Triffin would gradually give up the idea of returning to Louvain for a PhD on location economics. He would stay in Harvard for three years and write a thesis in pure theory, *General Equilibrium Theory and Monopolistic Competition*, under the supervision of Schumpeter, along with Leontief and Chamberlin.

Triffin left for Harvard in the summer of 1935. In his first report for the CRB, he was euphoric about the United States and Harvard University. The report started with a description of New York, where the ship arrived. Triffin fully agreed with the French novelist Céline: "C'est une ville debout" (It's a city standing). "The impression is so new that all attempts at a more detailed description fail to convey any meaning to those who have not fallen under the spell of the city itself."[8] The trip continued to New England, which Triffin described as "a large park." Moreover, to his surprise, the houses were not made of concrete or steel, but of wood. His destination, Boston, was, in his view, "a large, European town . . . too European even to inspire in us the same love as New York did."

Triffin was utterly delighted by Harvard, especially Adams House, the college where he was living:

And Harvard? Red bricks, white stones, changing ivy, lively squirrels, a peaceful atmosphere which makes work so much easier and more agreeable.

What of more trivial matters, such as lodging and eating? I am so enthusiastic about Adams House that I could not but strongly advise anyone who comes here to seize the opportunity of entering one of the Houses, if the opportunity is offered to him. Previous reports had told the story of the Houses, and their advantages over Conant Hall and Perkins Hall, reserved for graduate students exclusively.

A homely atmosphere in the common rooms, musical room, dining room, et cetera, a magnificent and so convenient library, perfectly modern apartments, and above all, the best choice of friends among the undergraduates, are things one should not miss.[9]

American universities are known for the quality of their libraries. Before the internet, the library was really the source of all information and of crucial importance for any university or research center. Triffin was full of praise for Harvard's Widener Library. "As to the library, no library in the world offers such conveniences, I think, as our Widener, the richest of all university libraries." In contrast to the restrictive policies of the European libraries to which he had become accustomed, Triffin lauded the welcoming nature of Widener, "free access to, and a reserved stall in, the stacks, the outside borrowing of books for a month, et cetera. Work is made so much easier this way."[10]

As far as his studies were concerned, Triffin took the decision to first study economic theory, instead of focusing on his PhD thesis: "However narrowly scholastic such a plan may seem, I am more and more convinced of the outstanding importance of a full theoretical preparation for any practical work." For Triffin, the program of the Harvard Economics Department was the best way to achieve this aim, "providing moreover some elements of mental discipline which, under the circumstances, are not necessarily to be despised." During the first term, he took four courses: Economic Theory by Professor Schumpeter, Recent Economic History by Professor Edwin F. Gay, Theory of Economic Statistics by Professors William L. Crum and Edwin Frickey, and Commodity Distribution and Prices by Professors John D. Black and John M. Cassels.

Schumpeter's Economic Theory course was, according to its description, focused on "the principles or tools of theoretical analysis as far as they are essential to all scientific work in Economics." Triffin quickly fell under the spell of Schumpeter and pure economic theory, a great contrast with Dupriez's empirically oriented business cycle approach to economics. As he wrote in his 1981 autobiographical article, "A few weeks at Harvard, however, sufficed to convince me that what I missed most was an adequate training in pure theory, then taught at Harvard by Professor Schumpeter whose broad culture in that field, and others, was as unique as his class showmanship" (Triffin 1981a: 241). In his CRB report, Triffin presented a vivid description of Schumpeter's way of teaching:

> Professor Schumpeter is the most fascinating person you could imagine. Due to his training in both Continental and English Economics, his course combines perfectly a rigorous logical exposition, and discussion of the broad implications of the subject matter, with a very searching study of the fundamental problems of value and distribution. These last aspects are along lines largely mathematical, at least if compared with the general teaching in Belgian and French universities. Occasionally other important subjects are touched upon. Most of the work has to be done outside the classroom and the reading assignments seem terrific to many students. Beside the assignments, the suggestions for further reading or studies will, I feel, keep me busy for a long time to come. Professor Schumpeter adores bringing before us new problems or new points

of view, discussing them briefly, indicating some books and articles, and then "dropping the subject, leaving it to your meditations in the dark of the night." In the ground covered in class, discussions coordinate, clarify, criticize the historical developments of the solution offered to the problem under investigation, always bringing the matter up to the more recent contributions.[11]

At the heart of economic theory, for Schumpeter, was general equilibrium theory. As observed by a fellow Harvard student, Paul Samuelson (1951: 103), Schumpeter was "surprisingly un-Austrian" in his approach toward economic theory, and much more Walrasian. In a retrospective article, Triffin (1950: 414) further emphasized that, for Schumpeter, economic theory was a method: "Economic theory doesn't answer our questions: it helps with asking them well, and, as a result, to organize them well. It is a working method, and not a ready-made list of recipes."

Moreover, Triffin decided to take Wassily Leontief's international trade class. He immediately felt attracted to Leontief and his course. "I have heard too much admiration of Professor Leontief's originality and profundity to miss his course of this year."[12] Like Schumpeter, Leontief, a future Nobel Memorial Prize laureate, was a European émigré. He was born in Russia in 1906 and had studied at the Universities of Leningrad and Berlin. In the mid-1930s, Leontief was the brilliant young mathematical economist. He published a series of papers on different topics (business cycles, international trade, marginal productivity theory, monopolistic competition theory, etc.), drawing heavily on his knowledge of mathematical economic theory. Leontief was very involved in the development of his "input-output" analysis for the United States, a type of gridline system, showing what individual industries buy from and sell to one another, presenting so an overview of the goods and services circulating in the economy. Leontief presented this as implementing empirically the vision of interdependence that had motivated Quesnay's *Tableau Economique* (Backhouse 2017: 119). With the so-called Leontief paradox, based on his empirical input-output system, he would later show that the United States exported labor-intensive products and imported capital-intensive products, questioning the Hecksher-Ohlin theory of international trade.

Triffin's work on his thesis was facilitated by "two fortunate circumstances." First, Harvard had secured Gottfried Haberler of Vienna for a course in international trade. Triffin had met Haberler in Louvain, a year prior to beginning his studies at Harvard, and stated in his CRB report that he would "appreciate the opportunity of listening to him." This was even more interesting as Haberler's approach to international economics was very different from Leontief's. Second, Harvard had launched a course in the very subject of Triffin's investigations, "The Location of Economic Activity." Triffin reported that he "found in this fact a confirmation of the interest of the field I have chosen, and the promise of welcome assistance in the framing of the theoretical preparation of my thesis."[13]

During the Christmas recess, Triffin attended the meetings of the American Economic Association in New York. It gave him the opportunity to meet some of the most famous economists in the United States like Frank Knight and Jacob Viner from Chicago, as well as John R. Commons, the father of institutional economics, and John M. Clark.

In the conclusion of his first, "immoderately long" CRB report, Triffin was full of praise for the "astounding friendliness and geniality" of his teachers. Triffin's formation extended well beyond the classroom. "Through informal luncheons or dinners, constant invitations to visit them at their offices, every opportunity is offered for discussions and guidance in a very enjoyable way. This easy intercourse, so precious to a foreigner, eager of knowing the country, is a characteristic of American education, but also, in a broader way, of all American life."[14] These interactions were a great boon to Triffin both professionally and personally and had important consequences for his path forward.

As is evident from his report, Triffin enormously appreciated Harvard and US academic life. So, he asked for an extension of his fellowship, which was granted. This made it possible for him to work on a PhD at Harvard. However, Triffin's decision to stay in the United States was not appreciated by Dupriez back in Louvain. As Triffin later observed: "As for Dupriez, I am hugely indebted to him for having involved me in his work and thus launched my career as an economist with my first publications in his Institute's review. But our relationship began to go wrong when I decided to extend my studies at Harvard and become the first Belgian to achieve a PhD there" (Triffin 1990: 16).

During the summer of 1936, as was the habit of the CRB fellows, Triffin made a grand tour in the United States. It was not only for leisure; he was also thinking of his thesis on the location of economic activity. He spent some time at Knoxville, interviewing some officials and visiting the installations of the famous Tennessee Valley Authority—a regional economic development agency for the Tennessee Valley, a region particularly affected by the Great Depression—a very symbolic achievement of Roosevelt's New Deal. He also visited some oil fields and steel factories, especially the Inland Steel plants at Chicago. Moreover, he went to several universities, like Princeton (where he stayed two weeks), Stanford, Berkeley, Madison, and Chicago. At Chicago, he stopped for about a month, taking advantage of the summer term organized by the university. It gave him the occasion to meet the Chicago economics faculty. "Through the unforgettable courtesy and friendliness of Professor Henry Schultz I was invited to register at the Quadrangle Club where I had every opportunity to meet the other professors in whose work and viewpoints I was interested, i.e. Professors Knight, Viner, Douglas."[15]

Back in Harvard for the new academic year, Triffin was, once more, "unable to resist the voice of the Sirens." As he observed, "Professor Schumpeter was hard to take leave of." Triffin registered with enthusiasm for his advanced course on business cycles, which "could not leave indifferent a student of Professor Dupriez." For his class work, he found inspiration in Belgium's interwar economic experience, especially the 1935 devaluation for which he had made the calculations. He wrote a paper on the effects of the business cycle and monetary overvaluation on the economies of the gold bloc countries during the years 1931–1935, focusing on Belgium. He also registered for Professor Haberler's International Trade course, one of his major subjects, for which he wrote a paper criticizing Cassel's PPP theories. He would draw on these papers for an article entitled "La théorie de la surévaluation monétaire et la dévaluation belge" (The theory of currency overvaluation and the Belgian devaluation), which would be published in Dupriez's *Bulletin de l'Institut de recherches économiques* (Triffin 1937; see Section 1.5).

Naturally, in his second year, he had to focus more closely on preparations for his thesis work. Here he changed topic, very much under the influence of Leontief. Moreover, Triffin followed Edward Chamberlin's "very stimulating" class on monopolistic competition. In those days, Chamberlin was regarded as the new up-and-coming economist at Harvard. Chamberlin was not so much interested in industrial analysis or statistical measurements; rather, he was involved in developing a more general theory of value (Mason and Lamont 1982: 423). In his January 1937 CRB report, Triffin reported on the change of direction for his thesis, a redirection that wove together the general equilibrium approach of Walras and Pareto and Chamberlin's monopolistic competition ideas:

I really began only to reap this year the first results of last year's preparatory work. The general complement of economic training I received at that time proves to be an incomparable asset. It has given my thoughts a very different direction, and I hope my thesis will show the trace of it. The blending of the continental approach to economics with the American outlook on the same problems seems to lead in a promising direction. This is especially true, I think, when the "general equilibrium" approach of Walras and Pareto is confronted with such modern developments of the theory of value as are due to Professor Chamberlin in his Theory of Monopolistic Competition.[16]

During this second year, most of his work was done in the form of readings and discussions in the field of economic theory, the area of his doctoral thesis. He was also granted a second extension of his CRB fellowship.

In 1937, Harvard recruited a new professor in political economy: Alvin Harvey Hansen. According to Paul Samuelson (1976), this would mark a new "age" at Harvard, as, after the age of Taussig and the age of Schumpeter, there came the age of Hansen. Hansen had written a doctoral dissertation on business cycles at the University of Wisconsin, the center of the American institutionalist movement, very much under the influence of Wesley Mitchell's quantitative empirical approach. Hansen would become one of the most eminent Keynesians in the United States. He would play a role not only in the development of Keynesian theories but also in popularizing them. One of his most well-known books was *A Guide to Keynes* (Hansen 1953). While there is a "myth" that Hansen converted to Keynesianism on the train from Minnesota to Harvard in September 1937, recent research shows that the "conversion" came later and was more gradual. At the end of the 1930s, Hansen was still reasoning very much in terms of business cycle theory (Backhouse 2017: 237; Mehrling 1997: 135). Hansen also had several advisory functions in the policymaking area. He became a good friend of Samuelson, to whom Triffin was close. Of particular importance for Triffin was that, in 1940, Hansen was appointed special economic adviser to Mariner Eccles, the chair of the Federal Reserve Board. Hansen would play an important role in Triffin's recruitment to the US central bank in 1942 (see Chapter 2).

Triffin returned to the University of Chicago in the summer of 1937. There he had valuable discussions with Frank Knight and Henry Schultz. He also attended advanced courses on economic theory and mathematical economics. Triffin admitted that Chicago had an excellent economics department. "Chicago is generally admitted to possess, after Harvard, the best department of Economics in this country (though I suppose the Chicago people would rather reverse my statement). In fact, men like Knight, Schultz, Viner, Douglas are enough to make an unusually strong department." However, Triffin clearly preferred Harvard. Two important factors for him were the library and the quality of the students at Harvard: "the weak point at Chicago is Harper Library: it will provide me with nightmares for the rest of my life. I also missed the stimulating atmosphere which is created at Harvard by the younger members of the department and some of the graduate students of exceptionally high standing. I suspect, however, that the summer crowd was an unfair sample of the Chicago students."[17]

It was only later that Triffin fully realized how privileged he had been regarding the quality of his fellow students at Harvard. "I also learned as much or more, as an economist, from *student colleagues* of mine in the most brilliant class that Harvard probably ever had (Paul Samuelson, Arthur Schlesinger, John Kenneth Galbraith, Shigeto Tsuru, Lloyd Metzler, Sidney Alexander, Richard Musgrave, etc.) than from the professors whose classes I attended (Schumpeter, Leontief, Hansen, Haberler, Williams, Chamberlin, etc.)" (Triffin 1981a: 254, original italics). One might note that Triffin adopted here a rather broad definition of "student" as Galbraith was a junior faculty member (Galbraith 1981). Moreover, another student at Harvard was John F. Kennedy, the future US president, whom Triffin would later be advising on international monetary matters (see Chapter 4). During his graduate studies, Triffin was especially close to Samuelson and Tsuru (a Japanese economist, who became president of the International Economic Association) and they often came to Adams House for dinner. The three were known as "the three Musketeers" (Backhouse 2017: 125).

Triffin had a keen interest in and curiosity about American life and society. The historian Arthur Schlesinger, later an adviser to President Kennedy, also lived in Adams House. He became a close friend of Triffin. In his autobiography, Schlesinger recalls that he learned much from two foreign graduate students, Triffin and Tsuru, who "were a little older and combined intellectual cosmopolitanism with a genuine zest for things American." He characterized Triffin as "a man of keen intelligence and altogether delightful dry humor" (Schlesinger 2000: 116). This genuine curiosity for other cultures was a constant in Triffin's character and approach. It would come very much to the fore in his Latin American missions for the US Federal Reserve Board in the 1940s (see Chapter 2).

During his third year at Harvard, Triffin focused completely on his doctoral work. "All my attention is now concentrated on my thesis." He attended courses only occasionally, "just to keep in touch with what is going on in the department." He had assembled all the material for his thesis and written down a large part of it in the form of papers. "I have reached the last and dull stage of my work when the only task that remains to be done is to put the whole thing in thesis form."[18] During this year, Triffin followed only research courses, consisting exclusively of individual discussions with Professors Schumpeter, Chamberlin, and Leontief.

In April 1938, Triffin finished the first draft of his thesis and, on the recommendation of the Department of Economics, he was allowed to present his "special" (i.e., the final PhD examination), bearing on the field of economics in which his thesis was written. Triffin completed his thesis in Belgium in the autumn of 1938 (it will be analyzed in Section 1.6). Triffin's doctoral work was very well appreciated at Harvard. In a letter to the CRB Educational Foundation, Joseph Schumpeter expressed very warm words on Triffin's thesis. "I take the opportunity to tell you that our friend Triffin has during the last half year developed still more favorably than I expected he would. His Doctor's thesis, which is now in shape and only requires expository elaboration, is a really remarkable piece of work and has greatly impressed all the members of this department who have read it. An amplified version of it in French should go far to establish him as an economist in his own country."[19]

In the summer of 1938, Triffin went back to Belgium. On board of the SS *Brant County*, off the coast of Newfoundland, he wrote his final report for the CRB. It started in a very nostalgic way: "The last of America is fading away at the horizon and I am finally beginning for the C.R.B. a final report that will be really final."[20] Triffin used this report to compare economics education in Belgium and the United States. He stressed the superiority of the American universities, especially, and rather to his initial surprise, in the field of economic theory:

> The first thing to be convinced of when you come here is that, in many fields of economics, your former training will be, by American standards, perfectly inadequate. Partly, this is due simply to a divergence in directions of interest, partly to a real superiority of the big American universities, where economics reached their independent status far earlier than they did in French-speaking countries. Personally, coming from Louvain, I found myself better prepared in the fields of Statistics, Business-cycles, Money and Banking. The gaps were most felt in the fields of International Trade, Economic History and Theory. The interest I found here in Economic Theory was a rather startling discovery, as I had always imagined a more direct, empirical attitude in the United States than in our country. The truth is at the exact opposite, at least as far as the big universities are concerned. This was one of the reasons that prompted me to give much attention to this field, so neglected today in Belgium and in France.[21]

In fact, Triffin was already feeling a second wave of Americanization, which would dominate the postwar period (Coats 1996). The first wave, in the interwar period, was very empirical and focused on business cycle theory (as discussed in Section 1.3). The second wave, in the postwar period, would be more characterized by the formalization of economic theory. European migrants, like Schumpeter and Leontief at Harvard, many fleeing

Nazism, would give a strong boost to economic theory in the second half of the 1930s in the United States (Hagemann 2000).

As already mentioned, Triffin much preferred Harvard to Chicago. Triffin adored the discussions with his fellow graduate students at Harvard, writing that "nothing is more stimulating than the atmosphere of discussions and lively interest in current literature, which results from the presence of a strong body of good graduate students." Triffin considered this "an invaluable asset for Harvard," where some graduate students were of an "absolutely unusual standing." Triffin further argued that Harvard's policy of giving instructorships or fellowships to many graduate students also bridged the gap between students and tenured professors, "contributing very much to the informality and friendliness of their relationships."[22] He was not alone with this opinion. Indeed, there were many complaints in the Chicago Department of Economics that their best graduate students left for the East and finished their graduate work at Harvard or Columbia, while very few students left Harvard or Columbia for Chicago. Later, Triffin was even very hard on Chicago, saying that he was "deeply disappointed by the intolerance and self-centered exclusiveness of the so-called Chicago School of economics, in search of faithful 'disciples' more than of true 'students'" (Triffin 1981a: 241). In the next two sections we will go into his two major publications during his time at Harvard.

1.5 THE THEORY OF CURRENCY OVERVALUATION AND THE 1935 BELGIAN DEVALUATION

In September 1937, Triffin completed an article on the theory of currency overvaluation and the recent monetary history of Belgium for the *Bulletin de l'Institut de recherches économiques* of Louvain University. The article was based on both his Louvain and Harvard experiences. In the article, entitled "La théorie de la surévaluation monétaire et la dévaluation belge" (The theory of currency overvaluation and the Belgian devaluation), Triffin went further into the theoretical and empirical background of the 1935 Belgian franc devaluation. In the first footnote of the article, Triffin acknowledged that he was drawing very much on notes that were discussed during seminars at Harvard. As mentioned, during the autumn of 1936, Triffin prepared two papers. The first concerned the relations between the effects of the business cycle and of a monetary overvaluation on gold bloc countries for Schumpeter's course. The second paper, prepared for Haberler's course, aimed to reinterpret Cassel's theories of PPP.

The article was in French and Triffin admitted that his knowledge of the language of Voltaire had deteriorated. "While in the process of writing it, I found out that my French had been going downhill considerably in the course of the last two years and it seems to have reached by now the same level to which I have been able to raise my English."[23] It was divided into three parts: (1) PPP and equilibrium on the foreign exchange markets, (2) a theory of currency overvaluation based on the domestic structure of prices, and (3) the Belgian devaluation of 1935.

Triffin started with a trenchant critique of Cassel's PPP theory (Cassel 1925). Triffin focused especially on the chapter "Deviations from purchasing power parities." His main criticism, in line with Dupriez's business cycle analysis, was that Cassel's theory was not suited to situations of disequilibrium and transition periods. "Based exclusively on the consideration, indeed essential, of static equilibrium positions," he said, Cassel "paid too little attention to the secondary phenomena that are characteristic of transition periods. It is precisely the study of these phenomena that proves to be the determining factor in the analysis of the former gold standard countries' problems" (Triffin 1937: 32).

Triffin pointed out that any estimation of exchange rate adjustment on the basis of the PPP theory required the implicit assumption that all internal price changes are equi-proportional. Consequently, he claimed that the PPP theory did not take into account the impact of transitory phenomena such as monetary disturbances on internal price movements. Triffin's fundamental criticism, in line with his 1935 article, was that Cassel did not look at the structure of prices in a country (see also Figure 1.1):

> And it seems to me that it is here that the major transition phenomena, characteristic of currency overvaluation, appear: this uneven flexibility of the various price groups causes the most serious dislocation in the country's economy, by disorganising relations between sales prices and cost prices. The producer's sales prices are wholesale prices, so quite flexible. Producers of standardised items, and notably industrial raw materials, are those whose revenue has been hit the hardest, but other wholesale prices are also going through an intense downward phase. From another angle, there is little sign of costs falling in the same proportion. The processing industries are obviously gaining an advantage from the extreme flexibility of raw materials prices, but this element is generally more than offset by the extreme rigidity of the other cost factors, namely wages and capital charges. (Triffin 1937: 37–38)

Triffin highlighted that relative prices can move for two completely different reasons. As heavily emphasized in economic theory, changes in fundamental factors such as technology and tastes will lead to divergent movements in prices of various goods and services. However, divergences

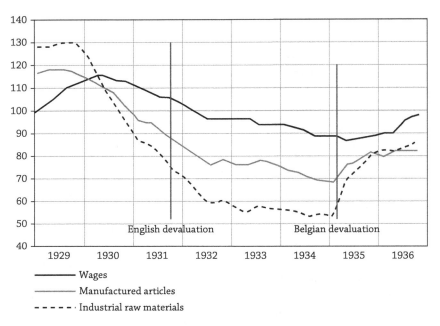

Figure 1.1 Flexibility of different types of prices, 1929–1936 (index 1927–1933 = 100).
Source: Triffin (1937: 37).

in price movements can also result from greater or lesser resistance of different categories of prices to a general movement of prices. Industries, he argued, "find their cost prices affected to varying extents by cyclical movements in prices, depending on the relative share that expenditure on more-business-cycle-sensitive raw materials takes up in their cost price, and by more rigid wage and capital charges." Triffin's conclusion was clear: "a general price movement tends to create new imbalances in the structure of production, rather than correcting old imbalances" (Triffin 1937: 38). Triffin also observed that, in the case of more differentiated goods, the imperfection of competition would curb the adjustment of prices. However, Belgium's exports were "des produits trop standardisés" (overly standardized products; Triffin 1937: 35). So, Belgium's pricing power in the international markets was very limited.

In the second part of the paper, Triffin demonstrated that the overvaluation of the Belgian franc, throughout the period 1932–1934, was reflected in the dislocation of the relationship between Belgian wholesale prices and costs (see Figure 1.1). Triffin pointed out that, since Belgium was specialized in the production of goods and services similar to those of international competitors (especially the United Kingdom), the sterling devaluation resulted in a rapid adjustment of the Belgian wholesale prices to the new international prices. However, domestic costs and prices were much less flexible. Consequently, profits in Belgian manufacturing were squeezed.

From a theoretical perspective, the dislocation in the structure of prices had serious consequences for the relevance of Cassel's theory in situations of disequilibrium. According to Cassel, the readjustment of wholesale prices would solve the disparity problem. In Triffin's view this was the moment at which difficulties really started, due to the uneven flexibility of the various price groups: "In this respect, the more perfect the adjustment of wholesale prices, the harder the situation producers find themselves in" (Triffin 1937: 38).

Like Taussig and Dupriez, Triffin also made a distinction between "sheltered" and "nonsheltered" sectors of the economy, with the sheltered industries operating mainly on the domestic market and relatively insensitive to international competition, and with the nonsheltered industries being subject to a much harsher international competition. Later, during the Great Inflation of the 1970s, this distinction would become very popular in the so-called Swedish model of inflation analysis (Lindbeck 1979). In the nonsheltered sectors of the economy, sales prices had to be aligned with world market prices, which had declined significantly in the 1930s, while costs were largely determined by domestic factors, which remained more stable.

Triffin then compared the profits in the nonsheltered and sheltered sectors of the Belgian economy (see Figure 1.2). The data revealed a

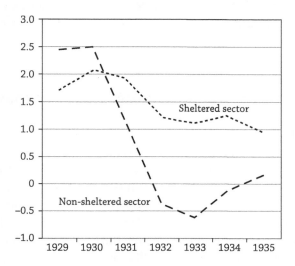

Figure 1.2 Profits of Belgian firms, 1929–1935 (in millions of Belgian francs).
Source: Triffin (1937: 40).

dramatic decline in profits in the nonsheltered sectors, while profits in the sheltered sector declined much less. In light of this, Triffin concluded that "the theory presented is once again clearly confirmed by looking at the chart. It reveals at a glance how the international group has been more badly affected by the events of 1931 [the devaluation of the pound sterling]" (Triffin 1937: 39). The Belgian economy's loss of competitiveness was thus not so much visible in the nonsheltered sectors' producer prices or the trade balance, but in a decline of profits in the nonsheltered sectors, a decline in production, and rises in unemployment. Moreover, the decline of industry had significant consequences for the financial system, as the banks made important losses on the loans they had given to industry. This was the direct reason for the March 1935 devaluation of the Belgian franc (see Section 1.2).

In the third part of the article, Triffin discussed the 1935 devaluation, for which he had made the calculations. He argued that, contrary to the deflation policy, a devaluation was the appropriate instrument to correct the dislocation of the structure of prices. Indeed, the devaluation, unlike the deflation policy, made it possible to rapidly adjust rigid prices. Moreover, the devaluation did not require any downward movement in prices. "The advantage of devaluation is thus: on the one hand, it leaves the imbalance for a shorter period; on the other hand, the price adjustment that it requires is upward rather than downward" (Triffin 1937: 42). Triffin concluded that the devaluation had, first, rapidly reduced the cost-price disparities with foreign competitors, especially the United Kingdom, Belgium's main competitor, and, second, it had allowed prices and wages to go up, compared to the earlier downward pressures under the impact of foreign competition and the deflation policy.

1.6 MONOPOLISTIC COMPETITION THEORY

While Triffin undertook important research on the Belgian economy during his time at Harvard, his dissertation, *General Equilibrium Theory and Monopolistic Competition*, under the direction of Schumpeter and with Leontief and Chamberlin also serving on the committee, dealt with a completely different issue. In the 1930s, imperfect and monopolistic competition theory had become very influential in the United States and in England with the seminal contributions of Chamberlin (1933) and Robinson (1933). It had its origins mainly in Marshallian partial equilibrium theory and brought the issue of economic power to the center of economic theory. In his work, Triffin tried to integrate monopolistic competition into general equilibrium theory, which was much more influential in economic thought on the continent of Europe and cherished by Schumpeter.

In March 1939, Triffin was awarded the prestigious Wells Prize for his doctoral thesis. The Wells Prize was instituted in honor of David A. Wells, a former US secretary of the Treasury. It is a biannual competition, open to seniors of Harvard College and graduates of any department of Harvard University, for the best essays in certain specified fields of economics. Thereafter, his thesis was also published in the prestigious *Harvard Economic Studies*.

In the preface to his book, *General Equilibrium Theory and Monopolistic Competition*, Triffin specified the respective roles of Schumpeter, Leontief, and Chamberlin in the development of his thesis, acknowledging that the original impetus came from Leontief. "Professor Leontief was the first with whom I discussed the problems to be investigated and the way in which they might be approached. I cannot overstress my indebtedness to him, as most of the present work evolved out of these preliminary, but fruitful and illuminating, discussions. While in the process of writing, I remained constantly in contact with him" (Triffin 1940: vii). Chamberlin followed the manuscript closely, "chapter after chapter," and Triffin emphasized that Chamberlin's remarks and observations were very valuable: "he kindly gave much time and attention to all the parts of the manuscript, and especially to those relating to the theories of imperfect or monopolistic competition." In fact, Triffin acknowledged: "Most of the modifications and improvements from the original to the present draft are due to his criticisms and suggestions." Schumpeter also read the whole manuscript. Schumpeter, to whom Triffin attributed his "interest in that branch of economic science," gave the manuscript his very close attention, with Triffin noting that it "bears everywhere the mark of his influence" (Triffin 1940: vii).

The book was divided into five parts: (1) the present state of monopolistic competition theories: Chamberlin, Robinson, Stackelberg, Pareto; (2) general evaluation and criticism of monopolistic competition theories; (3) the theory of external interdependence; (4) competition and the shape of the cost curve; and (5) the theory of profit.

In his final report for the CRB, Triffin summarized his work, emphasizing that his aim, very much in line with the approaches of Schumpeter and Chamberlin, had been to put imperfect competition theory firmly into the general equilibrium version of value theory and to present a more unified and generalized statement of monopolistic competition theory:

> The subject on which I have been working ("Monopolistic Competition and General Equilibrium Theory") embraces virtually the whole of value theory. It is an attempt to compare the latest doctrinal developments in Anglo-American economics with the general equilibrium theory of value developed on the continent by Walras, Pareto, etc. It is hoped that, on the basis of such comparisons and criticism, a more unified and generalized statement of the theory has been achieved, and that a number of uncertainties and contradictions have been eliminated. A new classification is presented in which the various types of competition are distinguished on the basis of a single criterion, with pure competition at one extreme and pure monopoly at the other, most actual cases belonging to the intermediary classes. A theory of profits is finally outlined, which, building up from Walras, Pareto, Schumpeter and Chamberlin, stresses both the dynamic and institutional aspects of profit: dynamic in their arisal, institutional in their appropriation. This serves as one more instance exemplifying the nature of the relationship existing between economic theory and social policy.[24]

Chamberlin's classes had a significant influence on Triffin. In his book, Triffin quoted approvingly Chamberlin's view that, with monopoly as the starting point, attention becomes focused on the "adjustment of economic forces within a group of competing monopolists, ordinarily regarded merely as a group of competitors" (Triffin 1940: 7). For Triffin, following in the footsteps of Chamberlin, the key issue in competition was "heterogeneity." This implied that there was no absolute monopoly, but that every "monopolist" had to confront the competition of many firms belonging to different industries. This shifted economics from the behavior of the industry, a key concept in Marshallian partial equilibrium economics, to that of the firm as the fundamental unit of analysis. Triffin then drew up a theory of monopolistic competition grounded in the general equilibrium approach. One of his main innovations was to introduce the concept of cross-elasticity of demand—the effect on the demand for one good resulting from a change in the price of another good—into a general equilibrium framework.

Triffin further developed a classification of market structures based on the competitive relationships between the firms, with monopoly/monopsony and competition on opposite sides. Triffin thus elaborated a systematic analysis of the various types of external interdependence between firms, analyzing the cases of pure competition, pure monopoly, and all the intermediate stages of monopolistic or imperfect competition. In this intermediate zone, Triffin made a distinction between product differentiation and oligopoly elements. Product differentiation makes the products of different firms imperfect substitutes for one another and gives rise to a declining sales curve for each firm. Oligopoly exists when the number of competitors is so small that changes in price or output of each one will have a significant effect on all the others. While the effects of product differentiation do not in themselves give rise to any indeterminacy, oligopoly is essentially indeterminate, as it introduces infinite series of actions and reactions.

Triffin's theory was devastating for Marshall's concept of industry. "The grouping of firms into industries, and the discussion of value theory within the walls of one isolated industry are perfectly valid and adequate procedures under purely competitive assumptions," he pointed out. Yet, he continued, they were "antiquated and entirely out of place in so far as monopolistic competition is concerned." His conclusion was clear: "Product differentiation robs the concept of industry of both its definiteness and its serviceability" (Triffin 1941: 188). The consequence was that economic theory lost its simplicity and definiteness. "Classical analysis was able to reach a high degree of simplicity and definiteness, owing to the use of a number of very drastic and limited assumptions: identity of each firm with an individual owner, purely competitive markets, perfectly free entry. As these assumptions are relaxed one after another, the theory gains in generality, loses in definiteness" (Triffin 1941: 189).

After the book's publication, various reviews were published in the main economics journals. Writing in the *American Economic Review*, John Ise described it as a "compact, thoughtful little book" (Ise 1940: 842). In his view, Triffin's summary of monopolistic competition doctrine had to be welcomed by economists "who have not time to read all the literature on the subject; and since it was checked by Professors Chamberlin, Schumpeter, and Leontief, and by others interested in the subject, it may be assumed to present the views of the writers discussed with reasonable accuracy." Ise also saluted Triffin's suggestion to abandon the concept of an "industry" and substitute it with "the whole collectivity of competitors," as all products compete, more or less, with any product. However, he questioned whether it had to replace Marshall's partial equilibrium approach, arguing instead that it might rather be complementary.

Milton Friedman's review of Triffin's book provided the first—but certainly not the last—occasion for him to cross swords with Triffin. Friedman (1941) strongly opposed the general equilibrium approach and defended the Marshallian approach. Friedman argued that most of the practical problems for which economists want to apply these theories are at the level of industries, not at the level of firms or of the economy as a whole. Consequently, as the concept of industry is so important and is not accounted for in monopolistic competition, Friedman argued that monopolistic competition theory was less relevant than the perfectly competitive model. Later, Friedman and Triffin would also have profound divergences on the reform of the international monetary system (see, especially, Chapter 4).

Margaret Joseph reviewed Triffin's book for the *Economic Journal*. Like several other reviewers, Joseph praised Triffin's overview of the theory of monopolistic competition and his capacity to synthesize the developments in economic theory "on both sides of the Atlantic." She characterized Triffin as "one of those economists who likes to keep his economics pure" (Joseph 1942: 358). "For those who regard economics as no more than an intellectual pastime or an exercise in logic," she said, "Mr. Triffin's book will be greeted with pleasure and complete satisfaction." However, Joseph regretted the complete absence of any approach toward economic policy. "Aesthetically and logically it is a fine piece of work. But for those—perhaps, naïve—idealists who look to the progress of economic science to point the way to more reasonable economic policies, the book is necessarily somewhat of a disappointment. It is distressing not so much that Mr. Triffin himself refrains from drawing any conclusions from his analysis, but that he is so entirely unaware that there are any conclusions to be drawn" (Joseph 1942: 359). This really illustrated how different Triffin's PhD work was from that which was to preoccupy him for much of his career, as all his other research was so strongly policy oriented.

Since the 1940s, the economic literature has largely acknowledged the originality of Triffin's contribution with respect to the seminal works by Robinson (1933) and Chamberlin (1933). For instance, his work was taken up by Perroux (1948) and Samuelson (1967) and figures prominently in Shackle's *The Years of High Theory* (1967), as well as in works by Backhouse (1985: 139) and Blaug (1997: 394). Moreover, as observed by Mosca (2013: 8), his work was very influential in all theories that aimed at building a theory of general equilibrium under monopolistic competition.

In the end, *General Equilibrium Theory and Monopolistic Competition* would make Triffin's reputation as a theoretical economist. However, it would be an outlier in his long career as a very empirical, policy-oriented economist, both before and after his doctoral work. But its effect on his path as an economist cannot be understated as it would shape his perception of economic phenomena, including in the monetary area.

1.7 A DIFFICULT YEAR IN BELGIUM AND RETURN TO HARVARD

After three years in the United States, Triffin returned to Belgium in August 1938. However, this would prove to be a difficult period in his life. Not only was he confronted with the problems of "reverse cultural shock," but also he had dire problems in finding an appropriate job.

In the first instance, Triffin still had to finish his Harvard thesis. He would do this in Flobecq (Wilson 2015: 132). At the end of October 1938, he completed the thesis and sent his work to his professors in Harvard, where it could be deposited in his cherished Widener Library. In February 1939, Triffin was officially awarded the PhD degree. He was the first Belgian to obtain a Harvard doctorate, something he would be very proud of.

However, life in Belgium was much more difficult for Triffin. In the autumn of 1938, he became a lecturer at the University of Louvain, teaching the course "Economie des transports, le commerce international et interrégional et l'économie agraire." But this was only an "enseignement accessoire," as Dupriez did not want to propose him for an appointment at the University of Louvain. Indeed, Triffin's relationship with Dupriez had significantly deteriorated. As Triffin explained in *Conseiller des Princes*, this deterioration was an important reason that he could not get a decent job in Belgium: "For a whole host of reasons, all of very different importance. The first, but by far not the least, was Professor Léon-H-Dupriez's disappointment that I had not taken up industrial location studies, that he had assigned to me, at Harvard." But this was only part of the problem, as Dupriez refused to acknowledge that Triffin's Harvard degree should excuse him from writing a second thesis "to gain a doctorate at Louvain" (Triffin 1990: 23). Triffin's hope that he could secure a job in the Economic Service of the NBB, like several previous CRB fellows, also evaporated. Indeed, the bank had already recruited many economists from the francophone Catholic University of Louvain and now wanted to broaden its recruitment.

In those days, Triffin was living a sort of hermit life. In a letter to Perrin Galpin of the CRB, he was very pessimistic about his life in Belgium, as respects both the chance of finding a job and the conditions for undertaking research, as he wrote to Galpin on January 4, 1938:

> About getting a job, I have unfortunately no further news to tell you, although I have been here for nearly half a year by now. At Louvain, hopes and half-promises are plentiful, but they are built upon macabre anticipations concerning the health of a dear old man who, I hope, will fool them for quite a time yet. . . .

Under the circumstances, you will not be surprised to hear that the enthusiasm with which I came back here after a three years' absence is rapidly wearing very thin. There is a French saying which I have just heard today: "au pays des promesses, on meurt de faim" [in the land of promises, one dies from hunger].... You will probably think that my letter shows an exaggerated pessimism, which is only a reflexion of the temporary difficulties and disappointments encountered in the last months. I do not think it is so. I am really afraid that outside of the National Bank, almost any job will mean a complete impossibility to pursue any activity of a scientific kind. Library difficulties and others are already in the way; with most of the time taken by office work. I do not see how it will be possible to avoid giving up all for what I have been working in the last three years. It is an outcome I am most reluctant to contemplate. The other aspects presented by the old continent in these days do not cheer me up. It is only now that I realize the meaning of American life and ideals.[25]

But the news from Harvard was much better. Not only was his thesis well appreciated, as shown by the award of the Wells Prize, but also he was offered a position as instructor in economics at Harvard University for three years. For Triffin, the choice was simple: "Harvard offered me a post as assistant, with decent pay—2.500 dollars a year—instead of the equivalent of less than 300 dollars that I could have got at Louvain as a library assistant and Professor of Transport—a subject that I knew nothing about!" (Triffin 1990: 24). So, after a completely disappointing year in Belgium, Triffin returned to the United States in the summer of 1939, accepting the position of instructor of economics at Harvard University for three years.

During this period, Triffin continued his theoretical research and published works related to his PhD thesis. In July 1939, Triffin was a visiting scientist at the Cowles Commission in Colorado Springs. The Cowles Commission was founded in 1932 by Alfred (Bob) Cowles 3rd, *Chicago Tribune* heir, who had become a Colorado Springs investment counselor (Dimand 2019). Disillusioned by the failure of forecasters to predict the Great Crash, Cowles promoted the use of formal mathematical and statistical methods in economics, initially through summer research conferences in Colorado and through support of the Econometric Society. In 1939, Triffin participated in its Fifth Annual Research Conference, presenting a paper entitled "Monopoly in Particular Equilibrium and in General Equilibrium Economics," later published in *Econometrica* (Triffin 1941). The Cowles Commission would play an important role in the development of economics and several of its collaborators were honored with the Nobel Memorial Prize. In 1939 the commission moved to Chicago and, in 1955, to Yale, where Triffin was then a professor (see Section 4.2).

When Triffin decided to go back to Harvard, he expected to find a more appropriate job in Belgium after a few years, whether at the University of Louvain or at the NBB. However, things turned out differently. Not only was there the German invasion of Belgium in the summer of 1940, but also on the ship to the United States he met the woman of his life. "The outbreak of war in 1940 made my return to Nazi-occupied Belgium unthinkable, and—most of all—I had met on one of the last trips of the *Normandie* a girl whom I loved at first sight, asking her to marry me after only six hours of conversation." Many of his friends were skeptical about this marriage, but, as Triffin observed: "This ship-board romance has—contrary to dire warnings—happily persisted now for 42 years and brought us three beloved and loving children and four very dear grandchildren" (Triffin 1981a: 241).

In 1942, Triffin moved on to a job on the staff of the Board of Governors of the Federal Reserve System in Washington. In the process, his research interests shifted completely, away from pure economic theory and toward international monetary economics. In his 1981 autobiographical article, Triffin himself observed that "when the opportunity came at the Federal Reserve, I gladly forgot monopolistic competition and pure theory. I have never regretted it" (Triffin 1981a: 242). He would become, for the rest of his career, a policy-oriented economist. However, imperfect competition theory and general equilibrium would shape his vision and approach to economics. In his perception of international monetary phenomena, he would be attentive to market power and economic interdependencies.

NOTES

1. van Zeeland, Mémoires, I.B., PVZA.
2. Report by Paul van Zeeland, PUA.
3. Janssen, Comment par une lente évolution la fonction monétaire de l'Institut d'émission est devenue dominante, AEJA.
4. Lettre de remerciement to P. van Zeeland, August 9, 1934, RTA.
5. Lettre d'acceptation de Triffin comme assistant, August 6, 1934, RTA.
6. Application for CRB fellowship by Robert Triffin, March 17, 1935, BAEFA.
7. Application for CRB fellowship by Robert Triffin, March 17, 1935, BAEFA.
8. Report by Robert Triffin, January 31, 1936, BAEFA.
9. Report by Robert Triffin, January 31, 1936, BAEFA.
10. Report by Robert Triffin, January 31, 1936, BAEFA.
11. Report by Robert Triffin, January 31, 1936, BAEFA.
12. Report by Robert Triffin, January 31, 1936, BAEFA.
13. Report by Robert Triffin, January 31, 1936, BAEFA.
14. Report by Robert Triffin, January 31, 1936, BAEFA.
15. Report by Robert Triffin, January 28, 1937, BAEFA.

16. Report by Robert Triffin, January 28, 1937, BAEFA.
17. Report by Robert Triffin, January 15, 1938, BAEFA.
18. Report by Robert Triffin, January 15, 1938, BAEFA.
19. Letter from Joseph A. Schumpeter to the CRB Educational Foundation, April 19, 1938, BAEFA.
20. Report by Robert Triffin, August 9, 1938, BAEFA.
21. Report by Robert Triffin, August 9, 1938, BAEFA.
22. Report by Robert Triffin, August 9, 1938, BAEFA.
23. Report by Robert Triffin, January 15, 1938, BAEFA.
24. Report by Robert Triffin, August 9, 1938, BAEFA.
25. Letter from Robert Triffin to Perrin Galpin, January 4, 1938, BAEFA.

CHAPTER 2

Money Doctor in Latin America

2.1 INTRODUCTION

Like many of his colleagues from Harvard and, indeed, economists from across the United States, Robert Triffin moved to Washington during World War II. Triffin started working at the Board of Governors of the Federal Reserve System in the summer of 1942. It is noteworthy that, at that time, the Federal Reserve System was still a relatively young institution. In fact, Triffin was two years older than the Federal Reserve System, which had been established in 1913.

Washington became a cosmopolitan place during the war, as many governments in exile had important delegations there to negotiate agreements with the United States. Paul van Zeeland (Triffin's Louvain professor; see Chapter 1) was there for Belgium and Jean Monnet and Robert Marjolin for France, and they became close friends of Triffin (see Chapters 3 and 5). Once the United States got involved in the war, federal agencies started hiring not only international specialists from US universities but also immigrants and refugees, especially to provide expertise on the countries they had left. Many academic economists joined the Federal Reserve Board. Nicholas Dawidoff, in his biography of his grandfather Alexander (Shura) Gerschenkron, went so far as to describe the Federal Reserve as "a university in exile, an economics department with no students," providing further a vivid description of the atmosphere at the Fed. "At meal times, the Fed's top floor cafeteria was packed with tweedy professors from Yale, Princeton, the University of Chicago, and it seemed some days, half the Harvard economics department, all of them avidly discussing the subtleties of fiscal policy with men whose speech bore thick traces of Hungary, Greece, Spain, Germany, and England (John Maynard

Robert Triffin. Ivo Maes, Oxford University Press (2021). © Oxford University Press.
DOI: 10.1093/oso/9780190081096.001.0001

Keynes and Sir John Hicks both made appearances at the Fed)" (Dawidoff 2003: 136–137).

Matters were also moving in a positive direction for Triffin on a personal level. He married his American sweetheart, Lois Brandt, on May 30, 1940, in New York. Two years later, he acquired US nationality and his first son, Nicholas, was born in Boston on May 30, 1942. His second son, Marc Kerry, was born in Washington on June 17, 1945. Later, when Triffin was in Paris, he had a third son, Eric, on June 29, 1951. While Lois was of Jewish origins (but not very practicing), the couple decided to give their children a Catholic education, but one that was very liberal and open, consistent with Triffin's own progressive Catholicism.

During his years at the Federal Reserve, Triffin worked mainly on Latin America and took part in several missions on monetary and banking reforms. They were part of the Roosevelt administration's Good Neighbor Policy and imbued by New Deal values. Triffin was an open and multicultural person, with both his Belgian and American background (see Chapter 1). As a progressive Catholic with a strong grounding in economics, he was the ideal person for this new type of monetary reform missions. Triffin himself described his reform proposals as "truly revolutionary at the time." He emphasized that the aim was to put monetary and banking policy at the service of the "overwhelming development objectives previously ignored in central bank legislation copied one from the other and trying merely to imitate a distant and largely inappropriate Bank of England or U.S. Federal Reserve model" (Triffin 1981a). This change in approach, from one size fits all to more customized structures, further reflected a more general change in economic paradigms, from classical economics to "Keynesian" economics (as seen in Chapter 1). The missions also had a significant geopolitical dimension. A key objective was to counter Nazi penetration, highly significant in Argentina where a part of the population had German origins and Juan Perón, the upcoming leader, had fascist sympathies. Moreover, the Latin American economy played an important role in sustaining the American war effort.

2.2 THE BOARD OF GOVERNORS OF THE FEDERAL RESERVE SYSTEM IN THE EARLY 1940S

Compared to continental European central banks, many of which had been founded in the early 19th century, the Federal Reserve System was established rather late in the day. The early monetary history of the United States was more than turbulent. While there were attempts to establish a central bank, they were not successful, showing the profound opposition to a centralized approach to central banking in the United States. This reflected deep currents in American society, "from deep-seated distrust of 'monied interests' to suspicion, bordering on hostility, between the country's South and West on the one hand and its Northeast on the other, to a strict constructionist interpretation of the Constitution that privileged the rights of the states over the federal government" (Eichengreen 2018: 361). Severe crises in 1893 and 1907, however, made clear that something needed to be done, and the Federal Reserve System was established in 1913. But it was a decentralized institution, with limited powers for the board in Washington and a strong role for the regional Federal Reserve Banks, especially the New York Fed. Certainly in times of crises, regional tensions and the flaws in the Federal Reserve's institutional structure would come to the fore, sometimes leading to heated debates on the regional reserve banks setting discount rates. The most serious disagreement occurred in June 1933, when, faced with a contagious run on the banks, the newly elected president, Franklin Delano Roosevelt, had no choice but to declare a bank holiday (Eichengreen et al. 2014: 15).

In 1934, President Roosevelt appointed a Utah banker, Marriner Eccles, to the chairmanship of the Federal Reserve System. Eccles only agreed to become chairman on condition that there would be greater centralization of decision-making for the board and its chairman (Meltzer 2003: 467). This implied breaking up the power of the regional reserve banks, and especially New York. Eccles himself was closely involved in drafting the 1935 Banking Act and setting up the Federal Open Market Committee, a crucial step toward the centralization of the Federal Reserve System. Power and authority thus shifted to the Federal Reserve Board in Washington, also involving board supervision over the reserve banks' foreign relations, a sensitive issue. Triffin, who worked mostly on Latin America, had to be attentive to relations with the other reserve banks, and not least the New York Fed.

As the board was expanding, there was a need for new offices. In 1937, the board moved into a new building on Constitution Avenue, bringing together all its employees in one place. Dawidoff painted a beautiful picture of it. "The Fed building had colored marble floors, intricate ironwork in the balustrades, gold-plated rest room doors, scalloped moldings, one of the only central air-conditioning systems in Washington, a recreation room, a free in-house barber, even a shoeshine man who came to your desk. That was all pretty swank by wartime standards" (Dawidoff 2003: 142).

One of Eccles's major objectives was to reinforce economic research at the board. Here, a key role was played by Emanuel Goldenweiser, director of the

Federal Reserve Board's Division of Research and Statistics. Goldenweiser was a Russian émigré with a background as a statistician. He became president of the American Statistical Association and the American Economic Association. In 1940, the board further attracted the eminent Harvard professor Alvin Hansen as special economic adviser.

With World War II looming, research on the economic impact of the defense program became a key topic, especially for Hansen (Nerozzi 2009). In September 1940, Hansen produced a tentative "Progress Report on Research Relating to the Defense Program and Its Impact upon the National Economy."[1] It was a broad-ranging memorandum covering a wide range of topics and issues. In the first instance, it analyzed the immediate magnitude and timing of the defense program and its effects on the various macroeconomic variables, such as national income and output, employment, investment, and public finances, as well as the dangers for bottlenecks, inflation, and labor unrest. It then went further into the financing of the program, giving attention to the Keynes plan for compulsory saving and direct monetary controls. Very much in line with Hansen's preoccupations on secular stagnation, the study discussed the postwar period. It analyzed issues relating to the postdefense slump, including "long-range proposals with respect to expansion, full utilization of resources, anti-depression policy, flexible tax structure, flexible program of public works, [and] a Fiscal Authority Planning Agency."

An important part of the memorandum concerned the impact of the war on foreign trade and US gold and foreign exchange policy, "especially in view of Germany's access to the gold and foreign balances of virtually the entire European continent." Of particular importance for this study was Hansen's conclusion that, in the event of a defeat of Great Britain and a break-up of the British Empire, the United States "would be more than ever centered on the Western Hemisphere. Indeed, this Hemisphere would probably be compelled to become largely self-sufficient." It thus underlined the strategic importance of Latin America, which would become Triffin's main area of responsibility.

The chief of the International Section of the Division of Research and Statistics was Walter R. Gardner, a New Englander, who had graduated from Brown and Harvard (Yohe 1990: 473). Like Triffin, he would go on to the International Monetary Fund (IMF) in 1946. A lot of the International Section's work was intended for use far beyond Washington. In early 1943, the board was asked to prepare handbooks on money and banking for the US forces, dealing with the European and Far Eastern countries to be liberated by the Allies. To take on this request, the board decided to expand the small International Section, mainly by recruiting economists of European origin, many of them refugees from Nazism, and so of "a somewhat different type than the average Board economist" (Stockwell 1989: 11). Among the recruits were Alexander Gerschenkron (born in Odessa, but educated in Vienna after fleeing Bolshevist Russia), Albert Hirschmann (from Germany), and Frank Tamagna (from Italy). Moreover, US economists, including Lloyd Metzler and Randall Hinshaw, were also recruited.

In the International Section, Triffin was in charge of work on Latin America[2] and undertook several missions there. The Triffin missions to Latin America represented a remarkable episode in US financial diplomacy. As argued by Helleiner (2009), they constituted a break, both in content and method, with the earlier approaches to international money doctoring, such as Kemmerer's Latin American missions (in the 1950s these US missions would be extended, for instance, to South Korea; Alacevich and Asso 2009).

Kemmerer, throughout his life, had been a staunch advocate of the gold exchange standard. In his work as a money doctor, he had overseen several currency reforms, typically with the establishment of the gold standard at its core (Kemmerer 1927: 4). Kemmerer had been Paul van Zeeland's professor at Princeton and influential in his doctoral thesis on the US Federal Reserve System and the initial stabilization plans for the Belgian franc after World War I (see Section 1.3). Kemmerer made a clear statement of his philosophy in his presidential address to the American Economic Association on December 29, 1926, "Economic Advisory Work for Governments." In his view, economic reforms were greatly hampered by economic fallacies, which involved a failure to understand fundamental economic principles. Stressing the importance of sound economic doctrine and basic economic principles, Kemmerer concluded:

> In economically new countries where accurate and wide-spread statistics are unavailable, and where the basis of financial reforms must be crude self-evident facts and basic economic principles, the best preparation for those who would formulate policies of financial reform is thorough and vigorous training in fundamental principles. Skill in making exact quantitative measurements is always valuable; but it counts for less on the world's economic frontiers than it does in economically more advanced places. Here the microtome is sometimes useful; but most pioneer work must still be done by the axe. (Kemmerer 1927: 4)

Kemmerer's advice, strongly grounded in economic principles, was very similar from country to country. As historian Paul Drake observed, "hardly a word in his [Kemmerer's] reports varied from Poland to Bolivia. In purely technical terms, he could have delivered most of his law by mail" (Drake 1989: 25).

This was in strong contrast to the US missions of the 1940s. US central bank officials, and certainly Triffin, not only rejected the classical liberal policies recommended by Kemmerer during the 1920s but also adapted their reform proposals to the economic and financial situation of each country and consulted with their Latin American counterparts. These elements were underlined by Gardner in his foreword to Triffin's monograph, *Monetary and Banking Reform in Paraguay*, published by the Federal Reserve Board in 1946 (Triffin 1946a):

> The main interest of the present study, however, lies in the recent adoption by Paraguay of new central banking legislation which marks, in two respects, a considerable departure from traditional patterns based on British and American experience. First of all, this legislation is specifically designed to meet the problems of a relatively small, agricultural economy, which is still in an early stage of development and which is particularly vulnerable to disturbances in international trade. Secondly, the central bank has been equipped with modern instruments of monetary control, reflecting recent developments in monetary theory and techniques that have not hitherto been systematically embodied in banking legislation. . . . Close contacts were also established with technicians from other Latin American central banks, thoroughly familiar with conditions and needs in that area. (Gardner 1946: iii)

But before discussing the Triffin missions, it is important to understand his basic view of the functioning of the Latin American economies.

2.3 TRIFFIN'S VISION OF THE LATIN AMERICAN ECONOMIES

Triffin's vision really comes to the fore in his contribution, "Central Banking and Monetary Management in Latin America," for a volume edited by Seymour Harris. The volume was very much based on contributions to Harris's Seminar on International Economic Relations at the Graduate School of Public Administration at Harvard University, and its roots in the spirit of the times is reflected in Harris's dedication of the book to "the continuance and expansion of the Good Neighbour policy" (Harris 1944: v).

After an overview of the history and structure of central banking in Latin America, Triffin focused on the special problems of Latin American monetary management. Triffin's analysis was very much in line with Dupriez's business cycle philosophy—illustrating that Triffin had not completely broken with Dupriez and his Louvain past—and to an extent Hansen's as well: focusing on the key determinants of the business cycle and the interaction with the monetary system (see Chapter 1). While in the older industrial countries the business cycle was largely determined by domestic savings and investment, Triffin argued that this was not the case in Latin America. In his view, the inflow or outflow of foreign exchange was the crucial driving force of the economic cycle there. "Domestic savings and investments are on a relatively minor scale, and the business cycle is dominated by the international movements of capital and by the fluctuations of imports and exports" (Triffin 1944b: 104).

In Triffin's view, this external dominance also had important implications for the classical theory of balance-of-payments adjustment. As discussed in Chapter 1, as early as the 1930s, Triffin had been critical of the classical theory, as it did not give much attention to situations of disequilibria. Here, Triffin would argue that structural factors, especially the dependence of Latin American economies on only a few export products, mostly raw materials, determined the evolution of their balance of payments. Consequently, the traditional price and cost factors played only a minor part in balance-of-payments trends in Latin America, a strong contrast to the older industrialized countries. Triffin felt that this had serious implications for the orthodox gold standard theory. "The essential weakness of the theory," he said, "is that the fluctuations of the balance of payments in Latin America are determined only to a minor extent by international cost comparisons" (Triffin 1944b: 108). For most Latin American countries, exports were dominated by one or a few agricultural products or industrial raw materials, "the supply of which may be determined by the vagaries of the weather and the demand for which is predominantly influenced by the state of the business cycle in the buying countries" (Triffin 1944b: 108). Consequently, Triffin emphasized the dependence of the Latin American economies on the business cycle in the industrialized countries.

In a later article, "Monetary Developments in Latin America," Triffin (1945) showed in detail how a few products dominated the Latin American countries' exports (see Table 2.1). This was so not only for the small economies but also for the largest economies, as the two leading export products—lead and gold for Mexico, meats and wheat for Argentina, and coffee and cotton for Brazil—accounted for more than 30% of total exports for Mexico and Argentina, and for Brazil even more than 60%. For Triffin, this reminded him of situations of imperfect competition.

Table 2.1 IMPORTANCE OF LEADING EXPORT PRODUCTS IN TOTAL TRADE
OF LATIN AMERICAN COUNTRIES, 1938

Country	Leading Export Products in Order of Importance		Percent of Total Export Trade From	
	First	Second	Leading Export	Two Leading Exports
South America				
Argentina	Meats	Wheat	23	36
Uruguay	Wool	Meat	44	66
Paraguay	Cotton	Meat	27	47
Brazil	Coffee	Cotton	45	63
Venezuela	Petroleum	Coffee	93	96
Colombia	Coffee	Petroleum	54	77
Ecuador	Cacao	Petroleum	23	39
Peru	Petroleum	Cotton	34	52
Chile	Copper	Nitrate	48	70
Bolivia	Tin	Silver	68	75
Central America				
Panama	Bananas	Cacao	74	85
Costa Rica	Coffee	Bananas	49	76
Nicaragua	Coffee	Gold	35	61
El Salvador	Coffee	Gold	87	92
Honduras	Bananas	Silver	59	75
Guatemala	Coffee	Bananas	61	90
Mexico	Lead	Gold	16	31
Island Republics				
Cuba	Sugar	Tobacco	70	77
Dominican Republic	Sugar	Cacao	60	74
Haiti	Coffee	Cotton	50	65

Source: Triffin (1945: 524).

Triffin then developed a further criticism of the orthodox gold standard theory. In Hume's price-specie-flow approach, the automatic adaptation of the money supply to fluctuations in the balance of payments was considered as perfectly normal and even desirable, as it would restore balance-of-payments equilibrium. As Triffin noted, "A favourable or an unfavourable balance of payments was taken as a sign of a fundamental disequilibrium in international price and cost levels, and it was assumed that the disequilibrium would be corrected by the domestic expansion or contraction brought about by the inflow or outflow of exchange" (Triffin 1944b: 108). But he disagreed completely with this view of things—or at least considered it inapplicable to the Latin American situation. As the balance-of-payments disequilibria in Latin America were not caused by price and cost disparities, movements in the money supply would amplify price and cost disequilibria. The gold standard was procyclical and exacerbated cyclical fluctuations.

For Triffin, the automatism of the gold standard prevented any control, "whether national or international," over monetary phenomena (Triffin 1947: 177). This also raised the issue of the availability of accurate and credible statistics to understand monetary phenomena. At the Federal Reserve Board, very much under the impetus of Goldenweiser, the Division of Research and Statistics was making significant efforts to improve monetary and banking statistics. In 1943, the board produced an important volume, entitled *Banking and Monetary Statistics* (Board of Governors of the Federal Reserve System 1943), running into 979 pages. In his introduction, Goldenweiser (1943) remarked that the volume was for the most part a "by-product of bank supervision and credit administration." He concluded by arguing that the series, even if they might "inspire awe, they should also inspire confidence. They are an augury that credit policy can be based in the future, as in the past, on fact rather than fancy."

While Triffin was part of a generation of economists with a Keynesian Weltanschauung, from a methodological point of view he was very much a "monetarist," emphasizing the importance of the money supply for economic developments. As a result, he was very interested in monetary and banking data. In his various articles and studies on Latin America, Triffin would present data and statistical analyses of changes in the money supply and its counterparts. Triffin (1945) provided, for the different countries of Latin America, a breakdown of the increase in the money supply that distinguished between "international" money (from increases in gold and foreign exchange reserves) and "domestic" money (from credit from the central bank or private banks). Here, his work was in keeping with the tradition of the Federal Reserve's monetary analyses (see Chapter 10 in *Banking and Monetary Statistics*, Board of Governors of the Federal Reserve System 1943) and pointed up the importance of international factors (balance of payments) for trends in the evolution of the money supply for most Latin American countries for the period 1939–1944 (see Table 2.2).

In further analyses, Triffin would produce statistical breakdowns of the counterparts of the money supply into three components: net international reserves of the central bank, the credit money of the central bank and Treasury, and the credit money of all banks other than the central bank. Triffin was not alone for this work. For example, for the study on Colombia, the detailed technical analyses of monetary and banking activity, both text and tables, were prepared by David L. Grove, one of

Table 2.2 CHANGE IN THE MONEY SUPPLY IN LATIN AMERICAN COUNTRIES FROM 1939 TO 1944 (IN MILLIONS OF LOCAL CURRENCY UNITS)

Country	Local Currency Unit	Total	From Gold and Foreign Exchange Reserves	From Domestic Factors
South America				
Argentina	Peso	3,338	3,024	314
Uruguay	Peso	168	252	−84
Paraguay	Guarani	34	27	7
Brazil	Cruzeiro	28,956	11,046	17,910
Venezuela	Bolivar	292	308	−16
Colombia	Peso	261	235	26
Ecuador	Sucre	453	426	27
Peru	Sol	692	95	597
Chile	Peso	3,863	1,671	2,192
Bolivia	Boliviano	1,326	839	487
Central America				
Costa Rica	Colón	109	62	47
Nicaragua	Córdoba	58	27	31
El Salvador	Colón	47	42	5
Honduras	Lempira	7	11	−4
Guatemala	Quetzal	14	14	0
Mexico	Peso	2,473	922	1,551
Island Republics				
Cuba	Peso	414	425	−11
Haiti	Gourde	16	26	−10

Source: Triffin (1945: 531).

Triffin's junior colleagues at the Division of Research and Statistics and also a Harvard graduate (Triffin 1946a: 25). Later, after Triffin left the Federal Reserve System, Grove would become the main person responsible for Latin America at the board.

In an early article, *Money and Banking in Colombia*, Triffin (1944a) had already given a detailed analysis of trends in the money supply and its sources in Colombia (see Figure 2.1). In the 1920s, the prosperity of export markets and the inflow of foreign capital led to a strong increase in international reserves. But the increase in the money supply was even greater as domestic credit expansion (central bank and commercial bank credit) also contributed to a strong inflationary expansion of money and credit. When, in 1929, the pendulum swung in the other direction, the

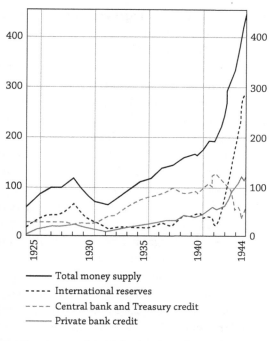

Figure 2.1 Sources of money supply of Colombia (in millions of pesos).
Source: Triffin (1944a: 61).

central bank was similarly unable to control the sharp deflationary impact of the adverse balance of payments and of the domestic contraction
in private banking credit. The gold standard functioned in a procyclical
manner and amplified the business cycle. It thus came as no surprise that,
in 1931, the gold standard broke down in most Latin American countries.
In the ensuing period, credit expansion, especially by the central bank,
led to an expansion of the money supply. With the onset of World War
II, the picture changed dramatically, triggering a boom in Latin American
exports. Consequently, international reserves expanded, leading to strong
inflationary tensions.

For Triffin, the policy conclusion was clear, and just the opposite of
the classical gold standard adjustment: "the proper policies to be followed
should be to offset and neutralize the effects of such erratic fluctuations
of the balance of payments on the domestic money market rather than
to magnify them through cumulative contraction or expansion" (Triffin
1944b: 108). Triffin categorically rejected any general or uniform approach
toward monetary policymaking in Latin America. In his view, the nature of
key monetary problems as well as the structure of monetary institutions

and markets and the efficacy of techniques of monetary control varied fundamentally from country to country.

This was reflected in Triffin's (1944b) overview of the structure of central banking in Latin America, where he distinguished four types of central banks: the discount banks (especially on the west coast), modern central banks (Argentina and Mexico), the all-purpose banks (like Guatemala or Paraguay, where Triffin would undertake important missions), and absence of central banking (like Brazil, Cuba, or Honduras).

Triffin described the central banks of the west coast (Bolivia, Chile, Colombia, Ecuador, and Peru), as well as those of El Salvador and of Venezuela, as "discount banks." He argued that they displayed "an extreme degree of orthodoxy which deprives them of any real control over the supply of money and credit" (Triffin 1944b: 96). The west coast central banks had received their organic laws from the Kemmerer missions of the 1920s. Triffin admitted that, as lenders of last resort, these central banks played a critical role in the avoidance of bank failures, which typically accompany a financial panic. However, Triffin was largely critical of the heritage of Kemmerer. He criticized not only the procyclicality of the gold exchange standard, which Kemmerer had introduced, but also the fact that Kemmerer's monetary policy framework was not suited for the type of financial markets of these countries:

> Monetary management, in particular, remained outside their sphere of action. The money was tied to a rigid gold or gold exchange standard, the only way in which the bank could influence it being the manipulation of the discount rate. Eligible paper, however, was scarce, and the discount rate soon proved a very illusory weapon of control, even more than in the older industrial countries with well-developed financial markets. (Triffin 1944b: 97)

On the contrary, Triffin felt that Mexico and Argentina had the most modern and powerful central banks in Latin America. He especially appreciated the Argentine central bank, "an outstanding institution among central banks not only in Latin America but in older countries as well." Raúl Prebisch played a key role in setting up the bank. Prebisch became the first general manager, serving from 1935 to 1943, and under his "brilliant leadership" the bank introduced new techniques of monetary management. An important role was also played by Otto Niemeyer, an executive director at the Bank of England, who had prepared the initial legislation (Niemeyer has become famous for having finished first among 104 candidates on the UK civil service entrance exam of 1906, with Keynes coming second).

The Argentine central bank had a wide range of instruments at its disposal, including open market operations. This made it possible for the central bank to neutralize the liquidity it created when buying foreign exchange. The bank was also responsible for the supervision of the private banks and for the exchange control system. According to Pérez Caldentey and Vernengo (2011), exchange controls, implemented through a system of auctions, are considered to be Prebisch's "most important contribution in the field of monetary economics."

The third category Triffin distinguished were the "all-purpose banks," in Guatemala, Paraguay, Haiti, Uruguay, Costa Rica, and Nicaragua. These were state banks of a rather heterogeneous character, mixing traditional monetary and central banking functions with commercial, agricultural, and even mortgage banking activities. Lastly, according to Triffin, in certain countries (Brazil, Cuba, Panama, Dominican Republic, and Honduras), the state banks could not be considered as real central banks as they did not have the power of monetary issue. In some of these countries the Treasury issued coins and/or certificates, and the US dollar circulated widely in most of these countries.

Triffin went on to discuss two other structural characteristics of Latin America, which imposed significant constraints on monetary policy: recurring deficits in public finances and the absence of well-developed financial markets. Consequently, it was mostly impossible for these states to finance their deficits via recourse to the general public or the private banks. The deficits had thus to be covered through foreign borrowing or monetary financing.

Given, then, the completely different economic and institutional environment of Latin America, Triffin was very critical of the traditional stabilization plans, as elaborated by the League of Nations in the 1920s. "The League's advice, however good in general, was primarily derived from the experience of the more stable and diversified economies of industrialized nations and could often be rightly regarded by less developed countries as impracticable or even irrelevant to their problems" (Triffin 1944b: 97). In Triffin's view, the success or failure of stabilization plans would depend very much on the willingness of monetary and financial advisers to "abandon generalizations and recommendations of supposedly universal validity." In this respect, Triffin was critical of exchange rate adjustments as an instrument of economic policy in the Latin American countries. He questioned the efficacy of a devaluation to correct balance-of-payments deficits, as these were highly specialized countries, with few export products, facing inelastic demand. Moreover, a devaluation in one country would probably be followed quickly by devaluations of the competitors, very much eroding the competitiveness effect of the devaluation. It is clear that Triffin's analysis was strongly shaped by his background in imperfect competition theory, as he portrayed the Argentine situation as one that "recalls the case of oligopolistic competition in which none of the sellers are usually able to profit for very long from price-undercutting policies" (Triffin 1944b: 112).

Triffin was positive about the use of direct quantitative controls on exchange transactions, and this would remain a constant element of his thinking (see Chapter 3). Triffin was aware that such ideas were "extremely controversial." He acknowledged that any system of exchange control was difficult to administer too. Moreover, there was always a temptation to use the system in a discriminatory fashion or for purposes that were not related to its original aims. But, in Triffin's view, policymakers were far too much influenced by the European experience, which, in his view, was much worse than the Latin American one:

> The position taken by many economists on this point appears to be inspired, to a considerable degree, by the study of European exchange-control regimes, in which aggressive or political considerations and discriminatory practices often played a much more important part than was the case in most Latin American countries. Latin American controls themselves were far from blameless, and I do not defend, any more than I reject, all controls *in globo*. (Triffin 1944b: 112, original italics)

Wrapping up his discussion, Triffin, who had become very much involved in the discussions of the international monetary system (see Section 2.5), discussed the main plans for the postwar international monetary order, especially those of Keynes and White. He acknowledged the importance of these plans for the Latin American economies but emphasized that domestic monetary stabilization would remain primarily the responsibility of the national monetary authorities. "Stabilization loans or long-term loans will be invaluable or worthless," he argued, "depending on whether they operate in a domestically stable or unstable monetary environment" (Triffin 1944b: 115). Elaborating frameworks for domestic monetary stability was indeed the crucial aim of the Triffin missions in Latin America.

2.4 TRIFFIN'S LATIN AMERICAN MISSIONS

The Triffin missions to Latin America would come to exemplify the new orientation of US financial advisory work. They were part of a broader ideological shift in US policy associated with Roosevelt's New Deal ideas, giving the state a more important role in the management of the economy. Key elements were skepticism toward the orthodox policies of Kemmerer and the old New York financial elite, as well as sympathy for efforts of Latin American governments to stimulate economic growth through state-led initiatives. As a pacifist and progressive Catholic, Triffin felt very much at ease with the ideals of the activist Good Neighbor economic policy and his sympathies lay with those in Latin America who promoted social and political reform.

With Eccles at the helm, the Federal Reserve Board wanted to establish its pre-eminence in the Federal Reserve System, and in the international arena too. This implied bringing into line the New York Federal Reserve Bank, which traditionally had a leading role in international missions. Moreover, there was a rivalry with the Treasury, which evidently was also involved in international monetary and financial relations.

With the start of US involvement in World War II in December 1941, power shifted to the government, just as in World War I. According to its official history, the Federal Reserve System came "under Treasury control" (Meltzer 2003: 579). It was also the Treasury, and especially Harry Dexter White, the powerful director of the Division of Monetary Research, that would elaborate the US plans for a postwar international monetary system, with the Federal Reserve System playing only a secondary role.

For the Federal Reserve Board, the first opportunity to step up its role in Latin America came in 1941, when the Cuban government asked the US State Department to provide advice on establishing a central bank (Helleiner 2009). At the time, Cuba had no central bank and its monetary system was dominated by the US dollar. Many of the ideas that Triffin put forward were already present in the advice offered by the Cuba mission. Key elements of the US mission's proposals were to demonetize the US dollar and create a new currency and central bank. The central bank was conceived not just as a lender of last resort, like in the old Kemmerer plans, but could also conduct a more activist monetary policy aimed at domestic needs. Even foreign exchange controls were part of the instruments for this new central bank.

During his years at the Federal Reserve Board, Triffin and his young family undertook several long missions in Latin America. He generally tended to visit several countries during a mission, sometimes staying as long as a few months in one country. According to Wilson (2015: 245), Triffin traveled to 18 of the 19 Latin American countries. Only Venezuela was missing. The focus of Triffin's first important mission was Paraguay. However, he received an urgent request from the Treasury to also take part in a Treasury-led mission to Honduras.[3] The head of the mission was

Edward M. Bernstein, the assistant director to White at the Treasury's Division of Monetary Research. In 1946, Bernstein would become the first director of the Research Department at the IMF, where he recruited Triffin to lead the Exchange Control Division (see Chapter 3).

Triffin's mission to Paraguay would become a significant success and would make Triffin's name as a "money doctor." In his study of Paraguay, Triffin (1946a: 16) emphasized that the Paraguayan monetary and banking reforms were a collective work. They were very much developed in Asunción, the hot and humid capital of Paraguay, with an important role played by Carlos A. Pedretti, the president of the Bank of the Republic of Paraguay. Moreover, they were widely discussed with central bank officials and economists, both in Washington and in various Latin American capitals. A crucial role was played by Raúl Prebisch, the former general manager of the central bank of Argentina, who stayed several months in Paraguay and became a close friend of Triffin. Triffin and Prebisch met for the first time in early 1944, during a series of seminars given by Prebisch at the Mexican central bank. Triffin invited Prebisch to work with him on the second part of the Paraguay project. The opportunity to work with Prebisch was of great benefit to Triffin, since, as observed by Dosman (2008: 193), few experts "possessed Prebisch's combination of language, practical expertise, and reputation."

In *The Life and Times of Raúl Prebisch, 1901–1986*, Edgar Dosman presented a vivid description of Prebisch's mission in Asunción. Pedretti and his colleagues were eager and attentive. Moreover, they were strongly committed to building an autonomous central bank with an efficient exchange control division, "against the long odds of political interference and corruption." Triffin was delighted with the results and tried to enlist Prebisch for further advisory work with the US Federal Reserve System in Latin America. Initially, Prebisch declined, as he wanted to stay in Argentina. Later, Prebisch was a consultant for the mission of Triffin and Henry Wallich in the Dominican Republic (Wallich and Triffin 1953: 25).

The monetary and banking reforms in Paraguay consisted of three main components (Triffin 1946a): a monetary reform, with a new monetary law; a central banking reform, with a new organic law for the Bank of Paraguay; and a new general banking legislation.

The first part of the reform was the new monetary law, which was put into place on October 5, 1943. The aim was to put an end to a chaotic monetary situation resulting from the coexistence of two monetary units: the theoretical gold peso and the actual paper peso. Both pesos were abolished and a new monetary unit, the "guaraní"—a reference to the indigenous people of Paraguay—was created. It was divided into 100 céntimos. Triffin was proud of the reform: "the guaraní was immediately accepted by the population" (Triffin 1990: 26).

The old paper peso had been tied de facto to the Argentine paper currency. Naturally, this implied that the Paraguayan peso not only was affected by difficulties originating in Paraguay itself but also suffered from the vicissitudes of Argentine monetary fluctuations. With the new law, a "composite exchange standard" was introduced (Triffin 1946a: 17). This standard defined external stability in terms of those foreign currencies that most affected the Paraguayan balance of payments. Initially, four currencies were taken into account: the Argentine peso, the pound sterling, the US dollar, and the Brazilian cruzeiro.

The second part of the reform, involving the establishment of the new central bank, emerged by Decree Law No. 5130 of September 8, 1944. On September 27, 1944, followed Decree Law No. 5286, on general banking legislation, which established the banking regime of Paraguay. The new central bank, the Bank of Paraguay, was divided into three departments: the Monetary Department, endowed with central banking functions; the Banking Department, which would operate as a commercial bank; and the Savings and Mortgage Department. In Triffin's view, this combination of functions was "imperative" given the structure of the Paraguayan financial system. Indeed, with one exception, all the Paraguayan banks were branches of foreign institutions, which were totally focused on foreign trade (Triffin 1946a: 18). Moreover, capital markets were nonexistent in Paraguay. This had two significant consequences: the absolute inadequacy of bank credit for economic life and serious difficulties in steering the money market through traditional central banking instruments. With its broad structure and missions, the Bank of Paraguay could correct for these deficiencies in the Paraguayan financial system.

Triffin further argued that, faced with similar problems, practically every Latin American country had created official or semiofficial credit institutions, to supply the types of credit that private banking was unable to provide. Indeed, one might add that these types of official or semiofficial credit institutions also existed in many European countries, such as Belgium (Buyst and Maes 2008: 19). Triffin (1946a: 19) also admitted that this broad central banking structure might lead to conflicts of interest, with commercial banking functions affecting monetary policy. However, he argued that the law had given the dominant role to the Monetary Department. Moreover, it had subordinated the bank's other departments to general policies, which were decided by the Monetary Board. The Paraguayan central bank was provided with a broad range of instruments of monetary and credit control, and these instruments, in Triffin's view, reflected "many fundamental innovations in the traditional routine of central banking" (Triffin 1946a: 20). Of crucial importance for Triffin was the integration, within the Monetary Department, of the banking supervision and exchange control functions. One might see here the influence of Prebisch, as this was also part of the Argentine experience. Triffin observed that a separation of the functions of banking supervision, exchange control, and central banking created many conflicts and problems of duplication. To combat these problems Triffin argued for a broad view of banking supervision. The aim of supervision should no longer be limited to protecting depositors. Instead, supervision should service the general objectives of monetary and credit policy, very much in line with Keynesian conceptions of economic policy. This was also the case for exchange controls. A further advantage of this broad approach was that the administration of exchange controls by the monetary authorities could prevent many abuses, "which are likely to develop when the controls are placed under the authority of a separate office, in which protectionist considerations may tend to predominate over monetary ones" (Triffin 1946a: 20).

The law further provided for a broad range of policy instruments, many quite novel for the time. The aim was to put the Bank of Paraguay in a strong position to control the money and foreign exchange markets, taking into account the specificities of the Paraguayan financial system. Among the instruments were the following:

- Foreign exchange controls. In Triffin's view, in- and outflows of capital had often been destabilizing, and certainly in Latin America. So, it was important to give the central bank the means to control them.
- Flexible reserve requirements (deposits of financial institutions at the central bank, calculated as a percentage of the liabilities of the financial institutions), with "drastic" powers for the Monetary Board on the rates of the reserve requirements and the type of liabilities concerned.
- The issuing and withdrawing of stabilization bonds. These bonds were liabilities of the central bank itself. They could be used to take the place of traditional open market operations, which were seriously hindered in Paraguay by the absence of a functioning government bond market.

As should be clear by this point, the monetary and central banking reforms in Paraguay implied a regime change: a shift away from monetary automatism to monetary management. This made it clearly necessary to provide adequate analysis and research to the monetary authorities. Accordingly, the research function of the Monetary Department was greatly reinforced and modernized.

The monetary reform in Paraguay was a great success, with Triffin himself often emphasizing the "revolutionary" character of the reforms. Other countries sought to replicate Paraguay's success, and several Latin American countries would ask the Federal Reserve Board for a "Triffin mission" for their central bank. This led to Triffin's involvement in important monetary and banking reforms in Guatemala, along with David Grove, and the Dominican Republic, with Henry Wallich, then at the New York Federal Reserve, which had the lead in that mission (in the 1950s Wallich would become a colleague of Triffin at Yale University; see Chapter 4). In his later life, Triffin would often go back to Latin America, undertaking important economic consulting missions.

Triffin's strongly held views on the need to tailor institutions and policies to country-specific situations shows through vividly in his reform proposals. In the Dominican Republic, the United States had had an important influence since the end of the 19th century. In the monetary area, this had been formalized, in June 1905, with the official adoption of the US gold dollar as the standard Dominican currency (its legal exchange rate for silver pesos was fixed at one to five). One of the key issues in the reforms was the transition from the dollar to the newly created Dominican peso. This also had consequences for the new monetary framework. As explained by Allan Sproul, the president of the New York Federal Reserve, "the legislation suggested by the Federal Reserve technicians and subsequently enacted places primary emphasis upon monetary stability" (Sproul 1953). So, as the shocks affecting the Dominican Republic were more of a domestic nature, the monetary framework was more focused on providing restraint against internal inflationary forces. This contrasted with Paraguay, where, as the shocks were more of an external nature, the monetary policy framework paid more attention to the exchange rate regime and foreign exchange controls.

Building on the success of the Triffin mission, the Federal Reserve Board also approved of an initiative for the preparation and publication of a series of studies on central banking in Latin America, in cooperation with these countries. Chairman Eccles sent letters to several governors of Latin American central banks, saying that he was pleased that the Federal Reserve project for the central banking studies had been well received and that he looked forward to the "invaluable collaboration" of the central bank concerned. "A similar reception to the project elsewhere," he noted, "indicates that the prospect of these studies is welcomed, that there is general willingness to cooperate in their preparation, and that they will therefore be of practical usefulness."[4] Triffin himself published two major studies for the Federal Reserve Board based on the work on these missions: *Money and Banking in Colombia* (Triffin 1944a) and *Monetary and Banking Reform in*

Paraguay (Triffin 1946a). In addition, his study on *Monetary and Banking Legislation of the Dominican Republic 1947* (Wallich and Triffin 1953) was published by the Federal Reserve Bank of New York.

A clear sign of the appreciation for Triffin's work was Goldenweiser's proposal in January 1944 of a significant increase in Triffin's salary, from $4,600 to $5,600 per annum. However, due to objections from the Personnel Committee, the increase was to be doled out in two phases.[5] The high regard in which Triffin was held at that time was further reflected in a request from White for Triffin to join the Treasury. Triffin declined the request, however. He was attached to his independence and he preferred to stay at the less influential Federal Reserve Board rather than join White's "regimented staff" (Triffin 1981a: 243). Triffin was indeed a monk in economist's clothing, strongly attached to his convictions, sacrificing even a more important position.

The Federal Reserve Board also supported the idea of periodic conferences of central banks of the Western Hemisphere. This could have important advantages, not only in terms of saving Federal Reserve resources for missions, but also in terms of macroeconomic benefits and prestige. The board was well aware of this:

> Specifically, these conferences should provide means by which the burden of furnishing technical assistance can be divided so that the Latin American central banks themselves can help one another instead of depending wholly on us. The conferences . . . should be useful to us, both in maintaining friendly relations with the rest of this hemisphere and in avoiding disturbance by our neighbours of our domestic credit and monetary conditions. . . . Our success will also work to the enhancement of American prestige and the cultivation of friendly and mutually helpful international relations.[6]

The first conference of central bank experts took place in Mexico City, from August 15 to 30, 1946. The conference was structured around three major themes: monetary and credit controls, balance of payments and foreign exchange problems, and cooperation among research departments of central banks. Even though by then he had left the Federal Reserve Board for the IMF (see Chapter 3), Triffin took part and presented his study on "National Central Banking and the International Economy" (Triffin 1946b). With the exception of Honduras, Panama, Cuba, and Haiti, all the Latin American countries were represented. The absence of Cuba was due to the fact that it did not yet have a central bank.[7]

According to Grove's minutes, Triffin and Prebisch largely dominated the discussions. A key issue was the nature of the business cycle. All the Latin

American delegates pointed to the crucial importance of developments in the United States for the economies of Latin America, with Prebisch eloquently distinguishing between "central" and "peripheral" countries. As Grove noted, "Dr. Prebisch's thesis is that the control of booms and depressions rests with the central and quasi-central countries, and that the peripheral countries can do relatively little to combat cyclical movements, although he admitted that unsound domestic policies of the peripheral countries could aggravate the situation." While it had already been evident from his first article in 1935 (see Section 1.3) that Triffin had clearly observed the effects of the business cycle in the industrial countries on the periphery, he did not completely agree with Prebisch. In Triffin's view, which was invariably close to the empirical reality, depressions were not always transmitted from the central countries. He also pointed to the supply conditions in the periphery. In his view, the depression in some of the agricultural countries in the late 1920s was caused by overproduction in these countries and not by falling demand in the central countries.

A second element of disagreement between Triffin and Prebisch concerned the definition of fundamental disequilibrium. This definition was not solely of academic importance, as it was also taken up in the IMF Articles of Agreement and required corrective actions by the authorities. Prebisch argued that fundamental disequilibrium should be defined in terms of cost-price relationships. Not surprisingly, with his background of the Belgian situation in the 1930s and general equilibrium theory, Triffin disagreed completely:

> Not all fundamental disequilibria manifest themselves in a disequilibrium in the balance of payments. It is most important to distinguish between the disequilibrium itself (or its causes) and its concrete manifestation in any given case. In accordance with the theory of general equilibrium, any disturbance in the economy of a country has repercussions and manifestations in various sectors. Thus, a disequilibrium which originates in external problems of international economic equilibrium may manifest itself not in a disequilibrium of the balance of payments, but in one which appears to be purely domestic, such as, for example, grave unemployment.

While Triffin and Prebisch enjoyed provocative discussions at the conference, they very much agreed on the topic of exchange control systems. They spoke about their experience in Argentina, Paraguay, and Guatemala. In their view, systems of exchange control were necessary in Latin America when cyclical evolutions in these countries were caused by fluctuations in the center countries.

2.5 TRIFFIN'S GLOBAL VIEW ON THE INTERNATIONAL MONETARY SYSTEM

During World War II, attention turned to the construction of a new postwar order. Roosevelt had an optimistic view of cooperation among the victors of the war. His aim was to build a new liberal world order (Van der Wee 1986: 347). The United Nations would become the political pillar of this new cooperative world order. With respect to the economic dimension, there was a broad consensus that it was imperative to avoid the competitive exchange rate devaluations and trade wars that had marked the 1930s. This vision was eloquently expressed by Morgenthau, the US Treasury secretary, at the Bretton Woods conference. He emphasized the importance of currency disorders in the downfall of the world economy and world order:

> All of us have seen the great economic tragedy of our time. We saw the worldwide depression of the 1930s. We saw currency disorders develop and spread from land to land, destroying the basis for international trade and international investment and even international faith. In their wake, we saw unemployment and wretchedness – idle tools, wasted wealth. We saw their victims fall prey, in places, to demagogues and dictators. We saw bewilderment and bitterness become the breeders of fascism, and, finally, of war. (as quoted in Daunton 2008: 3)

In the negotiations over the economic and monetary pillars of the new world order, the Treasury had the leading role for the United States. It strongly defended the US position as a creditor country. Treasury Secretary Morgenthau was also profoundly convinced that Germany should not become an industrial country again. Morgenthau himself had at best a minimal background in economics. Gladys Straus, a prominent New York donor, using a stereotype to which US financial circles were apparently not immune at the time, said that Roosevelt had managed to find "the only Jew in the world who doesn't know a thing about money" (as quoted in Steil 2018: 90). At the Treasury, Harry Dexter White took up a dominating role in the Bretton Woods negotiations. His parents were Lithuanian Jewish migrants who had escaped tsarist pogroms. White studied economics at Harvard with Taussig, Harvard's most influential economist in the early 20th century (see Section 1.3), receiving a PhD for his dissertation on *The French International Accounts 1880–1913* (White 1933). Like Triffin, he also received the Wells Prize for his doctoral dissertation. After some time in academia, he went to the Treasury in 1934 on the invitation of Viner (Steil 2013: 22), becoming director of the Division of Monetary Research and assistant Treasury secretary. Like many others in the United States, White was firmly anticolonial and considered Great Britain as a colonial empire. Though critical of British interests, he was sympathetic toward those of another US wartime ally; indeed, White's vision involved a much closer US relationship with the Soviet Union.

On the economic front, the new postwar world order consisted of arrangements for orderly finance and trade. The discussions on the monetary issues were concluded at the mountain resort of Bretton Woods in New Hampshire, in June 1944. There was a shrill contrast between the life-and-death struggles of the war, with the allied landing in Normandy, and the sometimes esoteric debates at the Bretton Woods conference. However, at stake in both was the kind of world order that would take shape in the aftermath of the war (Lamoreaux and Shapiro 2019). The Bretton Woods international monetary system was based on stable exchange rates and gave a prominent role to the US dollar as an international reserve currency. Moreover, two new institutions were established, the IMF and the International Bank for Reconstruction or Development (or World Bank). To promote free trade, and to avoid trade wars, the United States proposed the creation of the International Trade Organization (ITO).

During his time at the Federal Reserve, Triffin was also involved in international monetary matters. As early as September 1942, when he had just started working at the board, Gardner showed Triffin a numbered photostat of the Keynes plan for the International Clearing Union (Wilson 2015: 242). On March 2, 1945, Triffin attended a special meeting of the Board of Governors at which White and Bernstein discussed the Bretton Woods agreements and their implications for national and international monetary policies.[8] Triffin was also at the inaugural meeting of the IMF and World Bank in Savannah in March 1946.[9]

At the Federal Reserve Board, Triffin worked on the International Trade Organization dossier. In a note dated January 14, 1946, entitled "Exchange Control and Quantitative Trade Restrictions," he made an analysis of the ITO proposals.[10] He described the ITO as a "natural and necessary complement" to the IMF and the International Bank for Reconstruction and Development. Indeed, for Triffin, with his focus on balance-of-payments adjustment, quantitative trade restrictions fulfilled broadly the same functions as exchange controls. However, quantitative trade restrictions were not dealt with in the Bretton Woods agreements, but were covered in detail in the ITO proposals, and these were "far more specific in character than those devoted to exchange control in the Articles of the Monetary Fund." In his note, Triffin pointed out that, during talks on the Bretton Woods agreements, there had been a wide consensus that quantitative trade restrictions would form an indispensable complement to the IMF's provisions on exchange control, as both types of instruments had been used for similar purposes and with similar results. "Thus the ITO proposals are of vital importance for the success of monetary as well as of commercial cooperation by the United Nations."

Triffin then asked the question whether the ITO proposals on quantitative trade restrictions were well adapted to these objectives. First, Triffin was skeptical of treating exchange controls and quantitative trade restrictions separately, especially for safeguarding balance-of-payments equilibrium. Second, to stamp out discriminatory practices at the roots, Triffin wanted to outlaw procedures of administrative rationing and allocation, substituting them for a flexible and impersonal system in which foreign exchange would be auctioned: "Traders may buy whatever they please wherever they please (presumably from the cheapest source of supply) subject only to the auction premia that would arise with respect to less essential categories of transactions." Later, Triffin also participated in the ITO negotiations in Geneva on behalf of the IMF (see Section 3.2).

During these years Triffin was also involved in the negotiations of US loans to European countries like Belgium and France. In a note to Governor Szymczak in January 1945, Triffin underlined that the fundamental problem of the Belgian economy related to the supply side and that imports of food and materials were essential. "The industrial machine cannot work if it is not fed. If fed, it can contribute much more than it absorbs."[11] In 1947, the United States would adopt this approach with the Marshall Plan, a massive recovery plan for the European economy (see Section 3.3). On the Belgian situation, Triffin further observed, in line with the views of van Zeeland, his former professor at Louvain, that "the monetary legislation may have erred in the direction of financial conservatism." He said that "the present financial leaders in the Government represent the same groups responsible for a similar and disastrous monetary policy in the years 1933-1935." The then Belgian finance minister was Camille Gutt, who would become the first managing director of the IMF, where Triffin would start working in September 1946 (see Chapter 3).

Participating in US loan negotiations to European countries would be very important for Triffin's network and career. Triffin was a member of the US delegation in the negotiations for the loan to France, representing the Federal Reserve. The French delegation was led by Leon Blum, the former prime minister who had just been liberated from a concentration camp. Jean Monnet, with whom Triffin would cooperate closely on European monetary integration (see Chapter 5), was a member of the French mission too. In the US delegation, the Treasury, especially Bernstein, had a leading role. In 1946, Bernstein would become the first head of research of the IMF and Triffin one of his first recruits (Black 1991: 55).

In the mid-1940s Triffin became more and more interested in the changing nature of central banking and wrote several papers on this topic. In his view, central banking in most countries (not only in Latin America) lagged far behind the evolutions in economic theory and policy, marked by two world wars, the Great Depression, and the Keynesian revolution. The prevalent pattern of central banking was still that of a banker's bank or lender of last resort, "molded, more or less slavishly, upon the traditions of the Bank of England." Triffin emphasized that these traditions were the product of a very special historical and geographical environment. "Transplanted into other times and other countries, they have proved as futile and worthless as a banana tree would be, if moved from a tropical land into an Arctic climate."[12]

Triffin argued that central banking statutes still largely reflected the 19th-century ideals of the gold standard. This implied that variations in the volume of money were "completely and rigidly" governed by the inflow and outflow of monetary gold. In Triffin's view, such automatism was incompatible with modern concepts of monetary management. For Triffin, in line with Keynesian thinking, monetary policy should be an integral part of economic policy. It should then be no surprise that Triffin was also critical of the traditional 19th-century notion of central bank independence:

> Isolation, and often aloofness, from the organs of political power have proved a source of weakness, rather than of strength, for the new central banks. The growing impact of government finances upon the money market makes it impossible to dissociate monetary policy from governmental financial, fiscal, and even economic, policies. Unavoidable conflicts are left unsolved, necessary coordination is ignored, and, in the end, the independence of monetary authorities merely means that they are barred from influencing decisions the consequences of which they will not be able to escape.[13]

Triffin further argued that the central bank nationalizations in Europe after World War II, like in the United Kingdom and France, were not enough to face the challenges of postwar economic policymaking. In his view, monetary policy responsibilities were far too dispersed among various agencies and ministries. "Consolidation and coordination remain an indispensable prerequisite for effective management, whether public, semi-public or private."

As in his Latin American missions, Triffin also paid attention to the operational side of central banking. In his view, the traditional instruments of monetary policy reflected the older philosophy of monetary automatism and were not adequate for the new challenges. "Monetary authorities are asked to build a Boulder Dam, and given as tools as spade and a trowel."

In 1946, Triffin published his first important essay on the international monetary system, entitled "National Central Banking and the International Economy" (Triffin 1946b). It included an extensive discussion of the role of the IMF in the new international monetary system. It was published both in the *Review of Economic Studies* and in *International Monetary Policies* (Post-war Economic Studies No. 7 of the Board of Governors). Triffin presented the study at various conferences, including the first conference of inter-American central bank economists, held in Mexico City in August 1946 (see Section 2.4), and the annual meeting of the American Economic Association in Atlantic City, New Jersey, in January 1947 (published as Triffin 1947).

It proved to be a very influential article. An eminent former Bank of Italy governor, Paolo Baffi, devoted significant attention to the article in his laudatio for Triffin for the first San Paolo Prize for Economics (see Chapter 7). Baffi claimed that Triffin pointed up the fundamental inconsistency between the stability of the international monetary system and national sovereignty in economic policymaking; "he was the first thinker ever to emphasize that recurring crises and unrest in external economic relations stem from a fundamental dilemma existing between national sovereignty in economic policy decisions and the measure of international incompatibility inherent in such 'atomistic decisions'" (Baffi 1988: 16). While one might debate whether Triffin was the first economist to formulate this dilemma, Baffi's statement clearly shows Triffin's influence on the economics profession and the central banking world.

In the introduction to the article, Triffin underlined how the world had changed with the Great Depression and World War II. In his view, managed currencies were unavoidable. The crucial issue was to reconcile national objectives with international balance. "Any attempt to enforce rigid solutions patterned after orthodox gold standard doctrines would be even more futile in the postwar period than it has proved to be in the interwar period" (Triffin 1946b: 47–48). The focus of Triffin's paper was therefore on reconciling domestic monetary policies with the prerequisites of international balance. This was not an issue under the gold standard as the domestic money supply escaped the control of national authorities. However, in the new postwar world, this was no longer an option, as countries were now much more attached to national economic policy objectives.

As in his 1937 article, Triffin was very critical of the classical theory, which ascribed balance-of-payments disequilibria to international cost and price disparities. He raised two main criticisms, in line with his earlier work on cycles and imperfect competition theory, reinforced by his experience in Latin America:

> These views of the mechanism of international adjustment under gold standard assumptions are open to grave question. First, they fail to distinguish between a fundamental disequilibrium in one country's international position and world-wide disturbances in balances of payments associated with cyclical fluctuations. Secondly, the explanation of the readjustment of a country's balance of payments is vitiated by the underlying and totally unrealistic assumption of near-perfect competition between nations of roughly equal strength and importance in world trade. (Triffin 1946b: 55)

Triffin then raised the question of whether the international monetary system in the interwar period was a gold standard or a sterling exchange standard: "in recent years many writers have emphasized the central position occupied by Great Britain in the nineteenth century functioning of the gold standard . . . but the concrete implications of that assertion have not been fully drawn" (Triffin 1946b: 58). Triffin argued, following the analyses of Thomas Tooke in the early 19th century, that changes in the discount rate also had significant effects on capital movements. Consequently, as Great Britain was the major center of world trade and finance, the British discount policy immediately affected not only the domestic economy and prices but also other countries, thus transmitting British cyclical fluctuations. Triffin was thus very close to the ideas of Prebisch regarding "center" and "periphery."

Triffin further underlined the asymmetric nature of the adjustment process as the discount policy of debtor countries did not have the same effect. "Capital tended to flow toward them in times of prosperity and away from them in times of depression, irrespective of their discount policy. The effect of such fluctuations in capital movements was to smooth down cyclical monetary and credit fluctuations in the creditor countries, but to accentuate them in the debtor countries. To that extent the financial centers could shift part of the burden of readjustment upon the weaker countries in the world economy" (Triffin 1946b: 60). According to Triffin's statistical evidence, the consequence was that a restrictive British monetary policy would lead to an improvement in Britain's terms of trade and balance of payments, as prices in other countries, especially producers of raw materials in the periphery, were more affected than those in Great Britain. Triffin argued that the "improvement in the British terms of trade in periods of rising discount rates should not be surprising, in view of the special position of Britain as a financial center for world trade. On purely a priori grounds, it would appear at least as probable as the opposite pattern contemplated by the classicists" (Triffin 1946b: 61). Eichengreen (1992: 48) later labeled this the "Triffin effect."

Triffin had already concluded in his first article back in 1935 that raw material prices were the ones most affected by the Great Depression (see Section 1.3). The dominance of the London discount market had serious implications for the international adjustment mechanism, propagating shocks in the center of the world economy to countries in the periphery:

> Thus, the problem became essentially one, not of disparities between one country and the others, but of a simultaneous upward or downward movement engulfing most other nations along with Great Britain. . . . The failure of British discount policy to effect the type of readjustments contemplated in classical theory is thus easily understandable. It was due primarily to the *international* character of the London discount market, whose expansion and contraction affected foreign prices as much as or more than British prices. It is also explainable by the fact that producers of agricultural and raw materials are more vulnerable to cyclical and credit fluctuations than is the British economy. The main result of "orthodox" gold standard policies under such circumstances was to spread throughout the world at large any cyclical disturbance arising in major industrialized nations. (Triffin 1946b: 62–63)

As observed by Haberler (1947: 87), earlier writers, like Ralph Hawtrey, had already observed this phenomenon. Triffin (1946b: 63) agreed with this assessment, but he argued that these earlier writers had not systematically elaborated on the idea. Triffin further emphasized not only Keynesian quantity-type adjustments but also, in line with his analysis of the Belgian situation in the 1930s, imbalances in the structure of relative prices too. "Balance of payments deficits would be corrected in the end, but mostly through a general contraction in income and economic activity, rather than through direct price readjustments. Furthermore, the accompanying price changes would leave in their wake a basically unbalanced structure of international prices when the cyclical depression subsided and more normal conditions were restored" (Triffin 1946b: 63). As in his earlier analyses of Latin America, Triffin also made an explicit link with imperfect competition theory. "Price deflation and devaluation spread from country to country without increasing export receipts, especially if world demand for a nation's exports is relatively inelastic." He believed that this situation offered a strong analogy to that of oligopoly, "where each effort by one seller to cut into the competitors' markets is thwarted by the competitors' price retaliation" (Triffin 1946b: 80).

In Triffin's view, all this had important policy implications: compensatory policies should be followed to the fullest extent possible, effectively putting global liquidity at the core of the international monetary system. It was necessary to have a "high level of international reserves, especially in raw material and food producing countries, and the willingness to spend these reserves liberally in times of crisis and to accumulate them during prosperous years." Triffin also had a clear ranking of policy instruments, preferring exchange controls to devaluation. "When reserves are insufficient," he said, "foreign or international assistance—such as is contemplated under the International Monetary Fund—will be necessary. Failing this, exchange control should be used as a third line of defense, in order to continue compensatory policies and avoid the greater evils inseparable from deflation or currency devaluation" (Triffin 1946b: 80).

Triffin was quite optimistic about the new international monetary system with the IMF at its core. He noted, "A more constructive approach toward the problem is now in the process of effective realization." He pointed to the newly created IMF as "specifically designed to promote international monetary stability through the concerted action of all member countries." He argued that the IMF had two important advantages: the financial resources at its disposal and its influence on member countries' economic policies:

> First, the Fund has the financial machinery to help the members to maintain free and stable exchanges by supplementing their gold and foreign exchange resources in case of need. . . . Secondly, the Fund will wield a degree of influence over policy decisions of member countries. In some cases, the Fund has only the power to make recommendations, or the right to be consulted. In others, such as parity changes or the establishment of exchange control, action by a member is subject to the Fund's authorization or approval. (Triffin 1946b: 46–47)

Furthermore, Triffin believed that the IMF might develop a leadership and moral influence "far beyond the scope of mere official, formal recommendations" (Triffin 1946b: 53). In his view, the IMF was especially well equipped to deal with cases of temporary balance-of-payments deficits. "It is precisely this situation which the International Fund is so well organized to meet," he argued. "The drain of reserves is arrested, or moderated, by an indirect extension of credit by the surplus countries to the deficit countries, through their accounts with the Fund. In this manner the deficit countries are enabled to avoid recourse to internal deflation, currency devaluation, exchange control, or other restrictive policies" (Triffin 1946b: 65).

At the Mexico central banking conference, Prebisch observed that Triffin's paper was very significant. He was pleased that an IMF official, formerly from the Federal Reserve System, was advocating a series of ideas that had been developed in Argentina from 1933 onward and that had been severely criticized by economists and officials from the "center" countries. Hansen too reacted affirmatively to Triffin's analysis, and when discussing international matters, he would often refer to Triffin's study. In *Monetary Theory and Fiscal Policy,* Hansen (1949) admitted that the goal of an international economy based on multilateral trade and free convertibility of foreign exchange was still far away, "and may not ever be wholly reached." Consequently, different types of controls, especially in times of temporary stress, were likely to stay. Hansen explicitly mentioned Triffin's system of selective exchange control:

> This system provides that when there is a shortage of foreign exchange, importers of commodities which are not on the "preferred" or necessary list must purchase foreign exchange in an auction market. The auction rate will be a depreciated rate. All "necessary" imports and all exports will be traded in terms of the official exchange rate. As soon as the emergency is over and sufficient exchange again becomes available to meet all requirements, the auction rate would then tend to move toward the official rate and might eventually disappear altogether. (Hansen 1949: 209; see also Hansen 1951: 600)

Hansen further agreed with Triffin's advocacy of exchange controls for dealing with balance-of-payments deficits caused by a depression in the center countries. "Should the drain on gold and foreign exchange balances prove to be too great, then either exchange control or Dr. Triffin's auction market (selective exchange control or partial depreciation) are to be preferred to out-right exchange depreciation" (Hansen 1949: 211).

Later, Kenneth Rogoff, when he was director of the IMF Research Department, admitted that the topic of exchange and capital controls was still an important and difficult issue. During the last decades of the 20th century, free market reforms and liberalization had gained considerably in importance, and in developing countries too. This trend came clearly to the fore in the so-called Washington Consensus, a term coined by John Williamson (1990). However, the Asian crisis at the end of the 20th century led to important debates and controversies (see Williamson 2003 for a beautiful retrospective appraisal of the Washington Consensus). Moreover, the IMF also raised questions about the liberalization of capital flows. As Rogoff put it, in a formulation that comes quite close to Triffin's philosophy: "These days, everyone agrees that a more eclectic approach to capital account liberalization is required. But what should it be? How can developing countries drink from the waters of international capital markets without being drowned by them? . . . [W]e should acknowledge that this is a tough question, and we should be humble about what we know and don't know" (Rogoff 2002).

With his openness and curiosity for other cultures, Triffin had been the perfect person to steer the Federal Reserve Board missions away from the traditional orthodox gold standard views. In 1946, Triffin, with this multicultural background and experience, was well suited for the IMF, which at the time was being set up. He was among the first recruits that Bernstein, the first head of the IMF Research Department, asked for. In a meeting of the Board of Governors, Chairman Eccles reported on a phone call of Bernstein telling him that "the Fund planned to have about one-third of its staff consist of American citizens, that it was hoped that these individuals could be the very best qualified individuals available," including Triffin. Governor Szymczak added that Triffin had been offered a "position in charge of exchange controls and that he would like to accept the offer."[14] A new chapter in Triffin's life was about to start, even though he would often go back to Latin America.

NOTES

1. Memo to Mr. Goldenweiser, September 1940, MEA, Box 100, Folder 9, Item 1.
2. Minutes of the meeting of the Board of Governors, May 27, 1943, FRBA.
3. Minutes of the meeting of the Board of Governors, May 19, 1943, FRBA.
4. Minutes of the meeting of the Board of Governors, December 16, 1943, FRBA.
5. Minutes of the meeting of the Board of Governors, January 29, 1944, FRBA.
6. "Foreign Missions of the Federal Reserve System," March 29, 1945, FRBA.
7. "Report on Mexico City Conference of Central Bank Experts" by David L. Grove, September 25, 1946, FRBA.
8. Minutes of the meeting of the Federal Reserve Board, March 2, 1945, FRBA.
9. Minutes of the meeting of the Federal Reserve Board, April 12, 1946, FRBA.

10. "Review of Foreign Development," January 14, 1946, FRBA.
11. Note from Robert Triffin to Governor Szymczak, January 31, 1945, Belgium Baron Boel's Memorandum, RTAY, Box No. 7.
12. Recent Monetary and Banking Reforms, Triffin, 1945, RTAY, Box No. 7.
13. Postwar Reform of Central Banking, Draft, March 20, 1946, Triffin, RTAY, Box No. 7.
14. Minutes of the meeting of the Board of Governors, June 28, 1946, FRBA.

CHAPTER 3

Architect of the European Payments Union

3.1 INTRODUCTION

Triffin went to the International Monetary Fund (IMF) in July 1946 to head up the Exchange Controls Division of the Research Department. In this function, he dealt with issues such as exchange controls, trade restrictions, and financial regulations, very much dossiers he had also followed at the Federal Reserve Board (see Chapter 2). Initially he was still very much involved with Latin America. However, his attention would shift more and more to European issues. Indeed, the reconstruction of Western Europe became the crucial policy issue in the immediate postwar period, especially with General George C. Marshall's Harvard speech in June 1947, laying out the "Marshall Plan."

Triffin was well aware that a period after a war offered a window of opportunity to construct a new and better world. However, this was not guaranteed, as demonstrated by the experience of the interwar period. Constructive statesmanship was necessary:

"A great war, such as the one from which the world has so recently emerged, does not end with the restoration of peace. It leaves behind it a host of problems which, if not faced boldly and imaginatively, may bring about nearly as much dislocation, destruction and human suffering, as military hostilities themselves. On the other hand, the universal acceptance of the need for reform also offers a wider field for constructive statesmanship than would usually be permitted in ordinary time. The postwar period can be one of reconstruction, extending

Robert Triffin. Ivo Maes, Oxford University Press (2021). © Oxford University Press.
DOI: 10.1093/oso/9780190081096.001.0001

beyond the immediate legacy of the war itself to the solution of even prewar problems and the modernization of overaged machinery and institution.[1]

In the postwar period, Triffin became more and more a partisan of a regional approach toward monetary reconstruction, something that was not very well appreciated at the IMF. Triffin's regional approach was in line with his pragmatic empirical approach, focusing on country-specific situations, which he had developed in his Latin American missions (see Chapter 2). At his own request, Triffin was appointed to lead the IMF Representative Office in Europe in 1948. In this position, he closely followed the negotiations for trade and payment agreements in Europe. In December 1949, Triffin joined the Paris office of the US Economic Cooperation Administration (ECA), which administered the Marshall Plan, as special adviser. In this capacity, he played a key role in both the preparation of the ECA plan that was proposed in December 1949 and the negotiations of the European Payments Union (EPU). Triffin was described as "a consummate financial technician, eagerly advancing ingenious and usually successful methods for solving the mechanical problems posed by an automatic clearing system" (Kaplan and Schleiminger 1989: 39).

One can note that, in a certain sense, Triffin was one of the first historians of the EPU. In 1951, Triffin was appointed to a professorship at Yale University. However, international monetary problems remained at the center of his preoccupations and his research was very much a reflection on his experience as a policymaker. With *Europe and the Money Muddle: From Bilateralism to Near-Convertibility, 1947–1956*, Triffin (1957) published one of the first studies on the EPU. It was a very influential book, figuring prominently in Margaret De Vries's official history of the IMF (De Vries 1969). Harry Travers, an official at the Organization of European Economic Cooperation, in a study for the Organization for Economic Cooperation and Development (OECD) on the EPU, called it "a brilliant exposé of the problems of balance-of-payments adjustment and of Triffin's analysis of the working of the international monetary system and his views on the reforms needed in that system."[2]

3.2 THE EARLY YEARS OF THE INTERNATIONAL MONETARY FUND

The inaugural meeting of the Bretton Woods institutions, which Triffin attended, took place in Savannah, Georgia, on March 8, 1946. There it was decided that the IMF, as well as the International Bank for Reconstruction and Development, would be located in Washington.

The first meeting of the Executive Board of the IMF was held on May 6, 1946. The temporary chairman was White, who had been appointed US executive director. A crucial issue, which had not been decided at Savannah, was the appointment of the first managing director. The general idea was that White would take on this role, as he had played such a crucial role in the establishment of the IMF. However, at the last moment, the United States held back his candidacy. The official reason was that the United States preferred the presidency of the World Bank. In reality, the Federal Bureau of Investigation (FBI) had identified White as a Soviet spy (Steil 2013). The discovery of Soviet spy rings contributed to growing American distrust in the Soviet Union and communism, with McCarthyism as its climax. Triffin too came to be questioned about his relations with "communists."

In the end, the Executive Board of the IMF elected Camille Gutt, the Belgian executive director, as the first managing director. Gutt (1884–1971) had a remarkable career in public service and business in Belgium. He had been a close collaborator of Emile Francqui, who, as a minister without portfolio, had succeeded in stabilizing the Belgian franc in October 1926. Gutt was appointed as minister of finance for the first time in November 1934. In February 1939, he was reappointed and remained in office until February 1945. As such, Gutt acted as minister of finance for the Belgian wartime government in exile. His name is associated with the so-called Gutt operation, a drastic monetary reform—by which the money supply was reduced by two-thirds—in October 1944 after the liberation of Belgium. The Gutt operation restored Belgium's competitiveness, which contributed to the recovery of the Belgian economy after the war, as well as sizeable surpluses in the Belgian balance of payments. Even so, there was an element of irony in Gutt becoming managing director of the IMF, as, during the war, he had been skeptical about the chances of universal international monetary cooperation. Instead, he favored a gradualist and regional approach between countries with similar levels of economic development (Crombois 2011).

Gutt was a strong advocate of exchange rate stability. As finance minister, he rejected firmly any currency devaluation, both on moral and on economic grounds. In his view, a devaluation was a breach of contract between the government and its investors as it imposed on them a change in the value of their assets. Moreover, the advantages of a devaluation would be short-lived as it would lead to an inflationary spiral. Gutt felt greatly betrayed by van Zeeland's 1935 devaluation, for which the young Triffin had made the calculations (see Chapter 1). In a little book on the subject, entitled *Pourquoi le franc belge est tombé*, Gutt (1935: 97) rejected van Zeeland's argument that the government had to choose between saving the banks or the franc. He argued emphatically that a government of national unity could have saved the franc, "a government that, above all prejudice of political party, economic formula, political or social creed, would have had only this programme: save the country, save the franc, by any means."

The 1935 devaluation marked a significant deterioration in Gutt's relationship with van Zeeland. It led to a deep climate of distrust and rivalry between the two Belgian statesmen, as "on a personal level nothing could reconcile Gutt and van Zeeland" (Crombois 2011: 25). The devaluation also deteriorated the atmosphere between the economics professors of Louvain and Brussels (Gutt's university). According to Wilson (2015), the atmosphere between Louvain and Brussels later improved, though Triffin would always remain cautious in his relations with Gutt and van Zeeland.

The basic organizational structure of the IMF was put together during the course of 1946. Initially, the IMF consisted of the Research Division, Operations Division, Legal Division, Secretary's Office, Comptroller's Office, and Administrative Services unit (Horsefield 1969: 114). By the beginning of September 1946, the staff had expanded to about 100 people, from 15 countries. The divisions were then restyled as departments, a nomenclature that has since then been maintained. In June 1946, the IMF moved into a building at 1818 H Street that it shared with the World Bank (and which is still the headquarters of the World Bank Group).

Triffin started out in the Research Department. As mentioned in Chapter 2, the first head of the Research Department was Edward Bernstein. Bernstein had done his undergraduate studies at the University of Chicago, before going to Harvard for a doctoral dissertation with Taussig. He went on to teach at the University of North Carolina. In 1940, he moved to the US Treasury, becoming chief economist in the Division of Monetary Research, focusing mainly on the balance of payments and wartime inflation. From early 1942, Bernstein assisted White in the US preparations for the postwar international monetary system. He also had a leading role in the negotiations for the US loan to France. The US delegation included Triffin, who represented the Federal Reserve.

At the IMF Research Department, Bernstein brought together a remarkable group of economists. He had a highly selective hiring policy, recruiting only economists with a strong economics background and training. For example, of the dozen or so "division chiefs" in the original Research Department, four had attended the Bretton Woods conference. One of them was Jacques Polak, then a young economic model-builder. Earlier during this time at the League of Nations in Geneva in the second half of the 1930s, Polak had been an assistant of Jan Tinbergen—the first Nobel Memorial Prize winner, together with Ragnar Frisch—and had even shared an office with him (Cramer and Fase 2011). Polak was also a member of the Dutch delegation at Bretton Woods. In 1958, he would succeed Bernstein as head of the Research Department.

The Research Department was composed of both geographical units, which covered a region of the world economy, and horizontal units, specializing in a certain theme on a worldwide basis. Triffin became responsible for one of the horizontal units, focusing on exchange controls and practices, as well as trade restrictions, in line with his work at the Federal Reserve.

In the initial organizational structure of the IMF, the Research Department played a key role. Until 1950, when new departments were created out of its regional divisions, the analytical work and policy recommendations came from the Research Department. As observed by Polak (1996: 215), the IMF is unique as an international organization, because professional economists play such an important role in it. "With few exceptions," he said, "those crowding around its cradle at Bretton Woods were economists, and prominent economists at that. The design of the institution came out of a debate among economists." The initial staff of the IMF consisted almost entirely of economists, "assembled in a single major department, the Research Department." In Polak's view, the Research Department was the core of the fund, "or, disregarding legal niceties, was the Fund."

Bernstein stimulated innovative work on such themes as exchange rates, the balance of payments, and the adjustment process. Faced with major economic problems after the war, IMF staff were under constant pressure to refine existing economic concepts and theories and to devise new ones. There was a lively atmosphere in the department, with vigorous discussions among its members. Polak (1996: 220) even argued that, in its early years, the department was, to some extent, an "intellectual commune." In his view, "the property rights to particular ideas were not solidly established and one staff member's ideas might first show up in another's paper."

Most of the theoretical work undertaken at the IMF was published in its *Staff Papers*, which has become a major economics journal, dating from 1950. Even before that, starting in January 1948, the IMF had been publishing a selection of its statistics in *International Financial Statistics*. From the outset, there was an analytical presentation of each country's monetary statistics in a "monetary survey." These included data on the money supply and on the foreign and domestic assets of the consolidated banking system, the main counterparts to the money supply. As observed by Polak (1994: xxiv), this survey was inspired by Robert Triffin's distinction of "money of internal and external origin," on which he had been working at the Federal Reserve Board (see Section 2.3).

Later, in the 1950s, the monetary statistics provided the jumping-off point for the fund's operational monetary programming and the monetary interpretation of the balance of payments, which became famous with Polak's article "Monetary Analysis of Income Formation and Payments Problems," published in the *Staff Papers* in 1957 (Romberg and Heller 1977). The approach emphasized the role of domestic credit creation (captured in net domestic assets [NDAs]) in the development of balance-of-payments imbalances. It would become the framework for the fund's policy analysis. In his autobiography, Jacques de Larosière (2018: 76), a former managing director of the IMF, tells how he "used to urge the Fund's young economists, when they were about to negotiate adjustment programmes with Member States, to stick the three golden letters—NDA—on the door of their hotel rooms to help them prepare for their meetings the following day."

During the early months of the IMF, before its operations could begin in earnest, a crucial issue was the setting of the initial par values of the member countries' currencies. Triffin was involved in this and wrote several papers on the issue, especially as applied to Latin American and European countries. Triffin was very much aware of the perilous character of the exercise. In a more theoretical memorandum, he argued that "we should be prepared for a fairly liberal attitude towards modification in parity during the next few years."[3] Triffin emphasized that this was not only because of potential initial mistakes in setting parities but also because of economic developments during the ensuing years. Triffin was very explicit on this for France. In his view, French economic policy in the immediate postwar years aimed not only at reconstruction but also, with the five-year plan, at modernization. Triffin further underlined that shocks to the French economy were typically of domestic origin, something that still sounds true today:

> The history of the inter-war period suggests that the economic structure of France shelters the country, to an unusual degree, from the impact of world economic fluctuations. The main difficulties of France have sprung, traditionally, from internal weakness rather than from external shocks. The analysis of the current French position seems to reveal that the main dangers to French stability again appear to be of an internal, rather than external, nature.[4]

Triffin warned that stabilizing the franc at the new parity would crucially depend on containing inflationary pressures in the French economy. "Present price and fiscal trends do not warrant any easy optimism in this respect."

In the following months, Triffin and his division were very much involved with the IMF's relations with the proposed International Trade Organization (ITO) and multiple currency practices, marking strong continuity with Triffin's work at the Federal Reserve Board (see Chapter 2). Triffin was a member of a staff group, headed by Bernstein, that had to analyze technical issues arising from the ITO charter and how it affected the fund. In a memorandum of October 1946, Triffin pointed out the potential points of conflict between the ITO charter and the fund agreement. He concluded that "conflicts of jurisdictions between the two institutions will remain unavoidable if their respective competence continue to be defined in terms of formal techniques rather than objectives." Triffin's way out of it was a clear distinction between the mandates of the two institutions: "the primary responsibility of the Fund lies in the field of monetary, exchange and balance of payments problems," he said, "the primary responsibility of the Organization in the field of competitive relationship between domestic and foreign producers."[5]

As far as multiple exchange rates were concerned, Triffin examined their application in various countries and analyzed their significance as an instrument of exchange rate policy. Given the variety of forms and purposes for which they were adopted, he suggested that they could not be considered "a simple problem that can be settled by immediate and standardized treatment." In Triffin's view, they required "in each case . . . a thorough investigation of the problem in conjunction with the member." So, the purpose of the IMF should be to eliminate, within the scope of the fund agreement, "harmful international effects without imposing unnecessary changes in countries' fiscal and economic system."[6] Between mid-1947 and the beginning of 1948, Triffin also joined fund missions to some countries, including Ecuador and Chile, to supervise their economic and monetary policy programs and to advise on monetary and financial reforms.

It was not long, however, before the situation in Europe began to occupy the fund's attention. The first major economic policy problem arose in January 1948, when France wanted to modify its exchange rate arrangements (Horsefield 1969: 200). Basically, the French government wanted to depreciate the franc against the dollar and let the dollar rate float. But, at the same time, it wanted to leave the rate for sterling and the other European currencies unchanged. This was naturally a problem for the IMF, which was completely upset that the French franc might have two rates. Indeed, the French proposal threatened the introduction of differential rates for a currency (depending on whether it would be bought or sold via the dollar or via sterling), leading to disorderly exchange rates and trade distortions. In an IMF memorandum, to which Triffin contributed, it was argued that the French proposal was incompatible with a system of convertible currencies and multilateral trade. "This will increase the difficulties of restoring a tolerable pattern of international payments in the post-transition period."[7] Some of Bernstein's later observations further confirmed the Research Department's commune-like way of working. "When the French made this proposal, I met with Jack Polak and Bob Triffin, my most imaginative economists, and we talked this question out in front of the fireplace at my house until we understood what the problem was. . . . I wrote the paper on this and it was signed by Triffin and me" (Black 1991: 65).

Triffin was also closely involved in monitoring the situation of the Italian economy. Like in several other countries, the money supply had increased significantly during the war and the threat of hyperinflation loomed. In June 1947, a new government was formed, without the communists and socialists, but with Luigi Einaudi—the governor of the Bank of Italy and one of Italy's most eminent liberal economists—as deputy prime minister and minister of the budget (in 1948 Einaudi became Italy's second president of the republic). The new government introduced a strong stabilization program. In early 1949, the IMF sent Triffin to Rome to report on the Italian economy. Triffin was very positive about the improvements in the Italian economic situation, even if he remained cautious:

> It is impossible not to be deeply impressed by the most remarkable progress realized in the last year and a half. In many ways, Italy is clearly and rapidly approaching a "pre-stabilization" stage in monetary and economic recovery. The progressive unification and stabilization of exchange rates, the extraordinary improvement in exports and in the balance of payments, the stabilization of domestic prices and wages and the near balance achieved for the first time between them, are the most obvious signs of this recovery.[8]

Triffin nevertheless pointed out that many problems still had to be solved, especially the high level of unemployment and the continuing budgetary deficits. He further observed that the slowdown in credit creation, the principal reason for the decline in inflation, was the result of two opposing tendencies: an expansion in official credit and a sharp contraction in new credits to business enterprise. But he questioned the sustainability of this process, emphasizing the need for budgetary discipline: "It seems doubtful, however, whether these two opposite trends (easy credit for the state and tight credit for business) can coexist for long without retarding economic development or creating irresistible pressure for the relaxation of present controls." Triffin thus welcomed the news that the government for 1949–1950 intended to cut the deficit from 452 billion to 159 billion lire.[9]

As he had done in Latin America (see Chapter 2), Triffin worked closely and effectively with national officials. He clearly acknowledged this in the introduction to his report. "Whatever interest may be found in this paper is entirely due to the extraordinary cooperation of the technicians at the Bank of Italy and the Exchange Control Office. Very special thanks are due to Mr. Carli, Mr. Baffi, and their assistants, who gave me the benefit of their studies and experience." The mission would lead to lifelong friendships, especially with Guido Carli and Paolo Baffi. Carli, who was governor of the Bank of Italy from 1960 to 1975, consulted Triffin for sensitive and confidential issues regarding the international monetary system (Carli 1993: 226). Also Baffi became governor of the Bank of Italy, from 1975 to 1979. Triffin and Baffi would have wide-ranging discussions, not only on economics and the reform of the international monetary system but also on religion. Triffin tried to convince Baffi of the merits of Teilhard de Chardin (a Catholic theologian who had a profound influence on Triffin; see Section 1.2). However, Baffi was not convinced. He wrote that he had done some reading of Teilhard, but his impression was that Teilhard "stretches the Christian message too far. I have derived much greater consolation from the perusal of St. Augustine's confessions, which mirror a moving mother-to-son relationship."[10]

3.3 THE EUROPEAN ECONOMY AND THE MARSHALL PLAN

After the war, European countries were confronted with enormous war-related damages and a complete dislocation of their productive capacities. The United States was the only source of capital equipment for reconstruction. As a result, European countries—which needed US capital equipment to increase their production—had massive balance-of-payments deficits. Consequently, European policymakers used bilateral agreements and exchange and trade controls to restrict their imports from the rest of Europe. Countries wanted to maximize the availability of dollars and gold that could be used to buy imports from the dollar area.

The dollar shortage was aggravated by overvalued official parities, set in December 1946 (Bordo 1993: 39). At that time, the IMF did not consider devaluation as an adequate policy instrument for European payments imbalances. In a speech he gave at Harvard, Gutt (1948) argued that exchange rate adjustments were not effective under the conditions prevailing in Europe, since balance-of-payments deficits reflected structural problems in the export industries. He further emphasized that a currency devaluation might trigger inflationary pressures. In his view, both the inflation resulting from domestic monetary and fiscal policies and the latent inflation—caused by keeping on wartime exchange restrictions and rationing—were a major cause of the continued and recurrent European balance-of-payments deficits.

There was much debate about these issues among economists at the time. Several, including Milton Friedman and Fritz Machlup, took a free market approach. They believed that economic reconstruction and the liberalization of trade in Europe could only come about by free market forces and the adoption of market-determined exchange rates. But others, like Triffin and Carli, who had also been one of the leading negotiators of Italy's entry in the IMF in 1947, emphasized that several structural factors impeded the successful operation of market forces in Europe's postwar economies. As Carli wrote in a retrospective assessment, "The low level of gold and dollar reserves and of industrial productive capacity sharply emphasised the fact that the prerequisites of a system of free convertibility and those of free international exchange did not exist in postwar Europe" (Carli 1982: 162). Later analysis would very much support this view (Milward 1987; Eichengreen 1993). Moreover, given the political instability in many countries, the "social consequences of such policies were considered to be a major deterrent to their implementation" (Carli 1982: 162). Of particular importance was that communist parties were very strong in the immediate postwar period. In Italy and France, they were even the biggest party.

Crucially, in 1947, the United States moved from a stance of doggedly defending its creditor prerogatives, under Morgenthau and White, to one of reviving global growth. The change in US policy was essentially based on a new perception of US geopolitical interests, with the Cold War taking center stage. It became increasingly obvious that Stalin had his own agenda. As future secretary of state Dean Acheson observed: "Only slowly did it dawn upon us that the whole world structure and order that we had inherited from the nineteenth century was gone and that the struggle to replace it would be directed from two bitterly opposed and ideologically irreconcilable power centers" (as quoted in Steil 2018: 11). The urgency of the situation was reinforced by the reality that America's natural allies in Western Europe were teetering on the edge of economic, social, and political collapse.

Roosevelt died in April 1945 and was succeeded by Harry S. Truman as US president. In March 1947, Truman made his famous speech, putting the containment of the Soviet Union at the center of US foreign policy. This marked a complete break with Roosevelt's "One World" vision. Marshall's Harvard commencement speech followed three months later. The Marshall Plan promised massive US support for the reconstruction of the European economies. It implied a continuing US presence, as well as a reindustrialized West Germany at the heart of an integrated, capitalist, Western Europe. Of course, the benefits to the United States here were not only geopolitical, as a strong European economy would constitute an important market for US exports.

Originally, the State Department's idea was that the economic aid under the Marshall Plan would avoid a large US military effort in Europe. But over time, and very reluctantly, Washington had to acknowledge that economic security could not take hold in Western Europe without physical security. *Time Magazine* journalist Frank McNaughton summed up the US administration's argument by saying, "Europe can't fully recover until the sickle is removed from its throat" (as quoted in Steil 2018: 320).

The Marshall Plan was enacted in April 1948 with the approval of the Economic Cooperation Act by US Congress. The economic thinking behind the Marshall Plan was radically different from that under the Roosevelt administration. A crucial difference concerned its regional approach, which contrasted with Roosevelt's global approach. The Marshall Plan required recipient countries to cooperate in allocating aid and in the process of liberalization of trade and payments. Accordingly, the Committee for European Economic Cooperation (CEEC) was established in July 1947, renamed Organization of European Economic Cooperation (OEEC) nine months later, with initially 17 member countries.

Bradford De Long and Barry Eichengreen described the Marshall Plan as "History's Most Successful Structural Adjustment Program" (De Long and Eichengreen 1993). In their view, the Marshall Plan accelerated European growth significantly through changing the environment in which economic policy was made. The conditions imposed by the United States, both formally and informally, opened up the European economies to trade and contributed to financial stability. The result was that the "Marshall Plan conditionality pushed governments toward versions of the mixed economy that had more market orientation and less directive planning in the mix" (De Long and Eichengreen 1993: 191).

A key development in the 1950s, to which the Marshall Plan contributed significantly, was the German economic miracle. This was an essential element in Western Europe's recovery and the resolution of the dollar shortage. Indeed, Western Europe's large dollar deficits after the war were very much a reflection of Germany's disappearance as Europe's main capital goods supplier. The massive reconstruction needs therefore had to be filled by the United States. In recreating a European division of labor, with Germany as an importer of raw materials and exporter of capital goods, the Marshall Plan contributed to resolving the dollar scarcity. The strong postwar recovery made for a stark contrast with the period after World War I, when European reconstruction had been a failure, with hyperinflation in certain countries, the Great Depression, the implosion of trade, distributional conflicts, and the rise of fascism, which Triffin had been living through as a young man (see Chapter 1).

The management of the Marshall Plan was conferred on a new US agency, the Economic Cooperation Agency (ECA). Its first administrator was Paul Hoffmann, a businessman who had previously been president of American automobile manufacturer Studebaker. His deputy was Richard Bissell, an economist and official who would later become a deputy director of the Central Intelligence Agency (CIA). Theodore Geiger, a US diplomat and economic historian, who had put together the first plan for a multilateral clearing union (to replace the bilateral trade and payments agreements between European countries), was appointed Bissell's special assistant. The Office of the Special Representative (OSR) in Paris was headed up by Averell Harriman, the famous banker, politician, and diplomat, and he took on Ambassador Milton Katz as his deputy. Henry Tasca, who had served earlier as US financial adviser in Italy and as alternate US executive director at the IMF, became the head of the Paris Trade and Payments Division. Tasca "promptly recruited Triffin" for a position at the ECA (Kaplan and Schleiminger 1989: 40), and Triffin's old Harvard friend, Arthur Schlesinger, joined the ECA Paris office too.

In the ECA, the Planning Group had produced proposals for setting up a clearing mechanism between European countries. According to Kaplan and Schleiminger (1989: 362), the earliest recorded proposal for a European clearing union was drafted by Geiger in September 1946, when he was an official at the US Embassy in London. It was further elaborated at a meeting between Geiger and Harold van Buren Cleveland in London. In their view, it was a first institutional step to promote closer European economic and monetary integration (Hogan 1987: 271). But the US government was not of one mind on the matter. While the ECA's ideas were supported by the State Department, they were not shared by the US Treasury, which was concerned that regional integration could be a challenge to the authority and responsibility of the IMF.

In the fall of 1947, Triffin wrote a study together with a colleague, Raymond Bertrand, analyzing the European payments and trade situation (Maes and Pasotti 2018). In this study, published as an internal IMF memorandum in December 1947, Triffin outlined a proposal for a multilateral clearing arrangement.[11] Triffin was very critical of the bilateral payments agreements, especially because of their impact on intra-European trade. He admitted that bilateral payments agreements allowed European countries to manage their external balances and conserve hard currency. However, they led to a bilateral balancing of intra-European trade as counties only granted small loans under the agreements and restricted the use of the proceeds of these loans to goods of the country providing the loan (Triffin 1947: 2). Such bilateral balancing involved discrimination among import sources as well as export markets, distorting European trade. The result was that countries purchased goods from countries with which they had a bilateral surplus or that were willing to grant further loans, rather than making purchases from producers offering the lowest price. Bilateral balancing might thus imply that countries diverted imports from lower- to higher-cost sources and from goods that would be essential to goods that would not be essential for reconstruction aims. The implication was that this bilateralism effectively slowed down Europe's economic recovery.

Triffin put forward three ideas (Triffin 1947: 3). First, further loans, beyond those provided under the existing agreements, were necessary to prevent trade from degenerating into barter deals. Second, credit should be provided on a multilateral basis to prevent countries from resorting to discriminatory practices just for bilateral balancing. Third, the credit lines to deficit countries should be limited in size, in order not to relieve them from reducing unnecessary imports. They should also be granted on a multilateral basis to prevent them from being used for less essential imports from the lending countries.

On this basis, Triffin proposed that European countries would substitute a multilateral agreement for the network of bilateral agreements, creating a European clearing union in which "the total credit commitments made by each country to other Clearing members would be paid into the Clearing in its own currency, and the country would receive an equivalent balance in the Clearing which it could then use to settle the current account deficits with *any* Clearing member" (Triffin 1947: 4, original emphasis). The payments would not be made on a bilateral basis but by debiting the paying country's balance in the clearing and crediting the balance of the receiving country. Triffin also favored the introduction of an intra-European unit of account, called "European dollar" or "interfranc," to express the balances in the clearing (Triffin 1947: 4). This would become a recurring theme in Triffin's proposals in the ensuing decades.

Triffin also argued that, compared to the existing bilateral system, multilateral clearing had the advantage of promoting fuller use of credit commitments. However, the European countries had a significant deficit with the US dollar area. This meant that external financial resources, to finance the net overall intra-European deficits, were essential to the viability of the multilateral clearing arrangement. Triffin suggested two sources of external financing. The first was the Marshall Plan. The second was the IMF. He believed the IMF could provide European currencies as well as dollars, if the Marshall Plan proved to be insufficient to cover European countries' dollar deficit (Triffin 1947: 8).

In the debate on the transferability of the European currencies at that time, Triffin's proposal for a European clearing union was very similar to the boldest proposals advanced within both the OEEC Payments Committee and the ECA (Kaplan and Schleiminger 1989: 34). Special attention was paid by Triffin to a system of incentives and deterrents. First, the common unit of account would work as an exchange rate guarantee for intra-European payments. Second, the introduction of a ceiling for debtor countries' drawing rights would encourage them to adopt policies to adjust payments imbalances. Finally, the involvement of the IMF in the financing of net deficits would provide further guarantees to both debtor and creditor countries.

However, Triffin's ideas met with resistance within the IMF, right from the start. This was very clear in the Managing Board, where the American representative, Andrew Overby, who came from the Treasury, was particularly skeptical (Horsefield 1969: 220). Triffin's memorandum was also criticized by Bernstein. Triffin did not take this lightly and even wrote to Bernstein that he came close to offering his resignation (Wilson 2015: 463). Bernstein replied that there was not "a bit of meanness" in his criticism, admitting that he was "a tough fellow on work."

As he was getting tired of the atmosphere at the IMF in Washington, Triffin requested to be sent on mission to Europe. In October 1948, Triffin was appointed to lead the IMF Representative Office in Europe under the job title of head technical representative of the IMF in Europe. The establishment of an IMF office in Paris was preceded by an experimental period in Brussels. Triffin, together with his wife and children, arrived in Brussels on February 14, 1948 (Wilson 2015: 478). The IMF delegation also included Georges Sallé and Triffin's secretary, Isabel Loyd. The delegation was given offices in the National Bank of Belgium. After eight years of marriage, Triffin's wife, Lois, would finally meet her father-in-law for the first time, as well as the rest of Triffin's family in Belgium. Triffin's uncle Adolphe would organize Pantagruelian dinners in his home, Avenue Paul Dechanel 257 in

Schaerbeek. Referring to the discussions about his new job title, Triffin revealed that, on the insistence of a "suspicious" Executive Board, the IMF had originally proposed: "Roving Technical Head of the IMF in Europe." Triffin then asked for stationery printed with his French translation of this as "Tête Technique Ambulante du FMI en Europe," So, finally, Triffin became the IMF's first "technical representative" in Western Europe.

During Triffin's time in Belgium, the negotiations for trade and payments agreements in Europe gathered momentum, especially after approval by the US Congress of the Economic Cooperation Act in April 1948. Triffin, ever the real hedgehog, produced several memoranda on these issues, arguing in favor of the IMF's involvement in the European payments agreements. In a memorandum he wrote in May 1948, Triffin stated that "it would be particularly unfortunate if the Fund remained aloof from a problem so essential to the fulfilment of its purposes."[12] In a subsequent memorandum concerning the intra-European payments negotiations, in February 1949, he further stressed how the fund was presented "once more with an opportunity to reassert its leadership in helping member countries" to achieve some measure of progress toward its mission.[13] In a note on one of Triffin's memoranda, Bernstein said he was "anxious" that the fund should actively encourage attempts at multilateralism in European payments.[14]

In line with his general philosophy, Triffin's memoranda paid close attention to the need to strike a balance between financing and adjustment of payments imbalances. More specifically, he suggested the so-called matching credit formula, under which payments would be settled partly through loans and partly in gold or dollars. Triffin later revised the formula, advocating a gradual increase in the cash element in the settlements, as deficit countries made cumulative use of credit facilities. The effect was that the ratio of gold payments to borrowing facilities would increase gradually when the borrowing ceiling was approached by debtors and vice versa for creditor countries. In Triffin's view, this system of settlements would support progress from bilateralism to regional interconvertibility. On the one hand, it "would give some incentive to all countries to limit their Western Hemisphere deficit and to maximise their European exports," while on the other, it "would facilitate some accumulation of monetary reserves which would help to restore currency stability and smooth out balance of payments difficulties after the termination of [the Marshall Plan]."[15] It also had the further benefit of recreating incentives for the correction of surpluses and deficits in intra-European trade:

> The obligation imposed upon surplus countries to refinance one half of their intra-European surplus exceeding the estimates would limit . . . the incentive to build up surpluses through a contraction in their imports from other

participating countries. On the other hand, the system would impose some hardship on the countries which fail to reach their estimated goals. This, however, appears necessary as an incentive to maximum efforts and as a discipline to stimulate adequate monetary and exchange policies.[16]

Triffin emphasized the need for policy adjustment at the national level, "through changes in fiscal, credit, and monetary policies, in exchange rates, etc." (Triffin 1949b: 447), and he suggested that creditor countries should take action to limit their surpluses through further liberalization of imports, while partner countries that encountered heavy balance-of-payments pressures should be released temporarily from such commitments.

But his proposals met with considerable criticism at the IMF, both at staff level and in the board. In a note commenting on Triffin's memorandum of November 8, 1948, Bernstein wrote that the policy recommendations represented the personal views of Triffin and not of the staff. In fact, he said, "The staff believes that considerable qualification of these recommendations is necessary before they can be accepted by the Fund as a basis for policy." The IMF Executive Board also refused to endorse Triffin's proposals, as a result of which he was only allowed to submit his March 1949 scheme to the OEEC as a "technical and personal proposal" (Horsefield 1969: 223). The effort to squelch his recommendations was an important factor in Triffin's decision to leave the IMF and move to the US Economic Cooperation Agency in Paris. But, before going into these issues, it is important to discuss how Triffin's ideas on exchange rates evolved.

3.4 TRIFFIN AND THE EXCHANGE RATE ISSUE

As seen in Chapter 2, Triffin's 1947 essay on the international economy revealed that he was initially quite optimistic about the role the IMF could play in the world economy. But he gradually became more critical of the IMF (Maes and Pasotti 2018), especially where exchange rate stability and liberalization were concerned.

Triffin acknowledged that Article XIV of the Bretton Woods statutes gave countries the right to maintain restrictions on payments and transfers for current transactions for a transitional period lasting five years. Yet, he believed that the fund's policy, which had to promote both exchange freedom and exchange stability, had been devoted mainly to the stability objective in the postwar years. According to Triffin, the fund's arguments for exchange rate stability had been right in the immediate postwar years. Exchange rates could not be used as a meaningful mechanism of adjustment for European balance-of-payments disequilibria as Europe lacked export capacity. Against this background, trade and exchange controls could be expected to reduce the outflow of foreign exchange and reallocate it to those imports that the economy most urgently needed. By contrast, exchange rate readjustments could fuel domestic inflation, given the excessive rates of monetary expansion during the war and the early postwar years (Triffin 1948).

Over the course of 1949, however, Triffin espoused the cause of exchange rate adjustments, thus going against the official IMF position in the process. In the summer, when exchange realignments of European currencies were discussed, Triffin wrote various memoranda in favor of exchange rate revisions. He became convinced that the exchange rates not only did not correspond to the fundamentals but also were impeding trade liberalization. He argued that "the liberalization of controls is inextricably tied, for most countries, with a revision of exchange rates. Pursuing either policy also means implementing the other." Triffin argued, "The accent should be put on the first, for the revision of rates would merely facilitate the relaxation of controls, while the relaxation of controls would compel exchange revisions" (Triffin 1949a: 185).

In Triffin's view, the IMF had not only to authorize the exchange rate revisions, as envisaged in the Bretton Woods statutes, but also to facilitate the process rather than "hamper it by cumbersome, and often unrealistic, requirements" to attain par values that were both stable and effective. He suggested that a new par value had to be determined after "a transitional period of experimentation" (Triffin 1949a: 185). Throughout this period, any member country would be engaged in a consultation process with the fund and the exchange rate might fluctuate. Specific rules had to be followed to avoid abuses of exchange flexibility and to preserve, in cooperation with the fund, the orderly character of adjustments. One can observe here a remarkable similarity between Triffin's 1949 proposals and those of the IMF in 1971. In both cases, the idea was to let exchange rates fluctuate during a transitional period, under IMF surveillance, to find new par rates.

Triffin further argued that his proposal would not require any formal revision of the Bretton Woods statutes. Moreover, it would provide for "some regionalization of the Fund machinery" at both policy and staff levels (Triffin 1949a: 188). At the policy level, the regionalization could be accomplished if the European governors of the fund would meet in Europe at frequent intervals, "with a high officer of the Fund who would ensure the proper liaison with the Fund's management and Executive Board in Washington." At the staff level, Triffin recognized that a step in the right direction of regionalization of IMF machinery had been taken with the appointment of technical representatives abroad. Yet, he recommended that the offices abroad should be expanded .

At this point, it is interesting to compare the views of Triffin and Friedman regarding exchange rates (Maes and Pasotti 2018). In the fall of 1950, Friedman had been a consultant to the Finance and Trade Division of the ECA. His famous paper, "The Case for Flexible Exchange Rates," had its origin in a memorandum for the ECA, which he also discussed with Triffin (Friedman 1950: 187 fn).

Friedman advanced two arguments in favor of flexible exchange rates: the freedom of each country to pursue internal stability and the attainment of unrestricted multilateral trade. With this second argument, he was close to Triffin's analysis of the European economy in 1949. According to Friedman, there was no way of predicting in advance the precise economic effects of reductions of trade barriers:

> All that is clear is that the impact of such reductions will vary from country to country and industry to industry and that many of the impacts will be highly indirect and not at all in the particular areas liberalized. The very process of liberalization will therefore add substantial and unpredictable pressures on balance of payments over and above those that would occur in any event. And there seems no way to decide on the appropriate final exchange rates in advance; they must be reached by trial and error. Thus, even if the ultimate goal were a new system of rigid exchange rates, it seems almost essential to have flexibility in the interim period. (Friedman 1950: 197–198)

A crucial difference between Friedman and Triffin was that Friedman was completely skeptical of Triffin's distinction between temporary and fundamental payments imbalances—also the philosophy underlying the IMF statutes—and the financing of temporary disequilibria. In Friedman's view, the financing of "small and temporary strains on balances of payments . . . is an understandable objective of economic policy." However, he continued, such a course "is not a realistic, feasible, or desirable policy." In Friedman's opinion, it was not easy to know whether strains in the balance of payments were temporary or permanent. Moreover, there was a tendency to rely too much on temporary financing. The result, he concluded, is that "Corrective steps are postponed in the hope that things will right themselves until the state of the reserves forces drastic and frequently ill-advised action" (Friedman 1950: 172).

In the early years after the war, the Western European economy recovered only very slowly and payments imbalances remained important. This ignited the exchange rate issue. Following heated discussions throughout the spring and summer, the United Kingdom devalued its currency by 30.5% on September 18, 1949 (Schenk 2010). The major European countries followed in quick succession with similar devaluations of their own currencies. These devaluations marked an important difference between the postwar and interwar period (Hetzel 2002). In the 1920s, the attempt to resurrect the gold standard, and especially the United Kingdom's return to the prewar parity, led to disastrous consequences, as predicted by that other Cassandra, John Maynard Keynes (1925), in his "Economic Consequences of Mr. Churchill." Like also Triffin, Keynes emphasized that the world had changed with World War I:

> The gold standard, with its dependence on pure chance, its faith in "automatic adjustments," and its general regardlessness of social detail, is an essential emblem and idol of those who sit in the top tier of the machine. I think that they are immensely rash in their regardlessness, in their vague optimism and comfortable belief that nothing really serious ever happens. Nine times out of ten, nothing really serious does happen—merely a little distress to individuals or to groups. But we run a risk of the tenth time (and are stupid into the bargain) if we continue to apply the principles of an Economics which was worked out on the hypotheses of *laissez-faire* and free competition to a society which is rapidly abandoning these hypotheses. (Keynes 1925: 262, original italics)

After World War II, the willingness to accept major devaluations of European currencies in 1949 was strikingly different with the attempts to return to the prewar parities in the interwar period. It was a precondition for the Bretton Woods system to function and to offer monetary stability. One might also note a crucial similarity in the approaches of Keynes and Triffin to economics: Triffin (1981a) too preferred to be wrong 9 times out of 10, if he could contribute to avoid catastrophe. The two men were both focusing on concrete policy issues and, like Keynes, Triffin was skeptical of the self-correcting forces of a market economy. Moggridge (1976: 161) argued that the notion that macroeconomic management is a crucial government function was perhaps Keynes's greatest legacy. Triffin would certainly agree with that.

3.5 TRIFFIN AND THE CREATION OF THE EUROPEAN PAYMENTS UNION

In the summer of 1949, Triffin was asked to join the ECA in Paris. As he was more and more in disagreement with the official IMF position, both on the issues of exchange rates and on European payments, he decided to accept the offer. So, in December 1949, he joined the ECA in Paris as special adviser on policy to Henry Tasca, the director of the Division of Trade and Payments. In this role, he contributed to both the preparation of the ECA plan that was proposed in December 1949 and the negotiations for the EPU. According to Bissell (1996: 62), the deputy administrator of the ECA, Tasca and Triffin were both "fascinated" by the construction of the EPU. The ECA Paris office was located in the Hotel Talleyrand (Talleyrand was one of France's most famous diplomats and had been minister of foreign affairs for both the French kings and Napoleon). It was situated at the Place de Concorde, between the Tuileries gardens and the Champs-Élysées.

In his farewell letter to Triffin, Bernstein regretted very much that Triffin was leaving the IMF. He again emphasized his colleague's creativity and imagination, saying that "I needn't tell you how much I regret your leaving us. I have always felt that the most important thing in an economist is imagination, and you brought us plenty imagination." Bernstein went on to tell Triffin that: "We shall miss you beyond question. Good ideas don't come from discussions in groups in which everyone agrees, they come from discussions in groups in which there is plenty of disagreement but a patience to listen and a willingness to learn."[17] But Triffin wanted more than an environment that tolerated disagreement; he wanted to see his ideas put into practice.

In the course of 1949, the ECA had become increasingly worried by the limited progress toward freeing up European trade and reducing Europe's dollar deficit. The ECA was also under pressure in Washington, especially from the Treasury. There was a lot of criticism in the State Department too. In August 1949, Hoffmann, the ECA administrator, came to Paris. Along with his staff, he prepared a speech, putting the emphasis on the urgent need to make progress toward European integration. However, the State Department did not like it at all. Triffin was among the persons who encouraged Hoffman to go ahead with the speech (Bissell 1996: 62). On August 16, 1949, Hoffman urged the OEEC heads of delegations to advance with the integration of the European economies:

> You must be aware of the importance that the Congress, and I might add the American people, set upon the integration of the European economy. . . . The time has come when we must have evidence of the European efforts to make good on their pledge of mutual aid. . . . There must be proof of accomplishment in the direction of genuine cooperation among the European nations to the end that Europe becomes a single market.[18]

This was not the only time that Hoffman was to sound this note. He made another frank speech, this time to the OEEC ministers, in October 1949. That Hoffman was issuing a stiff challenge was clear from the response of Hubert Ansiaux, the Belgian representative, to Hoffman's speech: "You are asking us to achieve in the next four years what, with past progress, we might achieve in the next 400 years."[19]

At the start of the EPU negotiations, in October 1949, Hoffman cabled Bissell in Paris, stressing that a robust institutional framework was necessary for trade liberalization. He pushed for a liberalization of trade and payments, which he believed would shift the attention of the European countries from symptoms of the issue, like trade restrictions, to the underlying causes, especially the lack of coordination of national policies. The potential benefits were clear to Hoffman: "This process of learning collectively, by experience, that supra-national authority is needed in order to have a freely trading area could be as important as the necessarily limited substantive accomplishments in liberalisation of trade and payments which we can anticipate through the OEEC."[20] At this same time, at the ECA headquarters in Washington, Albert Hirschman was busily drafting a memorandum sketching the main lines of a monetary authority for a federated Europe (Adelman 2013: 271).

With mounting pressure in the United States, it was important for the ECA to obtain pragmatic, concrete results. In a letter to the then British chancellor of the Exchequer Sir Stafford Cripps, Hoffman stressed the importance of this:

> ECA was under continuing and mounting pressure to bring about the "unification of western Europe." There was no agreement as to what was meant by this phrase, although the notion was gaining momentum that there should almost overnight be brought into being a United States of Europe. This being a case, it seemed to me imperative that the OEEC adopt a programme more practical in concept and that once adopted we exploit that programme in order to bring U.S. expectations down to a realisable goal.[21]

The United States' pressure revived the EPU negotiations. In the closing months of 1949, plans for the new payments scheme were circulated within the OEEC. The two most important proposals came from the ECA and the OEEC secretariat. There were quite a few similarities between the two proposals. Both plans suggested setting up a clearing mechanism, so that each member country would be expected to seek a balance with all members of the union as a whole, thus minimizing the need for dollars to settle imbalances. Moreover, each country would have access to credit from the union to accommodate temporary fluctuations in the country's position and permit some leeway for adjusting economic policies to regain equilibrium. Yet, the ECA plan was more sophisticated (Kaplan and Schleiminger 1989: 31). It included provisions that would press member countries to adopt monetary and fiscal policies conducive to a balanced intra-European position. The ECA plan also provided for an authority with discretionary powers over member countries' national policies. In Travers's opinion, this "revolutionary set of proposals . . . owed much to the lucidity and ingenuity of the main author, Robert Triffin."

Triffin himself remained unhappy with the IMF's choice not to engage with the European payments problems. He argued that it had resulted in "a generalised distrust in IMF policy and machinery" in international monetary cooperation and consultations (Triffin 1949a: 183). Triffin continued to press for IMF involvement in the EPU at both the IMF and the OEEC. In a letter to Camille Gutt, the managing director, he wrote: "The only immediate action that would make sense would be for you to come to Paris with a broad delegation of authority, not necessarily to commit the Fund, but to enter into close contact with the OEEC Secretariat and national delegations at the highest political level, and pave the ground for an intelligent discussion of the problem at the Board at a later stage." Continuing to push this point, Triffin added, "I have not the slightest doubt about the need for a close working relationship between the Fund and the European clearing. I have pressed this point myself at every occasion."[22]

Triffin was still in contact with Bernstein, who followed developments in Europe closely. Bernstein wrote to Triffin, praising him for his role in the negotiations. "I have been following with great interest the developments of the European payments plan and I hope something constructive will come out of it. I can tell from this and that how large your role has been. In fact, I can generally segregate the Triffin from the non-Triffin side of almost any scheme."[23] In his reply, Triffin summarized the essential lines of thought in the ECA. The initial plan reflected two very different trends of thought. "Some people here conceive of it as a natural and desirable development of previous intra-European payment plans, while others here think of far more ambitious schemes for a European super central bank or even for a quick monetary unification of the Continent." Triffin further observed: "The latter ideas were reflected primarily in the provisions about management and were viewed with considerable scepticism by most countries."[24]

Triffin also fiercely defended the EPU plan, stressing that the alternatives were worse: "Most of all, I think we should never lose sight of the most likely alternative to a successful negotiation of a EPU plan. I am certainly worried as much as you are with the dangers of premature convertibility, or with the danger of freezing purely regional convertibility scheme, but I am also concerned with the likelihood that the failure of EPU might merely mean the continuation of a purely bilateral and most uneconomic system of trade balancing in Europe." In all of this, Triffin's "general equilibrium" approach came to the fore. He never looked at countries in isolation, but he put them in their context. "I have absolutely no quarrel with the insistence placed on the need for internal monetary stabilization," he said, "but it must also be realized that mere internal stability cannot insure convertibility, as long as other countries retain all of their bilateral arsenal of controls."[25]

The United Kingdom strongly opposed the EPU proposals up to May 1950. Indeed, the EPU posed serious problems for the United Kingdom (Daunton 2008). The British economy had been badly hit by the war and faced serious balance-of-payments problems. The British government was anxious to maintain the sterling area and the pound's status as a reserve currency (Schenk 2010). It also wanted to maintain the system of imperial preference and Britain's identity as a major imperial power. Multilateralism and convertibility posed major difficulties here. Fundamentally, for the British government, the EPU negotiations were a perilous equilibrium exercise between America, Europe, and the British Empire.

Despite all of these challenges, the EPU went ahead. It was established on September 19, 1950, originally designed as a two-year transitional arrangement, renewable on a yearly basis (OEEC 1950). The EPU had two key features. First, there was a multilateral compensation system under which, at the end of each month, the surpluses and deficits of a member country in its trade with all the other European countries were offset to produce a single net position toward the union. The effect of this was to make all the European currencies interconvertible, an essential condition for free trading. Accordingly, each country's net balances with each other member country were reported at the end of every month to the Bank for International Settlements, which canceled out offsetting claims. Any remaining balances were consolidated, leaving each country with liabilities or claims against the union as a whole, as the ECA plan had proposed. The second feature was a quota system under which countries moving into deficit with the union received credit from it to cover part of their deficit. However, they were obliged to settle an increasing proportion of their deficits by gold or dollar payments. Similarly, surpluses of the creditors were settled partly by credit granted by the creditor to the union and partly by gold or dollar payments by the union to the creditor.

Furthermore, a single monetary unit, the EPU unit of account, was adopted so as to have a common denominator for all the accounts deriving from the settlements among the central banks. Triffin played a key role in these negotiations. The financing of net settlements would be provided by a grant of $350 million of Marshall aid to the EPU. As later observed by Carli, "the failure of the monetary compensation agreements on a European level was thus salvaged by the injection of dollar funds and by Triffin, who was the catalyst that converted the whole plan into what became the European Payments Union" (Carli 1982: 163).

The management of the EPU was conferred upon the Managing Board, composed of financial experts. When a member country threatened to exhaust its quota, the EPU Managing Board could advise and recommend corrective policies after reporting to the OEEC Council. The board could also extend supplementary loans to countries that had exhausted their EPU quotas, attach conditions to their provision, and monitor domestic policy adjustments. In addition, officials from countries receiving exceptional credits were required to attend the monthly meeting of the EPU board for questioning and submit monthly memoranda for the board's review.

As already mentioned, the EPU needed a monetary unit (in which all accounts could be denominated) for both the compensation mechanism and the multilateralization of net debts or claims to be able to function properly. This was a sensitive issue, as the choice of this unit would also determine the exchange rate guarantee attached to the union's credit operations (Triffin 1957: 172). The EPU agreement created a special EPU unit of account, initially defined by a gold content equal to that of the 1950 US dollar. This gold content could be changed at any time by a decision of the OEEC Council. However, the unanimity rule for OEEC decisions made any such change highly improbable: the creditors would always have an interest in vetoing a devaluation and the debtors an interest in vetoing an appreciation of the EPU. So, it was stipulated that no country could veto a change equivalent to (or smaller than) the appreciation or depreciation of its own currency. This effectively implied a definition of the EPU unit of account in terms of the member currency that remained most stable (in terms of gold).

Triffin played a key role in these negotiations. In January 1950, the issue of a unit of account was the topic of intense negotiations. In a meeting of the financial subgroup, Tasca argued that it was desirable, in the eyes of US Congress, not to have the dollar as the unit of account for the EPU. Instead, he argued for a different unit of account. There then followed a discussion whether this could be an existing currency. Triffin intervened forcefully in the debate, arguing against the adoption of an existing currency:

> Mr. Triffin maintained that it was totally erroneous to tie the unit of account to another currency. The currency to which the unit was related should be defined in terms of gold, thus leaving it open to the participating countries to follow

uniformly a change in the gold value of the currency to which the unit of account was related. The maximum guarantee to the creditors needed only to be a guarantee that any depreciation of the unit of account in relation to gold should be no greater than the depreciation of the creditor's currency. This gold guarantee assures that the creditor is no worse off than it would have been in a bilateral system where the debtor's obligations would have been in the currency of the creditor.[26]

Triffin's proposal was largely accepted. Later, he claimed paternity for the formula and pointed to its significance for the future of European monetary integration. His aim had been to "define a form of exchange guarantee that might be used later to encourage a resumption of capital movements in Europe, and a monetary unit that might be adopted in future agreements on European economic integration" (Triffin 1957: 173). Travers summarized the work of the main protagonists in the EPU negotiations, Triffin, Ansiaux, Marjolin, and Figgures:

> The difficult process of getting all the OEEC countries to agree on them was greatly helped by Triffin's continuing inventiveness, on the ECA side, by Hubert Ansiaux's political sense and negotiating ability, as the Chairman of the OEEC Trade and Payments Committee, and by the technical brilliance and capacity for finding effective compromise solutions of Robert Marjolin, the Secretary-General of OEEC and Frank Figgures, the Head of the OEEC's Trade and Payments Directorate.[27]

Even Bernstein congratulated Triffin on the EPU and his work: "I hear a good deal about you and the fine work you are doing to get the U.S. and all the Europeans to work together in the EPU. My own feeling is that an excellent job has been done with the EPU and that it is destined to be a great constructive factor in Europe. Let me hear now and then about how things go with you."[28]

With the EPU, Triffin introduced a new geographical entity into his analysis: the region, which occupied that important space between the nation-state and the world economy (Maes and Pasotti 2018). He considered monetary regionalism, not only as a solution to Europe's internal imbalances, but also as an effective mechanism for dealing with dollar scarcity. Besides, the regional solution of returning to currency convertibility was less risky than a global approach.

But not everyone saw things as Triffin did. The EPU was initially confronted with a goodly amount of diffidence on the part of the existing international institutions. Notwithstanding Gutt's plea for active IMF involvement in European matters, the EPU was considered by many IMF

Executive Board members as being at odds with the philosophy of monetary reconstruction embodied in the Bretton Woods agreement (de Vries 1969). The Bank for International Settlements also had a "fairly ambiguous" attitude toward the EPU (Toniolo 2005: 333). On the one hand, it provided the technical skills and banking functions because of its clearing agent role, while on the other hand, it believed that the EPU was against the restoration of free exchange markets.

When the EPU was established, Triffin was appointed alternate US representative on the Managing Board. In fact, the Managing Board had a two-tier structure.[29] Each member was accompanied by, or could be represented by, his alternate. The group of alternates met between the board's sessions to clarify issues and work out solutions for technical questions. As part of this process, they drew up papers analyzing the issues and setting out the conflicting national views and options.

The US representative on the Managing Board was Hubert F. Havlik. Havlik had been a professor at Columbia University in the 1930s, teaching courses on economics and government, especially government regulation of industry. After some time in the War Production Board, he moved to the State Department, where he became chief of the Lend-Lease Division. In an interview, Havlik remarked that he was rather surprised that he was appointed US representative, as he had not negotiated the EPU agreement. He also revealed that Triffin was disappointed by this decision:

Well, this agreement was negotiated by Tasca, Triffin, et al. It was with considerable surprise that I heard from Tasca and Katz that they wanted me to sit as United States Representative on the Managing Board, as I had not negotiated the agreement. But they explained that I was a person who had demonstrated capacity in the other payments agreements and that what was required was the presence of a person in whom the United States had top administrative confidence. . . . Triffin was appointed as my alternate on the Managing Board. He was disappointed, partly because he felt he had negotiated the agreement, was well-known in Europe, etc.; also he did not know me well. But then we worked together for a period of about two years before he resigned to go to Yale University, and we had a relationship of very good mutual cooperation. He was an entirely dedicated person, dedicated to his principles of fostering an establishment of a central monetary system of some sort—essentially, I think, a kind of international central bank. But we got along. We had some problems; I think sometimes he felt, maybe, that I was not flexible enough, and sometimes I felt that he was too flexible.[30]

The decision to appoint Havlik, as well as Havlik's own comments, suggests that Triffin was distrusted in some US circles. It was an important factor for Triffin to accept, in 1951, a professorship at Yale University (see Section 3.7).

With the communist invasion of South Korea on June 25, 1950, the nature of the Marshall Plan changed drastically. Rearmament and other military issues came to dominate the agenda of the Western countries. A single-minded focus on European recovery was no longer the main priority.

3.6 THE GERMAN PAYMENTS CRISIS

A few days before the EPU agreement took force, the EPU had to face its first test with the German payments crisis. Even though production and exports had increased rapidly after the 1948 currency reform, the German economy lagged behind most other EPU countries, as its postwar reconstruction had started much later. Moreover, US aid was being scaled down, as a result of which German imports shifted substantially from the dollar area to the EPU area, widening Germany's EPU deficits. All of this contributed to a rapid exhaustion of the German EPU quota (Kaplan and Schleiminger 1989: 99).

As it grappled with the German payments crisis, the EPU board, in October 1950, called on the opinion of two independent experts: Alec Cairncross, who was economic adviser to the OEEC, and Per Jacobsson, who held the same position at the Bank for International Settlements (Clement 2006: 29). In their report, Cairncross and Jacobsson argued that, given the right policy mix, Germany's payments position would improve significantly over the months to come. In November 1950, the EPU Managing Board recommended a temporary line of credit accompanied by a program of financial and economic readjustment policies to be adopted by Germany under EPU supervision. The program included commitments to maintaining the existing exchange rate, abstaining from any deficit financing, and raising taxes. Moreover, it implied that the other EPU countries should endeavor to liberalize trade in goods of interest to Germany, grant generous quotas to German goods not on their free list, and refrain from seeking unreasonably large quotas for their own exports to Germany.

Early on, the results of this program were disappointing. At the time, there were heated discussions and disagreements, even among the Americans. In his interview, Havlik revealed that he and Katz were taking a harder line against US participation in the special loan, while Bissell and Triffin were arguing for more flexibility:

> But Katz put his neck on the line in talking with Bissell. He insisted and he won his point. But that put me and Triffin in a very difficult position, with a crisis

which almost cost me my health. The EPU Managing Board was thrown into long discussions, and there was a considerable amount of tension. Triffin was very anxious to provide some additional financial assistance and probably some of the Europeans pressed him. So, eventually, when I had to say at the Managing Board that the United States would not provide any additional assistance for the European Payments Union or to the Germans for settling the German debit balances, that was received like a cold fish.[31]

Havlik admitted that this episode offered a stern test of the cohesiveness of the Managing Board of the EPU. "For a time," he said, "it looked like those things would shatter." Moreover, it created considerable tensions between Havlik and Triffin and led to further discussions, in the OEEC secretariat too. Herbert Giersch, then a young economist in the OEEC Economics Division, raised the issue of whether it might not be appropriate to discuss the desirability of a German devaluation. His head of division, W. Brian Reddaway, a student of Keynes in Cambridge, brought the matter to Marjolin's attention.[32]

The OEEC then decided to temporarily suspend trade liberalization. This effort was put under the supervision of a group of independent experts to preclude a scramble for German import licenses and to ensure an allocation of licenses that would minimize the harmful impact of German restrictions on the weaker OEEC members. Triffin pointed out the "revolutionary character of this decision" as "it involved a renunciation by each country of its bilateral bargaining strength and sovereignty for protecting its national interests in the middle of a dangerous crisis" (Triffin 1957: 182). In the end, the measures had a significant impact on the German balance of payments. Consequently, the special loan was repaid and exchange controls were removed. By the spring of 1953, Germany had become the largest creditor in the EPU (Kaplan and Schleiminger 1989: 107). A strong German balance-of-payments position would remain a constant in the ensuing decades and this would put Germany in a strong position in European monetary negotiations.

Even if Triffin had favored more flexibility, the Managing Board's handling of the German payments crisis was in line with his own vision for the sustainable functioning of an international monetary system. It combined the provision of international liquidity as temporary relief—to avoid the need for severe restrictions on exchange transactions that would have deeply affected other EPU economies—with economic policy coordination among EPU countries.

The German case illustrated how the EPU system worked and the extent to which it genuinely involved taking collective decisions on an individual country's economic policies.[33] It established the role of the Managing Board as an international forum where national economic policies were examined and where international agreement was reached on whether a country's policies were in the general interest. Indeed, the German case established many of the principles that became major features of the EPU system and were favored by Triffin, notably:

- While the maintenance or restoration of a country's internal and external economic equilibrium was primarily its own responsibility, the country also had to take into account the interests of all the member countries, making progress toward their common goals.
- Trade and payments developments were very closely linked. They had to be dealt with together and by complementary measures and policies in both areas.
- Multilateral and nondiscriminatory trade and financial flows, as free from restriction as possible, were of fundamental importance. A country should justify and obtain the consent of the other member countries whenever it failed to maintain the agreed degree of freedom.
- If a country had significant imbalances within the EPU, the board had to examine not only the country's external policies but also its domestic policies. Countries should be prepared to cooperate in a full examination of all aspects of their economic policies.

Two particular aspects of crisis management were emphasized in the later literature (Kaplan and Schleiminger 1989: 116). The first was the use of macroeconomic policies, something that was highlighted in the *Federal Reserve Bulletin* in December 1951 and by Triffin himself (1957: 182). The second aspect was the advantage of a cooperative approach developed under an effective (regional) institution. As Triffin (1957: 182) later observed, it left "a deep impression on other countries," facilitating acceptance of their responsibility in resolving balance-of-payments problems. It also helped to reconcile a tightening up of the EPU settlement rules with further progress toward trade liberalization (Triffin 1957: 208). Later analyses of the EPU would support this idea (Eichengreen 1993; Oatley 2001).

With time, the management of the German payments crisis was widely recognized as a success. In Triffin's words, it endowed the Managing Board "with prestige and authority far beyond the most optimistic expectations of the promoters of the EPU Agreement" (Triffin 1957: 182). The way in which the German payments problems had been surmounted became a model for the crises the EPU had to confront. It also demonstrated that the (European) region could be an appropriate level for effective crisis management.

For Triffin, in line with his earlier analyses, the German crisis also showed the importance of the availability of sufficient international liquidity for a country with temporary balance-of-payments problems. In a later note, Triffin pleaded for the constitution of a very large EPU fund for special assistance operations. "This technique proved invaluable in the German case, and will become all the more necessary as debtors exhaust their quota and need temporary support for readjusting programs, if we are to avoid a brutal restoration of quantitative restrictions."[34] He further remarked that Bissell would have been in favor, "but only to support the creation of a supercentral bank by the Pleven Plan countries." However, according to Triffin, that idea was "completely premature and naïve" at the time (April 1952).

During these years Triffin also developed creative and imaginative ideas regarding the relationship between the IMF and the EPU. In a note of May 1951, he launched the idea, in line with his ideas about a regionalization of the IMF, that the EPU might become a sort of "European Branch" of the IMF. The IMF would then become a rediscounting agency for the EPU, rather than lending directly to individual EPU countries.[35] However, he admitted that such discussions were "obviously premature at this stage." In a letter to Bissell, in July 1951, Tasca summed up the EPU's achievements. He first presented the broad US objective as an effort "to improve Western Europe's ability to balance its own dollar payments and receipts at high levels of economic activity." He further stressed the liberalization of trade and payments, while also paying attention to the political dimension. "We have tried to achieve this result at politically acceptable standards of living," he said, "and with a minimum of resort to trade or payments restrictions, by obtaining an improved allocation of Europe's resources."[36]

Tasca also very clearly specified the limits of the EPU program: it was temporary and had to stay within the United States' global vision, in which the IMF had a key role. As Tasca pointed out, "the IMF's supreme jurisdiction with respect to the maintenance of a viable pattern of exchange rates, plus declining U.S. aid, offers the final assurance that the EPU area cannot isolate itself from the dollar area for any significant length of time." Along the same lines as Triffin (and later De Long and Eichengreen 1993), Tasca put strong emphasis on the institutional and cooperative elements of the EPU and the improvement in resource allocation:

> The discussions which have led to the present state of agreement on EPU have
> been of great value in providing working experience in European cooperation

and unity of action. Furthermore, the agreement itself will continue to provide more valuable experience of the same kind. I am confident that I need not belabour for you the important political and psychological boost which this agreement can give to European and Atlantic morale.

I might summarize our views by saying that we are not so naïve as to think that the EPU agreement will, like some miracle drug, cure all, or even any, of Western Europe's major economic problems. However, we do believe that it provides the type of institutional arrangements which are a necessary part of the economic environment if United States and European economic policies and developments over the next several years are to lead to a satisfactory attainment of the substance as well as the form of the objectives which we have set for ourselves. The economic success of the EPU agreement cannot be measured only in terms of the amount of gold which flows in intra-European settlements or in terms of the hardness of the EPU settlement schedules. Rather it must be measured in terms of the improved quality of trade which it produces, and in terms of related improvements in the pattern of European resource use, bringing increased output and productivity. The political measures are, I am sure, quite apparent to you.[37]

Triffin and many other people involved in the negotiations and management of the EPU would look back with nostalgia on the EPU experience. Marjolin, for example, strongly praised the spirit of cooperation, not to say complicity, at the EPU:

> There developed during the years 1948 to 1949 a close collaboration, which resulted often in life-long friendships among three groups of people: representatives of the ECA, European national representatives, and the Secretariat. Having gone through the experience of many other international organisations, I can say that the Marshall Plan experience was unique. Between the three groups I mentioned above, there was not only cooperation, but a kind of complicity to make the endeavour a success. National representatives, for instance, would often exchange information on the instructions they had received from their capitals and discuss the best way of side-tracking those which constituted a danger in relation to achieving the common purpose of European recovery.[38]

3.7 TRIFFIN'S SEARCH FOR A DESTINATION

During his years in Paris, Triffin was uncertain about his future prospects and was exploring different job opportunities. One of the options was a return to academia. He discussed this with Chamberlin in Harvard, who made him an informal offer for a short-term appointment there for the academic year 1950–1951.[39] Triffin turned it down, however, as he had just accepted the ECA position in Paris.

Triffin also considered a return to the IMF in Washington, after his leave of absence for the ECA. He discussed the matter with Overby and Irving Friedman, the assistant to the deputy managing director. Friedman, in May 1950, sent him a letter, saying, "I understand from Overby, as well as from our conversation in Paris, that you are thinking seriously about coming back to the Fund and more particularly to the Exchange Restrictions Department."[40] He then informally offered Triffin the position of assistant director of the Exchange Restrictions Department. Wary because of his previous experiences, Triffin replied that it depended very much on the IMF's attitude toward the EPU. He added that it was a difficult issue to discuss by mail and he hoped that Friedman would have an opportunity to come to Paris, so that they would be able to "talk about it more freely and adequately over a glass of champagne at the Champs Élysées."[41]

Of far greater interest to Triffin was the letter that he received on May 3, 1951, from Lloyd Reynolds, a former classmate of Triffin at Harvard, offering him the position of director of the Institute of International Studies at Yale University. Reynolds emphasized that, with respect to teaching, Triffin "could do as much or as little" as he wished, which would leave Triffin significant latitude for consulting work and policymaking activities. Triffin replied to Reynolds in a letter of May 8, 1951. Initially, he took a quite reticent position, saying that he was reluctant to leave his job "at this juncture." He considered his work at the ECA as "fascinating" and believed that the prospects for the future were very promising. In his view, the EPU had worked extremely well but the present organization was "only the forerunner of much bigger things to come in the way of European monetary integration and its linkage with an effective system in international monetary cooperation." Given this, he "would have liked to be present—and helpful—at the birth."[42] However, Triffin admitted that the Yale offer was "extremely tempting." Finally, there was also the question of timing. "I don't want to be a 'quitter' here," he said, "and I obviously could not leave OSR overnight. There are also some very practical problems involved in moving my family and in winding up two households (one here in Paris, and another in Washington)." Triffin also asked Bissell for advice, stating that he was "honestly very hesitant about it."[43] He asked him both about the situation in Yale (Bissell had obtained his PhD at Yale in 1939) and the potential to "build up EPU." Bissell took a month to reply, assuring Triffin that he was still determined to "strengthen the EPU" and to make it "a permanent institution which will advance us toward the goal of a single

European currency."[44] Moreover, he mentioned that, if Triffin stayed another year at the ECA, MIT "would be very much interested in you."

As early as the end of May, less than one month after the initial offer, Triffin decided to accept the Yale position, and he moved to New Haven in September 1951. As he was leaving the ECA so quickly, he agreed to assist the ECA further, especially in the renegotiation of the EPU agreement the following summer. Early in July 1951, Triffin replied to Bissell that he had already made up his mind to accept the offer from Yale. He admitted that he certainly felt "very blue about leaving EPU, and about missing also MIT where I have very close friends." In his letter, Triffin summed up the accomplishments of the EPU:

> As for EPU, I think we have every reason to be proud of the accomplishments of this first year. I am most impressed, not only with the financial side of it (which reduced our financing of gross intra-European deficits from 30% in the previous period to 7%) and with the trade objectives obtained, but also with the extraordinary influence and prestige which the Managing Board has developed in spite of all the opposition and pessimistic forecasts preceding its creation. Not only have all its decisions been unanimous, (as you know they could be taken by simple majority) but no action was ever delayed by lack of agreement in the Board. Moreover, the Board members individually have expressed most forcibly individual views often at variance with their governments' policies, and have been most successful in gaining their governments' acceptance to the Board's views, rather than vice versa.[45]

Triffin continued that his "main regret" in leaving the ECA was that he would no longer be able to help in developing the ECA position in the forthcoming negotiations. The stakes here were significant, as he noted: "We shall be facing very big problems of the permanent shape of EPU, of its link to the outside world and to the IMF, of its potential development toward a common reserve fund, and even possibly a joint central banking institute for Europe." Triffin further emphasized that it was important not only that the right decisions were taken but also "that they be taken as much as possible by the Europeans rather than under ECA dictation."[46]

The evidence suggests quite strongly that, during his Paris days, Triffin was torn between his policymaking work and a return to academic life. One of the reasons for his disappointment with policy work was probably that he felt that his qualities and the contributions that he could make, especially if given a more substantial role, were not sufficiently recognized, as when he was passed over for the position of US representative on the EPU Managing Board in favor of Havlik (as seen in Section 3.5). This raises naturally the issue of why Triffin was overlooked. It is clear that there was a certain suspicion toward Triffin; one of the primary reasons was that he was considered to be too close to the Europeans. This came clearly to the fore in a note from Frank Tamagna of the New York Federal Reserve Bank, in which he criticized Triffin's proposals to give more financial resources to the EPU on the grounds that they might be detrimental to the position of the IMF:

> Without passing on the details of the Triffin proposal, I would like to comment on the apparent concern with the inadequate resources of EPU and the proposal for a bigger EPU fund. . . . The solution offered, of raising additional resources so as to provide EPU with ample means, would seem to raise serious political difficulties, including objections from those groups in the U.S. Government which have steadily insisted that EPU would tend to become a permanent institution which, by fostering a regional system, would hamper the objective of world-wide multilateralism. Without excluding considerations for larger resources for EPU, it seems that the same objective could be achieved if the resources of the Monetary Fund could become available in those cases where the EPU resources would prove inadequate. I agree with Bob Solomon that "Triffin would no doubt agree" with this position, but the fact that this is not explicitly stated is likely to be construed as another attempt by Triffin (or the defenders of the Triffin proposals) to strengthen EPU and eliminate the Fund from any European arrangement.[47]

Naturally, for Triffin the relationship between the IMF and the EPU was a complex one and his ideas evolved through time (see Section 3.6). However, one can note that a few years later, in a secret letter to Monnet, Triffin would indeed argue that one advantage of a European Reserve Fund was that it would make the European Community more independent from the IMF (see Section 5.4).

The suspicion about Triffin also may have had some roots in concerns that he had communist sympathies. Naturally, as a pacifist and a progressive Catholic, he would make for a good suspect. Triffin did in fact have to justify himself for his contacts with several people who were suspected of communist sympathies, including his mother-in-law. In an official testimony at the US Embassy in Paris in July 1954, the high days of McCarthyism, Triffin admitted that his mother-in-law had had communist leanings. However, Triffin argued that, despite some "foolish" associations, she was a loyal American. Moreover, the relationship between Triffin's wife and her mother was not so close:

> That with respect to the activities of my mother-in-law, Mrs. Zelma Brandt, I know that she has been a "joiner" of causes for a number of years. She at one

time joined the America First Committee, which I understand was suspected of having Fascist overtones. I have found that it is a part of her character to be opposed to generally accepted opinions and she expressed this by joining such organizations. I knew that she was connected with some Communist organizations because when she attempted to join the ADA which I understand is an anti-Communist organization Mr. Arthur Schlesinger contacted me and asked me if she had stopped such activities. I wrote and told him that I felt sure she is a loyal American despite some rather foolish associations in the past. I felt that if they accepted her application she might find some contentment. That I knew that my mother-in-law visited the Soviet Union and in fact that she tried to persuade my wife who was then fifteen years of age to go to school in Russia which my wife refused to do. I would state that the relationship between my wife and her mother is not particularly close, chiefly because of emotional difficulties between them and that my wife has never been under her mother's domination or influence since our marriage.[48]

The final result of Triffin's agonies and maneuvers was that he left for Yale but stayed on as a consultant to the ECA. This was not too bad for him. He returned to the academic world, recovering his intellectual freedom, but he stayed involved in policy work, which he adored. This shows Triffin as a clever and agile negotiator. It also shows that he was willing to sacrifice powerful positions to preserve his independence.

3.8 TRIFFIN'S RETROSPECTIVE VIEW OF THE EUROPEAN PAYMENTS UNION

The EPU led to heated discussions among economists, including both policymakers and academics (Maes and Pasotti 2018). Two issues very much dominated the debates: whether the EPU was a discriminatory trade and payments area and whether the EPU was a monetary gimmick.

Viner, in his 1950 book *The Customs Union Issue*, played a central role in these discussions. He questioned whether a customs union would necessarily be a movement in the direction of free trade. In Viner's view, the primary effects of a customs union were shifts in production, "and the shift can be either to lower- or to higher-cost sources, depending on circumstances" (Viner 1950: 44). Viner analyzed the impact of a customs union on trade flows, introducing the concepts of "trade creation" and "trade diversion." In the case of trade creation, there is a shift from domestic supply to supply from the customs partner. This will increase economic welfare as higher-cost domestic sources of supply are replaced by lower-cost imports from the customs partner. In the case of trade diversion, there is a shift in supply from a nonmember country to a member country. This has a welfare cost as lower-cost sources of supply are replaced by higher-cost supplies in the partner country. Basically, a customs union will be welfare creating when the trade-creating effects outweigh the trade-diverting effects. Viner also discussed other repercussions of customs unions such as terms of trade effects and economies of scale.

When the EPU was established, many economists believed that it created a discriminatory trade and payments area, which would be at odds with the philosophy of the postwar international system. During a conference in the early 1950s at Princeton University, several delegates expressed "strong doubts" as to whether the EPU would remedy structural imbalances rather than perpetuate them. Ragnar Nurkse, then at Columbia University, argued that he was rather suspicious of proposals about stabilization loans or clearing pools. "To my mind," he said, "they are methods of concealed relief or aid based on the wrong criteria. Countries will get help that are not the most deserving recipients" (as quoted in Knorr 1952: 28).

Triffin offered the rebuttal. He pointed up how successfully EPU members had liberalized trade among themselves. He insisted that the EPU had actually made for less discrimination. This was in contrast to Viner's argument that it was theoretically possible for overall discrimination to be raised by the skillful removal of discriminatory practices within a regional bloc. However, Triffin acknowledged that the EPU discriminated against dollar imports, but he also claimed that the gradual liberalization of intra-European payments would boost European competitiveness. "It certainly forced the higher-cost countries within the EPU region to compete with the lower-cost members," he said, "and this is an indispensable preparation for full convertibility." All this contributed to the readjustment of the European cost and price pattern vis-à-vis the United States, thereby alleviating "dollar scarcity," the fundamental imbalance in the world economy.

Later, Triffin (1957) objected to the criticisms based on Viner's (1950) "trade-creating" and "trade-diverting" categories to analyze the effects of a customs union on trade flows. Triffin pointed out that the presumption of trade-diverting and trade-creating impact must be assessed by considering the actual circumstances surrounding the regional agreements. He nevertheless acknowledged that the EPU "entailed a certain degree of discrimination against non-EPU members." However, he argued that cooperation in the EPU agreement was extended to an area where countries were highly interdependent and their trade accounted for nearly 60% of world trade. This allowed efficiency-enhancing arbitrage to operate strongly, minimizing price distortions. He also affirmed that price distortions were further minimized by the fact that the economies of Europe, notwithstanding their troubles, possessed a number of important industries that allowed intra-EPU trade to drive prices down to the levels established by the lowest-cost producers. Indeed, the United States was not always the lowest-cost producer of particular goods, as, "for many categories of goods, the lowest European prices which [domestic producers] had to meet— Swiss prices for some goods, Belgian or German prices for others, etc.— were probably as competitive as those of any third countries, including the United States" (Triffin 1957: 207). In the later literature on customs unions, these elements, like a large economic area and more competitive economies, were singled out as factors favoring trade creation (Robson 1987: 22). Moreover, Triffin argued that one should also look at the "dynamic" effects of the EPU. "The trade-creating and trade-diverting effects of regional integration," he said, "cannot be fully appraised by looking only at the immediate and direct trade concessions incorporated in a regional agreement. Indirect policy and incentives are far more significant for arriving at a broad judgment of the overall impact of the agreement on future trade patterns" (Triffin 1957: 262). In the EPU agreement, "indirect policy and incentives" were related to the provision of stabilization credits by the creditor countries to the debtor members of the system; the willingness of the creditor countries to speed up their own liberalization measures beyond the formal commitments agreed to by all members, and to release temporarily from such commitments partner countries that encountered heavy balance-of-payments pressures; the willingness to submit to international discussion and scrutiny the whole range of their economic policies; and the existence of a highly effective machinery for continuous consultation and negotiation among members.

The role of the EPU in postwar European reconstruction has been emphasized in the literature. Milward argued that the EPU, and the European Coal and Steel Community, were the "pillars of the reconstruction" of Western Europe (Milward 1987: 470). The EPU was designed "not just to permit but also to encourage national policies of expansion" (Milward 1987: 487). Eichengreen too comes to the conclusion that "the EPU was critical by virtue of its positive spillovers for domestic and international political economy. These spillovers in turn contributed importantly to the post-war growth process" (Eichengreen 1993: 95). According to Eichengreen, the discriminatory features of the EPU, which many economists emphasized at the time, did appear to have affected the direction of international trade. However, accompanying policies and fortuitous circumstances minimized the negative side effects, and "the EPU offered the best of both worlds" (Eichengreen 1993: 117).

A second criticism argued that the EPU was a monetary "gimmick" and that it might, by rendering prevailing maladjustments easier to bear, prevent the real problems from being tackled. As Viner argued:

> All these devices, though there are better and poorer ones, do not of themselves solve any problems. They may cover up the problem and create new problems. They will solve problems only if their manipulators are constantly bent on making these gimmicks unnecessary in the future. There is always the danger that these devices are sold to the world as true solutions and will thus free responsible leaders from the obligation to search for genuine, even though perhaps only partial, remedies. . . . It is a gimmick literature. It presents gimmicks as genuine solutions and thus creates a diversion from really creative effort. (as quoted in Knorr, 1952: 29)

Geiger, who had developed the first plans for multilateral clearing, also criticized Triffin on this point. He shared Viner's fear that the monetary arrangement proposed by Triffin, "though no doubt likely to work better than existing arrangements, would work so well as to obscure many of the basic problems that must be attacked. It would obscure them not permanently, but it would obscure them long enough to permit fundamental disequilibrium to grow" (as quoted in Knorr, 1952: 30). This is naturally a classical dilemma for a central bank: monetary accommodation gives other policymakers time to tackle the basic problems of economic imbalances, but also diminishes the urgency to do so.

Triffin did not deny these dangers. He was in agreement that the fundamental issues behind the payments imbalances were not of a monetary nature. But he was concerned with what could be done until such time as the fundamental problems could be tackled effectively. As usual, he was interested in ways of "solving some of our very concrete monetary problems of the moment." In Triffin's view, the EPU was a concrete way to make progress with the liberalization of European trade and payments. As he put the matter in 1952:

> Basic problems are rarely solved overnight. I reject, however, the defeatist conclusion that as long as those basic problems are not solved, there is no use in doing anything at all to adjust ourselves to existing disequilibria in the best possible manner. . . . Call it gimmick, if you want. Say that it detracts attention from the basic problem, and that problem is not simply a monetary one. All that is true, but the fact that a better monetary arrangement is no panacea still does not mean that you can live without any monetary arrangement—or gimmick— whatsoever, or that an absurd monetary arrangement, which needlessly

reinforces bilateralism and discrimination, is then preferable to a monetary arrangement which preserves the maximum of transferability and multilateralism. (as quoted in Knorr 1952: 30–31)

Moreover, Triffin stressed the importance of a pragmatic, step-by-step approach, but based on a bold vision. In his view the key issue was "to know in what general direction we want to move, and then to find out what the next steps are which are feasible now." Nor, he said, should one "attempt to predict to the last detail . . . because the exact nature of these final arrangements will depend a great deal on the successes and failures we have met in approaching them." Instead, "We must keep our plans sufficiently broad and flexible to adjust them continuously in the light of experience" (as quoted in Knorr 1952: 44–45).

The EPU experience showed that multilateralism in trade and payments required cooperation among countries based on mutual commitments and binding rules. In Triffin's view, this was not feasible on a worldwide basis. "It is possible only among countries which are highly interdependent . . . keenly conscious of their interdependence and able to understand each other's problems and policies. These factors—different in degree, but not in kind, from these underlying a fuller political union—explain the success of, and justify the need for, regional cooperation in trade and payments" (Triffin 1954: 212). These elements clearly point to the EPU as a separate geographical entity, as compared to countries or the world economy. Triffin further emphasized the relevance of an institutional framework, giving countries incentives to cooperate and to observe the rules of the system. For him, the Managing Board and the unit of account were indispensable elements of the EPU.

The EPU was to shape Triffin's approach toward reform of the European and international monetary system. While he also developed proposals for a global reform of the international monetary system, he put the emphasis on regional monetary integration, with Europe as one of the pillars of a multipolar international monetary system. This will be discussed in the next chapters.

NOTES

1. Triffin, "Postwar Reform of Central Banking," Draft, March 20, 1946, Triffin, RTAY, Box No. 7.
2. Travers's book draft, 1983, OECDA.
3. Triffin, "The Use of Purchasing Power Parity Theory in the Study of Postwar Exchange Rates," October 16, 1946, p. 5, IMFA, Collection Executive Board Documents (CEBD), Research Department Memorandum (RDM) 362266.

4. Triffin, "Initial Par Values, France," October 30, 1946, RTAY, Box No. 6.

5. Triffin, "The New Proposals for an ITO Charter," October 1, 1946, IMFA, CEBD, RDM 362245.

6. Triffin and Brenner, in consultation with Pazos and Del Canto, "Multiple Currency Practices," January 3, 1947, p. 5, IMFA, CEBD, RDM 272734.

7. Bernstein and Triffin, "Economic Aspects of the Problem of Cross Rates," RD-503 Revised, International Monetary Fund Research Department, Staff Memorandum No. 169, RTAY, Box No. 7.

8. Triffin, Italy's Progress in 1948, RD-804, March 4, 1949, BIHA, Baffi Papers, Pratiche, no. 30, f.1.

9. Triffin, Italy's Progress in 1948, RD-804, March 4, 1949, BIHA, Baffi Papers, Pratiche, no. 30, f.1.

10. Letter from Baffi to Triffin, October 7, 1963, BIHA, Baffi Papers, Pratiche, no. 1, f.1.

11. Triffin 1947, with R. Bertrand, "The Unresolved Problem of Financing European Trade," with conclusive remarks by Bernstein, December 29, 1947, Staff Memorandum No. 160, IMFA, CEBD, RDM 270821.

12. Triffin, "Multilateralization of European Payment Agreements Among Fund Members," May 7, 1948, p. 1, IMFA, CEBD, RDM 294415.

13. Triffin, "January 1949 Sessions of the OEEC Supervisory Sub-Committee and Intra-European Payments Committee," February 17, 1949, p. 8, IMFA, CEBD, RDM 292637.

14. Triffin, "The OEEC Plan for the Financing of Intra-European Payments, 1948–1949," November 8, 1948, IMFA, CEBD, RDM 293173.

15. Triffin, "The Multilateralization of Drawing Rights," Staff Memorandum No. 312, p. 6, January 28, 1949, IMFA, CEBD, RDM 292639.

16. Triffin, "The Multilateralization of Drawing Rights," Staff Memorandum No. 312, p. 6–7, January 28, 1949, IMFA, CEBD, RDM 292639.

17. Letter from Bernstein to Triffin, January 17, 1950, RTA.

18. Travers's book draft, 1983, OECDA.

19. Travers's book draft, 1983, OECDA.

20. Travers's book draft, 1983, OECDA.

21. Travers's book draft, 1983, OECDA.

22. Letter from Triffin to Gutt, January 17, 1950, original emphasis, RTA.

23. Letter from Bernstein to Triffin, April 18, 1950, RTA.

24. Letter from Triffin to Bernstein, April 26, 1950, RTA.

25. Letter from Triffin to Bernstein, April 26, 1950, RTA.

26. Minutes of the eighth meeting of the Financial Subgroup of the Executive Committee's Working Party No. 3, January 11, 1950, OECDA.

27. Travers's book draft, 1983, OECDA.

28. Letter from Bernstein to Triffin, April 23, 1951, RTA.

29. Travers's book draft, 1983, OECDA.

30. Interview Havlik, June 20, 1973, HSTLM.

31. Interview Havlik, June 20, 1973, HSTLM.

32. Memorandum, March 23, 1951, OECDA.

33. Travers's book draft, 1983, OECDA.

34. Letter from Triffin to Ansiaux, April 14, 1952, RTAY, Box No. 16.

35. Triffin, "Possible Outline of IMF-EPU Cooperation," May 11, 1951, RTAY, Box No. 16.

36. Letter from Tasca to Bissell, July 3, 1951, RTA.

37. Letter from Tasca to Bissell, July 3, 1951, RTA.
38. Travers's book draft, 1983, OECDA.
39. Letter from Chamberlin to Triffin, November 25, 1949, RTA.
40. Letter from Friedman to Triffin, May 19, 1950, RTA.
41. Letter from Triffin to Friedman, June 6, 1950, RTA.
42. Letter from Triffin to Reynolds, May 8, 1951, RTA.
43. Letter from Triffin to Bissell, May 7, 1951, RTA.
44. Letter from Bissell to Triffin, June 21, 1951, RTA.
45. Letter from Triffin to Bissell, August 2, 1951, RTA.
46. Letter from Triffin to Bissell, August 2, 1951, RTA.
47. Note from Tamagna, July 1, 1953, OECDA.
48. Triffin testimony, US Embassy Paris, July 14, 1954, RTA.

CHAPTER 4
Bretton Woods Cassandra

4.1 INTRODUCTION

In 1951, Triffin became a professor at Yale University. Notwithstanding his return to academia, he retained a very strong interest in policy issues, especially regarding the international monetary system (IMS). At the core of his preoccupations was the liquidity position of the IMS, a strong continuity with his 1946 essay "National Central Banking and the International Economy" (see Section 2.5).

Triffin's view on international monetary liquidity was very much shaped by the evolution of national monetary systems, where gold had gradually lost its functions in favor of a managed currency. This was also a key theme of his professors at Louvain (see Section 1.3). Triffin often emphasized this point himself. "The historical trend toward the national displacement of commodity money by fiduciary money, and toward the increasingly centralized orientation and management of the latter by national authorities, will be duplicated in the international field by a similar displacement of gold reserves by fiduciary reserves" (Triffin 1967b: 134).

Triffin had a very optimistic and very Keynesian belief in a better way of managing the world economy. In his view, an international currency was "an aspect of the adjustment of the former tribal, feudal and national institutions . . . to the ever-changing realities of a more and more interdependent world" (Triffin 1967b: 134). It was part of his broader historical perspective, which emphasized the "long march of mankind toward its unity and a better control of its own fate" and was very much in line with the teleological ideas of Teilhard de Chardin that Triffin had embraced during his time at university (see Section 1.2). In a debate in Paris, Jean de Largentaye, who translated Keynes's *General Theory* into French and had

Robert Triffin. Ivo Maes, Oxford University Press (2021). © Oxford University Press.
DOI: 10.1093/oso/9780190081096.001.0001

been one of the French negotiators at Bretton Woods, described Triffin as the "prophet of the International Central Bank" (Conseil économique et social 1967: 134). This was certainly true, as Triffin was not a nationalist but a world citizen and a passionate crusader for a true IMS.

Notwithstanding this optimistic world view, by the end of the 1950s, Triffin had become ever more worried about the United States' international reserve position. This was due to the US gold losses and increase in dollar liabilities. In his view, the United States' balance-of-payments deficits and the ensuing continued deterioration in its net reserve position would undermine foreigners' confidence in the dollar as a safe asset. The Bretton Woods system was therefore not sustainable, leading Triffin to formulate his famous dilemma:

> The gold exchange standard may . . . help in relieving a shortage of world monetary reserves. It does so only to the extent that the key currency countries are willing to let their net reserve position decline. If they allow this to happen, however, and to continue indefinitely, they tend to bring about a collapse of the system itself through the gradual weakening of foreigners' confidence in the key currencies. (Triffin 1960: 67)

Triffin so established his reputation as the Cassandra who predicted the end of Bretton Woods. But Triffin was an "optimistic" Cassandra. He believed in a reform of the IMS. Like Keynes, he sought a more international solution for the world liquidity problem, a true "internationalization" of the foreign exchange component of the world's international reserves. While Triffin correctly predicted the breakdown of Bretton Woods, the 1970s did not bring a depression, like the 1930s, but high inflation, in large part due to strongly expansionary US economic policies. In this chapter, the focus is on the development of Triffin's ideas in the second half of the 20th century, considering his position both in the academic debates and in the discussions among policymakers. But before that, it is important to take a look at life in Yale and Triffin's reaction to the Vietnam War.

4.2 YALE AND THE VIETNAM WAR

Triffin arrived at Yale University in September 1951. At the time, Lloyd Reynolds was building up the Yale Economics Department. He was chair of the department from 1951 to 1959 and he more than doubled the faculty, from 31 to 65 professors (Sadeghi 2005). In 1950, he had attracted James Tobin, a future Nobel Memorial Prize winner (Dimand 2014).

In 1951, not only did Triffin come to Yale, but also so did Henry Wallich (with whom Triffin had worked on the Dominican Republic; see Section 2.4) and William Fellner. Fellner was a Hungarian immigrant and also a policy-oriented economist (he was a member of the Council of Economic Advisers from 1973 to 1975). He was also active in international economics. Yale needed to reinforce international economics as it had lost several members of its Institute of International Studies, as well as funding from the Rockefeller Foundation, to Princeton.[1] In the 1960s, together with Triffin and Fritz Machlup, Fellner would become one of the animators of the Bellagio Group on the reform of the IMS (see Section 4.5). In 1955, Reynolds succeeded in a major coup with the Cowles Commission's move from Chicago to Yale (Triffin had been a visiting scientist at Cowles in July 1939; see Section 1.7). In fact, the Cowles Commission in Chicago had tried to recruit Tobin as its research director. After Tobin's refusal, and with growing conflict—methodological, ideological, and personal—between the Cowles Commission and the emerging Chicago school of Milton Friedman, the Cowles Commission left Chicago (Dimand 2019). As part of the commission's move (it was renamed the Cowles Foundation at Yale), several eminent economists joined the Yale Economics Department, though some left after a few years. Of particular importance for Yale were Jacob Marshak and Tjalling Koopmans (Shiller 2011). Koopmans, a Dutch immigrant and former student of Jan Tinbergen, was a future Nobel Memorial Prize winner. Marshak had been a student of Eugen Slutsky in Kiev, a PhD student in Heidelberg, and the founding director of the Oxford Institute of Statistics. Very much like Sir John Hicks (1935), he conceived of the theory of money as embedded in a theory of asset markets and of choice under risk (Dimand and Hagemann 2019; Maes 1991). He would have a significant influence on Tobin's work on portfolio theory—for which Tobin would be awarded the Nobel Memorial Prize—and the Yale monetary school.

At Yale, Triffin was especially close to Tobin and Reynolds (interview Kerry and Eric Triffin). Triffin and Reynolds knew one another from their time at Harvard, as both PhD students and instructors. Triffin also got along well with Reynolds's wife Mary, with whom he shared a love for good red wine. As Triffin (1990: 39) recounted about his decision to move to Yale, "I gave Lloyd and Mary my assent at one of the best restaurants in Paris, as we were enjoying a Nuit-Saint-Georges 1937, which—to my total surprise—Mary identified after only a moment's hesitation, something which I could not have done myself. They are both still among our dearest friends". Triffin was also very close to Tobin. They shared the same fundamental approach to economics, even though Tobin was technically more adept. As observed by Shiller (2011), Tobin was "moral"; he viewed economics as a means of strengthening growth and employment. Like Triffin, Tobin was a monk in economist's clothing.

At Yale, Triffin made two important contributions to the life of the university (Tobin 1988). First, he founded (and fostered) a graduate program in International and Foreign Economic Administration, designed to give economics training to promising young or middle-aged people already in government service, particularly in central banks. The program focused on economic development and international economic relations, and Triffin invited James Meade, a future Nobel Memorial Prize winner who was then at the London School of Economics, to deliver the opening lecture.[2] Many of the Yale program's alumni came to occupy positions of influence in central banks, ministries, and international organizations, and the program thus contributed to Triffin's worldwide network.

Then, in 1967, Triffin became master of Berkeley College, one of Yale's twelve undergraduate residences. As observed by Tobin (1988): "He and Lois dedicated themselves to their 300-odd adopted adult children, who revered them with great affection." It was a turbulent period, with civil rights protests (against discrimination of African Americans), the Vietnam War, and student unrest and revolt. But, as noted by Tobin, "Robert's sympathetic understanding of students' concerns and values, exemplified by the altruistic undertakings of his own sons, was an important factor in maintaining peace and civility in his college and throughout our campus." As a convinced pacifist since his studies in Louvain (see Section 1.2) and a person open to other cultures, Triffin could indeed connect with the students of the 1960s. Moreover, his wife, Lois, captured the spirit of the times. Always nonconventional and already a yoga fanatic in the late 1940s, she set up a Zen center at Berkeley. Throughout their life, their sons were involved in altruistic undertakings, something they regard as a legacy of their father and mother.[3] As young adults, Kerry and Eric were organizing buying clubs to pool food orders and buy wholesale. This project developed into a true food cooperative, with all the members working in the store for one hour a month. Later, they and several friends started a collectively operated natural foods and vegetarian restaurant. The restaurant hosted poetry nights, folk music, and other progressive activities. The Triffin family took the lead in a petition against an interstate highway exit ramp as it would destroy two local parks. Against all expectations, they succeeded with their protests and the exit ramp was redesigned. Being master at Berkeley allowed Triffin to try out a plan for group representation, inspired by the Paris events of May 1968. It is noteworthy that his original plan for "a participatory democracy with full representation of the voters" appeared on the front page of *Le Monde*, France's leading newspaper, on July 9, 1968.

With the election of John F. Kennedy as president, the 1960s started with high hopes for progressives in the United States. Triffin himself played a role in Kennedy's team of economists (see Section 4.5). However, the Vietnam War and the ensuing student protest led to growing disappointment in Kennedy among progressives, including Triffin. Later in life, Triffin was very explicit about this. "At first, like most people, I was enthused by his [Kennedy's] social programs and plans for racial harmony. Later, I came round to de Gaulle's view that Kennedy wanted to make people happy in spite of themselves, even if that entailed using force, and that he was motivated by crude anti-communism. Wasn't the great hero of Kennedy actually James Bond?" (Triffin 1990: 30).

The Vietnam War would lead to deep and painful divisions in American society. The Triffin family was completely united against the war and the escalation of the US participation in it. Theirs was an activist opposition, as they took part in several protests against the war. A major issue, at the universities too, was the military draft, which more and more young Americans tried to avoid. Triffin was critical of the draft and he strongly backed his eldest son Nick's application as a conscientious objector.[4] He also supported the young men who turned in their draft cards, a clear act of civil disobedience (a principle that had earlier been advocated by Einstein in the 1930s; see Section 1.2). This led to agonizing discussions with some of his old friends, including Eugene Rostow, the former dean of the Yale Law School, who had become President Johnson's under secretary of state for political affairs. In a letter of October 1967, Rostow made the sources of his disagreement with Triffin crystal clear: "Bob, there is a line between protest and anarchy. In a democratic society, and in other societies governed by law, the ultimate component of the Social Contract is the citizen's moral obligation to obey the law, and to seek change in law and policy only by legal means. It is arrogance—and worse, it is lynch law—to say that citizens can decide for themselves what laws to obey, to evade the draft, or to incite others to do so."[5] In January 1973, Triffin and several of his Yale colleagues wrote an open letter to President Nixon. The so-called Yale group charged President Nixon with the failure of the Paris peace talks and accused him of attempting to extract from Hanoi a surrender by "unrestrained intimidation through terror bombing." The group asserted: "The foundations of our democracy have been shaken by Mr. Nixon's usurping of the powers of Congress, by his attempts to curb freedom of the press and television and by his unwillingness to explain himself to the American people."[6]

By contrast, a much more enjoyable moment during Triffin's period at Yale was the visit by the Belgian king and queen, Baudouin and Fabiola, in

1976, when they stayed for a week at Berkeley College. The king was interested in getting to know the United States better. He chose to do this during a private visit, not an official one, and Triffin noted that "the King preferred to stay with us rather than with the President of Yale so that his contact with the University would be as 'normal' as possible" (Triffin 1990: 67). This worked out very well and the king and queen took most of their meals at a student table at Berkeley College. The king had meetings and seminars with eminent Yale professors, very much focused on US economic and political issues. The queen had a specific program, specially geared to her interests, especially the differences between Belgium and the United States regarding children's education and health care. Moreover, when visiting New Haven, "she made a point of including the poorest districts which visitors are not usually shown" and also visited the food cooperative where Triffin's sons Kerry and Eric were involved.

Triffin's work at Yale left him time for foreign lectures and consultancy work, which was also excellent for the renown and prestige of Yale University. From 1958 to 1961, Triffin was a professor at the Graduate Institute of International Relations in Geneva. He also participated in a number of missions, the focus of which was often on regional monetary integration. In the mid-1950s, he was a consultant to the United Nations Economic Commission for Latin America, when the first steps were being taken to reorganize and simplify the region's existing system of payment arrangements. Together with Pierre Uri, Triffin also undertook several missions for the United Nations Economic Commission for Asia and Far East. Typically, Uri focused on the trade aspects and Triffin on monetary cooperation.[7] In August 1960, when the newly independent state of Congo was negotiating the liquidation of the Central Bank of Belgian Congo and Ruanda-Urundi, Triffin was a consultant to the Congolese government.

One of Triffin's first missions was to Iran, for the United Nations in 1952, together with Gutt and Jorge Sol (an old colleague and close friend from his days at the International Monetary Fund [IMF]). During his visit, Triffin met Prime Minister Mossadegh, who had nationalized the oil industry. Gutt wrote a short poem, called "The Cocktails," during this mission, highlighting Triffin's statistical work:

> The cocktails that we loved too much
> The compliments that your eyes drank in
> The waltzes with Lefébure
> All very bad for the stomach
> Yet, the harmful vapors,
> A ransom to pay for golden Martinis,

Will fly out the window when you know
That thirty-seven single people

Good dancers, affluent, astute-looking
—The statistic comes from Triffin—
Await, with beating hearts, the time

When you can get out of bed.
(This sonnet is called Oh the illusion of time!
"Working at Bank Melli")[8]

4.3 EUROPE AND THE MONEY MUDDLE

Back in the academic world, Triffin produced his first important book in 1957, entitled *Europe and the Money Muddle: From Bilateralism to Near-Convertibility, 1947–1956*. It was very much based on his earlier experience as a policymaker, especially in Paris with the European Payments Union (EPU).

Contrary to what the title might suggest, the book was really optimistic about the situation in Europe. In a key table, Triffin (1957: 87) had assembled the core statistics of the European economy (Table 4.1 offers a selection of Triffin's indicators). They showed significant increases in production, in both agriculture and industry, compared to both the prewar period (1938) and the immediate postwar period (1947). Moreover, Europe's

Table 4.1 EUROPE*: INDICES OF RECOVERY, 1947–1955

	1947	1955
GNP Volume (1938 = 100)	91	144
Agricultural production	83	128
Industrial production	88	169
Domestic capital formation	102	174
Volume of exports	59	156
Volume of imports	98	127
Balance on Goods and Services	−7.2	1.4
(in billions of US dollars)		
A. With the United States	−5.4	−0.1
B. With other countries	−1.8	1.5

* The European countries of the Organization for European Economic Cooperation
Source: Triffin (1957: 87).

exports had expanded enormously and the balance of payments had swung from a substantial deficit in 1947 to a surplus in 1955. Even with the United States, the balance of payments was close to equilibrium, compared to a significant deficit in 1947, the period of "dollar scarcity."

In stark contrast to the post–World War I period, inflation had been brought under control. In line with his monetarist methodology (see Section 2.3), Triffin stressed that this "final abatement" of both internal inflationary pressures and balance-of-payments deficits was conditional upon the restoration of overall monetary balance. Three factors were crucial: (1) the end of credit monetization; (2) the absorption of the monetary overhang (the massive increase in the money supply during the war, when price rises were limited due to controls and production was focused on war aims)—the overhang was wiped out by monetary purges, production increases, and price increases; and (3) the adjustment of exchange rates to the new pattern of international prices (Triffin 1957: 85).

Triffin emphasized very strongly that Europe's recovery was based on sound fundamentals, in terms of both price stability and the creation of a strong productive basis through massive investment. The recovery was much stronger than a mere reconstruction of war-time destruction and damages. "Large-scale investment," he said, "combined with monetary readjustments, have brought to European economies a degree of strength and vitality which contrasts sharply not only with the near bankruptcy of 1947 but also with the relative stagnation and recurrent monetary instability of the pre-war era" (Triffin 1957: 85–86).

Always in touch with the facts, Triffin was one of the first economists to point out that the period of "dollar scarcity" was over. With the growing US balance-of-payments deficit, the European countries had been able to boost their international reserves, while those of the United States declined. Triffin even became quite optimistic about the distribution of international reserves in the world, with one significant exception, the United Kingdom, "whose gold reserves and dollar holdings continue to fluctuate widely from year to year and provide only a fractional cover for foreign-held sterling balances" (Triffin 1957: 270). However, even for the United Kingdom, the situation had improved as sterling liabilities had declined in the postwar years.

In the book's conclusions, Triffin emphasized that the enormous improvement in the reserve position of European countries was primarily the result of a vast redistribution of the net reserve position from the United States to the rest of the world (Table 4.2). Gold and dollar holdings outside the United States had risen by more than $12 billion since 1949. However, only $2.6 billion of this increase came from additions to the world's monetary gold stock. The overwhelming portion of the increase—nearly $10

Table 4.2 GOLD RESERVES AND DOLLAR HOLDINGS, 1938–1955
(IN BILLIONS OF US DOLLARS, AT THE END OF THE YEAR)

	1938	1949	1955
I. **World (Gold)**	26.3	35.4	38.0
II. **United States (Net = A – B)**	12.4	16.3	6.5
A. Gold	14.6	24.6	21.8
B. Dollar balances	2.2	8.2	15.2
III. **Other (Gold plus Dollar Holdings)**	13.8	19.1	31.5
A. International	–	3.3	4.0
B. Foreign countries	13.8	15.8	27.5
Of which:			
1. Continental Western Europe and dependencies	7.3	6.3	13.6
2. Sterling area	3.9	2.8	4.0

Source: Triffin (1957: 311).

billion—reflected gold losses and increases in short-term liabilities on the part of the United States. Triffin observed the vulnerability of this process: "It is evident that such a movement could not continue indefinitely without eventually undermining confidence in the dollar itself" (Triffin 1957: 297), a clear formulation of the Triffin dilemma.

Moreover, Triffin had not forgotten how, in the 1930s, the gold exchange standard had fallen apart. In his view, the vulnerability of the gold exchange standard to sudden shifts from one currency to another or from foreign exchange balances into gold had been amply illustrated by the events of the early 1930s. In support of his case, Triffin reminded his readers that "Massive conversions of foreign-held sterling assets into gold and dollars—particularly by the Bank of France—played a large role in the sterling crisis of September 1931." The result was "a generalized flight into gold and a drastic contraction in the foreign exchange component of international monetary reserves" (Triffin 1957: 295–296).

The implication in Triffin's view was that the IMS needed reforming. He therefore proposed a system based on deposit accounts at the IMF. In line with his ideas for the EPU, he also included an exchange risk guarantee for the deposits at the IMF:

The solution of this dilemma should lead us to explore more fully than has been done up to now the possibility of broadening the basis of the gold exchange standard and of protecting the system against erratic and unnecessary shifts from one reserve currency into another and from reserve currencies into gold. This could be done by inducing or requiring all countries—or at least all major countries—to maintain an appropriate proportion of their international monetary reserves in the form of a deposit account with the International Monetary Fund. Such accounts would be fully usable in international payments and would carry an exchange risk guarantee with respect either to gold or to an internationally defined unit of account. They could be drawn upon at any time to make payments in any currency whatsoever, or even converted into gold, as long as the proportion of the country's international deposits to its total reserves is maintained above the minimum agreed to. (Triffin 1957: 299)

Triffin believed that such a system would preserve the advantages of the gold exchange standard while eliminating the major sources of weakness that caused its demise in the early 1930s. Reserve-holders would be protected against unilateral devaluation or inconvertibility decisions on the part of the reserve center countries, and the latter would not be forced into unilateral actions by sudden and unpredictable withdrawals of foreign funds from their financial markets. The safeguards would also stimulate the revival of international currency confidence and of "normal" rather than "hot money" capital movements from one market to another.

In line with his earlier 1946 essay, "Central Banking and the International Economy" (see Section 2.5), Triffin emphasized in his conclusions that the enormous expansion of state intervention in economic life was incompatible with the restoration and maintenance of convertibility on the basis of uncoordinated national policies of independent sovereign states. "A collective organization and effective internationalization of the present gold exchange standard," he said, "are particularly essential in this respect, if we are to eschew the well-known pitfalls unanimously denounced by economists and sadly demonstrated by events in the early 1930s" (Triffin 1957: 303). Armed with his EPU experience, Triffin also considered regional monetary integration as a fallback position in the event of problems at the world level. "Closer cooperation and integration, on a regional scale, is equally indispensable to organize a 'defence in depth'—rather than a mere 'Maginot line'—against the spread of deflation, restrictions, and bilateralism," he argued. Moreover, as in his 1946 essay, he stressed the limits of national sovereignty for the modern world economy. "The fundamental dilemma of international economic relations in this twentieth century lies in the inadequacy of national sovereignty as a framework for policy decisions and their administrative implementation in an interdependent world" (Triffin 1957: 303). Triffin would become an economist statesman of interdependence, arguing for a more "rational" IMS. However, many would argue that he would show a continuing naivete toward national sovereignty, especially regarding powerful nations, like the United States.

4.4 GOLD AND THE DOLLAR CRISIS

Triffin went on to elaborate the ideas of *Europe and the Money Muddle* in *Gold and the Dollar Crisis*, the book that made him famous. The focus was on international liquidity and the vulnerability of the IMS. For Triffin, these were two closely interrelated and urgent questions. His initial focus was on the level of international liquidity in the world economy, but this quickly led to a broader issue, "the vulnerability of a world monetary system whose operation becomes increasingly dependent on one or a few *national* currencies as major components of *international* monetary reserves" (Triffin 1960: 19, original italics).

The main body of the book (published in 1960) reproduced, with only minor changes, the texts of two articles that Triffin had published in 1959 in the *Banca Nazionale del Lavoro Quarterly Review*, "The Return to Convertibility: 1926–1931, and 1958– . . . ?, Or Convertibility and the Morning After" (Triffin 1959a) and "Tomorrow's Convertibility: Aims and Means of International Monetary Policy" (Triffin 1959b). The introduction of the book was Triffin's Statement to the Joint Economic Committee of the US Congress on the International Monetary Position and Policy of the United States on October 28, 1959 (Triffin 1959c).

In line with the teachings of his professors at Louvain (see Section 1.3), Triffin took a broad perspective on the evolution of the monetary system. In his view, World War I and the Great Depression had completely changed the role of monetary reserves. He considered that the universal disappearance of gold coins from active monetary circulation had fundamentally modified the role of central bank reserves. Their main function was no longer to preserve the overall liquidity of individual central banks, "but to permit the financing of short-run deficits in the country's external transactions" (Triffin 1960: 33). Consistent with his earlier analyses, Triffin made a distinction between two types of balance-of-payments deficits that had to be financed by international reserves. The first consisted of reversible deficits, which reflected temporary fluctuations in foreign revenues and expenditures. The second case concerned fundamental disequilibria, calling for corrective action, but for which the adjustment would take time. This implied a need to finance temporary deficits. For someone so deeply affected by the experience of the 1930s, the alternative was gloomy. "In both cases, an insufficient level of reserves will force the deficit country to resort to otherwise unnecessary measures of deflation, devaluation or restrictions" (Triffin 1960: 34).

As in his 1957 book, Triffin observed that the world's liquidity requirements were increasingly being met by the growth of foreign exchange reserves, especially dollar balances. He was exceedingly concerned by this. He again turned to the interwar period and the experience with the sterling exchange standard (see Figure 4.1). In his view, the growth of foreign exchange reserves during and after World War II repeated, but on a much larger scale, their similar expansion after World War I. Foreign exchange reserves had then risen from an estimated 16% of total reserves in 1913 to 38% of reserves in 1928. In Triffin's view, this trend was encouraged by policymakers at the international monetary conference in Genoa in the spring of 1922. An important reason was a shortage of gold. However, Triffin also strongly emphasized the role of the United Kingdom. "It was also propagandized throughout the 1920s by the United Kingdom, whose very low reserve position was considerably eased by foreign accumulation of sterling balances" (Triffin 1960: 56). The British return to convertibility in 1925 was thus significantly eased by the maintenance of short-term sterling balances by foreign countries in the London market. In Triffin's view, this was a very fragile construction. He thought the British position was highly vulnerable as funds could move in and out due to changes in relative interest rates and/or changes in exchange rate expectations. Moreover, the return to gold at the prewar rate made sterling highly vulnerable on the foreign exchange markets. The financial crisis of the 1930s put further pressure on the pound. "The final blow came in the summer of 1931, when the development of the world crisis

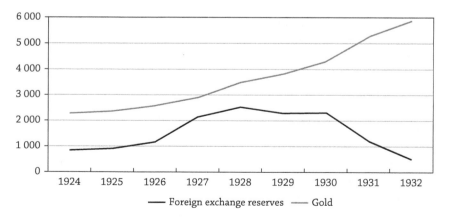

Figure 4.1 Triffin's nightmare. Gold and foreign exchange reserves, 1924–1932 (total for 24 countries, in millions of US dollar).
Source: Nurkse (1944: Annex 2).

put into difficulties the Credit Anstalt of Vienna, triggering a financial panic which spread rapidly throughout Central Europe and led to further and massive withdrawals of funds from London" (Triffin 1960: 57). The ensuing devaluation of sterling in September 1931 had devastating implications for the global monetary system and international liquidity. It marked both the end of the sterling exchange standard and an implosion of international liquidity. As Triffin described the process, "The conversion of pounds into gold and dollars was accompanied and followed by similar conversions of dollars into gold. The foreign exchange component of the world's monetary reserves was nearly wiped out in the process, except for the countries of the sterling area" (Triffin 1960: 57). This dramatic fall in international monetary liquidity contributed to the Great Depression.

By the end of the 1950s, Triffin was becoming more and more worried about the United States' international reserve position, as the country was losing gold and its foreign dollar liabilities were increasing (see Figure 4.2). Strongly influenced by the experience of the pound sterling in the 1930s, Triffin's view was that the continued deterioration in the US net reserve position would undermine foreigners' confidence in the dollar as a safe medium for reserve accumulation. "The time will certainly come, sooner or later," he said, "when further accumulation of short-term foreign liabilities will either have to be slowed down or substantially matched by corresponding increases in our already bloated gold assets. If this were not done on our own initiative, foreign central banks would do it for us by stopping their own accumulation of dollar assets and requiring gold payment instead for their overall surplus with the United States" (Triffin 1960: 63). This was precisely the policy followed by Charles De Gaulle in France in the

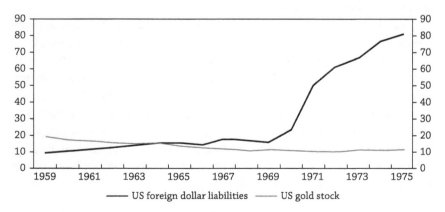

Figure 4.2 US gold stock and foreign dollar liabilities, 1959–1975 (in billion dollars).
Source: International Monetary Fund, International Financial Statistics.

1960s, under the influence of Jacques Rueff (Solomon 1982). For Triffin, the conclusion with regard to international liquidity was clear: "further increases in dollar balances cannot be relied upon to contribute substantially and indefinitely to the solution of the world illiquidity problem" (Triffin 1960: 63). So, in Triffin's eyes, the gold exchange standard was not sustainable, leading to his famous dilemma:

> The gold exchange standard may . . . help in relieving a shortage of world monetary reserves. It does so only to the extent that the key currency countries are willing to let their net reserve position decline through increases in their own gross reserves. If they allow this to happen, however, and to continue indefinitely, they tend to bring about a collapse of the system itself through the gradual weakening of foreigners' confidence in the key currencies. (Triffin 1960: 67)

Triffin did not fear a dollar collapse but the return of a liquidity shortage and a repeat of the gloom and doom of the 1930s. In his view, the growing inadequacy of world reserves would lead to a "new cycle of international deflation, devaluation and restrictions, as it did after 1929" (Triffin 1960: 70).

Of course, Triffin knew that deflation was not the only solution to his dilemma. Logically, the opposite could also be the case, with inflation as the result. He was very explicit on this in his 1967 testimony to the US Congress: "if foreign countries continue to be willing to take large amounts of gold and sterling in future years it might very well be that . . . well, there will be no worldwide shortage of reserves. You might even have inflationary problems in this case" (Triffin 1967a: 144). With the experience of the 1930s still fresh in his mind, Triffin was extremely skeptical that the other countries would continue to accumulate US dollars (which, however, they would continue to do; see Section 4.6).

One might naturally ask the question of whether Triffin was actually the first to come up with the "Triffin dilemma." Eichengreen (1992: 203) argued that Feliks Mlynarski had already formulated it in his 1929 book *Gold and Central Banks*. Mlynarski emphasized that the accumulation of foreign exchange reserves was the key feature of the gold exchange standard, but these reserves were "nothing other than an accumulation of short-term credits granted to foreign countries by the banks which apply this system" (Mlynarski 1929: 79). And, as foreign deposits were growing relative to the gold stocks of the reserve currencies, convertibility of the reserve currencies was threatened:

> The banks which have adopted the gold exchange standard will become more and more dependent on foreign gold reserves, and the banks which play the

part of gold centres will grow more and more dependent on deposits belonging to foreign banks. Should this system last for a considerable time the gold centres may fall into the danger of an excessive dependence on the banks which accumulate foreign exchange reserves and vice versa the banks which apply the gold exchange standard may fall into an excessive dependence on gold centres. The latter may be threatened with difficulties in exercising their rights to receive gold, whilst the former incur the risk of great disturbances in their credit structure in case of a sudden outflow of reserve deposits. (Mlynarski 1929: 89)

Mlynarski (1929: 12) also observed that advocates of a "managed currency" like Keynes (1927) were concerned about certain vulnerabilities of the gold exchange standard, especially the "hoarding" of gold by France.

Also, other economists at the time were critical of the Bretton Woods system. In his analysis (though not in his policy conclusions), Triffin was close to the French economist Jacques Rueff, who was very influential, especially with De Gaulle. In his autobiography, Rueff talked explicitly about his friendship with Triffin and the similarities in their analyses: "I must pay homage to my friend Robert Triffin, a Yale University professor," Rueff said. "He too had warned of the risk that the gold exchange standard posed for the stability of the West. But while we agreed on the diagnosis, we differed fundamentally about the choice of remedy" (Rueff 1977: 430). In the 1930s, Rueff had already been a staunch opponent of the gold exchange standard, which he felt permitted reserve-currency countries to live beyond their means, as they could borrow in their own currency to finance balance-of-payments deficits "without tears." In the 1960s, it became commonly referred to as the "exorbitant privilege," about which French Finance Minister Valéry Giscard d'Estaing complained (Eichengreen 2011: 4). The idea that reserve-currency countries could live beyond their means was also an important element in Triffin's analysis of the Bretton Woods system. Rueff also strongly criticized the fact that international liquidity was crucially dependent on the dollar and sterling balances: "Can one seriously allow the immense weight of the international monetary system to rest on the currency of two countries with constant balance-of-payments deficits? This situation is truly preposterous, and what is worse, it can only disappear through the elimination of the gold-exchange standard that produced it" (Rueff 1972: 110).

On the policy front, Rueff argued for the liquidation of the foreign exchange component of the Bretton Woods system and a return to a gold standard system. During the interwar period, Rueff had already played an influential role in the French policy of converting foreign currency reserves into gold, increasing the French share of world gold reserves from 7% in

1926 to 27% in 1932, and according to Irwin (2010), these French policies accounted for 30% of world deflation in 1930 and 1931. In the 1960s, Rueff inspired De Gaulle's criticism of the US dollar and the French government's threat to liquidate its dollar balances. Triffin, on the contrary, was strongly against a return to the gold standard, arguing, "We may distrust the management of man over his own affairs, but neither God nor Gold will manage them for him" (Triffin 1965a: 354). Triffin thus shared Keynes's distrust in mechanical systems based on gold, which Keynes (1923: 138) had described as a "barbarous relic."

Like Keynes, Triffin believed there was a more rational way of managing the IMS. He also joined Keynes in seeking a more "international" solution for the world liquidity problem, one that was in line with the development of national monetary systems:

> The most promising line of approach to a long-term solution of the problem lies in the true "internationalization" of the foreign exchange component of the world's international reserves, protecting the world monetary system from the instability resulting from arbitrary shifts from one reserve currency into another or into gold. Such a solution should be regarded as the normal culmination of one of the techniques used in the past to adjust the monetary system to the requirements of an expanding economy, i.e. the gradual withdrawal of gold coin from active circulation, and its concentration into the monetary reserves of national central banks. (Triffin 1960: 71)

For Triffin, there was an almost perfect analogy with a national banking system: "Just as the development of national banking systems served to offset a deflationary pressure . . . [t]he substitution of a credit mechanism in place of hoarding would have repeated in the international field the same miracle . . . of turning a stone into bread" (Triffin 1960: 91).

The similarities between the views of Triffin and Keynes on this score are striking (Maes and Pasotti 2018). Both argued for a multilateral clearing system with an international authority and an international currency. A key objective was to establish an IMS where balance-of-payments adjustments would be more symmetrical between deficit and surplus countries.

Behind the shared ideas of Keynes and Triffin on the reform of the IMS, there was a common vision or Weltanschauung, marked by the experience of the Great Depression, which questioned the self-equilibrating character of the free market economy. Both Keynes and Triffin were in favor of a "managed currency" to replace the gold standard (Triffin 1968a). They both drew a parallel with the experience of national banking systems, which shored up credit in the economy, thus turning "stone into bread." One might further note that Keynes, like Triffin, was a convinced pacifist and had an optimistic view on the progress of humanity.

Yet, while Keynes and Triffin shared this vision of a "true" IMS, with a world currency and a world central bank, there were nevertheless differences. Keynes's (1943) proposal for a clearing union was an official government document, setting out the British position in the negotiations for the new postwar IMS. It focused on the worldwide IMS and paid significant attention to the availability of credit for debtor countries (like the United Kingdom). As the title of the third volume of Lord Skidelsky's biography of Keynes clearly argued, Keynes was *"Fighting for Britain"* (Skidelsky 2001; in the US edition, the title became *Fighting for Freedom*). Triffin, in contrast, wanted constraints on increases in international liquidity. He was also more skeptical about the use of the exchange rate as an economic adjustment instrument and he highlighted the close link between trade and international payments. This would become part of a continental European tradition of emphasizing the connection between a common market and exchange rate stability (see Chapter 5). A further difference is that Keynes, with his profound knowledge of the United Kingdom's sophisticated banking and monetary system, was a severe critic of the quantity theory of money, toward which Triffin was sympathetic (several of Triffin's close friends were rather surprised by this and found it quite odd). But Triffin used the quantity theory in analyses of balance-of-payment imbalances, as in the case of Latin American countries in the 1940s, as a pragmatic tool of analysis (see Section 2.3). He would also advocate a pragmatic money supply rule to orient and limit the growth of international liquidity.

A very important difference between the two "economist statesmen" was that Triffin, as a "defense in depth," was a partisan of a regional approach. So, at times when Triffin appeared very pessimistic about the possibilities of a global reform of the IMS (when he was at the IMF in the second half of the 1940s or after the breakdown of Bretton Woods), he would lean toward a multipolar international monetary system, with Europe as a crucial pillar. This is also a topical issue in modern-day debates. For instance, Bini Smaghi (2012) and Eichengreen (2011) are also quite in favor of a multipolar system and, with the advent of the euro and the renminbi, see signs of such a system emerging.

In *Gold and the Dollar Crisis*, Triffin developed his earlier ideas for a system of deposit accounts at the IMF:

> Let the United States, the United Kingdom, and other major countries bar the use of their national currency as monetary reserves by other countries. Give all countries, instead, the choice of keeping in the form of international,

gold-convertible, deposits at the International Monetary Fund, any portion of
their reserves which they do not wish to hold in the form of gold. Attach to these
reserve deposits at the Fund exchange rate guarantees that would make them a
far safer medium for reserve investment than any national currency holdings,
always exposed to devaluation, inconvertibility, blocking, or even default by the
debtor country. Let them, finally, earn interest at a rate to be determined, and
varied from time to time, in the light of the Fund's earnings on its own loans and
investments. (Triffin 1960: 10)

The IMF deposits could be used by member countries for all their international payments (Triffin 1960: 90). The various features of these deposits,
combining the earning incentive of foreign exchange holdings with the
safety incentive of gold holdings, were to ensure strong and continuing demand for the deposits. However, to take account of initial diffidence and
inertia, and to guarantee the system against the vagaries of sudden and
unpredictable shifts between gold holdings and IMF deposits, all countries
had to agree to hold a proportion of their gross monetary reserves in the
form of IMF deposits. Triffin proposed an initial minimum deposit ratio
of 20% to launch the new system. The new deposit system would also take
the place of the "exceedingly complex and rigid" system of national quota
contributions to the IMF capital.

Triffin was convinced that a sustainable IMS required more than just the
ample provision of international liquidity to finance temporary disequilibria.
It was also necessary to coordinate economic policies so that long-run equilibrium in each country's balance of payments could be preserved. The IMF
had an important role to play here. The new system of IMF deposits would
give the IMF not only more financial firepower and so more possibilities
to intervene in the event of temporary disequilibria but also more leverage
and negotiation power to promote policy adjustment in problem countries
(Triffin 1960: 146). In more general terms, Triffin took a skeptical view of
the loss of sovereignty that his proposals might imply. He considered that
national sovereignty was always subject to limitations, not so much because
of legal agreements or international commitments, but due to economic
imperatives, especially the balance-of-payments constraint.

Triffin recognized that his plan was designed on the model of the
Keynes plan. Indeed, he considered the Keynes plan "to this day, far superior to any of the practical alternatives offered to it" (Triffin 1957: 107).
Triffin's sympathy for Keynes was well known. In a presentation for fund
trainees, Oscar Altman called the Keynes proposals "the father, if not the
father and mother, of the proposals by Professor Triffin."[9] Triffin's proposal
for replacing national currencies with an international reserve asset, such

as IMF deposits, was similar to Keynes's idea for bancor issued by an international clearing union (ICU). At the same time, Triffin was keen to point out the differences between his plan and that of Keynes, whose clearing union had unlimited lending capacity, as all members had to accept bancor transfers in full settlement of any balances due to them from any other member. This implied that creditor countries had to accept any decision of the clearing union about lending operations and that they had no political or bargaining power that could derive from direct negotiations with borrower countries.

Triffin also believed the IMF would have a central role in the shift of the IMS away from gold and toward a more fiduciary and managed system. In many ways, its functions would be "similar in many respects to those of the national central banks' credits operations" (Triffin 1960: 115). The IMF would play the role of a clearing house for settlements among central banks, very much like the EPU. "Foreign currency balances acquired by a central bank would be deposited to its Fund account and debited from the account of the debtor of such balances" (Triffin 1960: 117). This implied the replacement of the existing bilateral lending procedures with a multilateral system with the IMF at its core.

IMF lending operations would fall into two broad categories. The first involved advances requested by the borrower country. While similar to IMF lending operations at that time, under Triffin's plan, they would be linked to an agreement between the fund and the member country regarding both the maturity of the loan and a policy program (Triffin 1960: 115). This implied a certain degree of discretionary power for the IMF over the borrower country's use of the lending, a type of conditionality. The second category of IMF lending operations consisted of investments in the financial markets of member countries, on the initiative of the IMF, but in agreement with the country concerned (Triffin 1960: 117). Triffin suggested that the IMF's operations should primarily target long-term investments for economic development. They could take the form of purchases of World Bank bonds or other securities of a similar nature. This last proposal raised technical objections. For instance, Roy Harrod (1961–1962: 117) doubted that underdeveloped countries could benefit, because they had no deep and liquid markets in which large-scale operations could be conducted. Harry Johnson, of the University of Chicago, observed that the annual amounts of money that would have to be channeled through the World Bank could be very substantial and might strain its administrative capacities (Johnson 1962: 387).

Triffin knew full well that his plan would be criticized for being inflationary, just like the Keynes plan for an international clearing union

(Pasotti 2012). To counter this criticism, Triffin argued that the IMF's annual lending should be limited to the amount necessary to preserve an adequate level of international liquidity. In contrast to the Keynes plan, however, Triffin envisaged limits to the overall lending capacity of the fund, and here, once again, his monetarist methodological approach came to the fore. His basic proposal was to limit the fund's net lending "over any twelve months period, to a total amount which would, together with current increases in the world stock of monetary gold, increase total world reserves by, let us say, 3 to 5% a year" (Triffin 1960: 11). However, in special circumstances, a higher degree of lending could be authorized, but this would require a qualified majority of votes: two-thirds, three-quarters, and ultimately four-fifths of the total voting power, or even unanimity (this idea has been taken up in the IMF's New Agreements to Borrow, established in 1998). So, under Triffin's plan, the IMF would play a crucial role in adjusting the expansion of international liquidity to world economic growth. Yet, the limits proposed by Triffin to the IMF's lending capacity were still considered too loose by some economists, who argued that the IMF could be transformed into an engine of potential international inflation (Altman 1961; Angell 1961; Yeager 1961). On the other hand, Harrod and Bernstein objected to the Triffin plan, because they feared that it would have a deflationary bias (Harrod 1961–1962; Bernstein 1962).

Triffin stressed two additional advantages of his plan as compared with the existing quota system. First, the accumulation by member countries of a portion of their monetary reserves in the form of IMF deposits would involve no sacrifice of liquidity for their holders, "and their amounts could be made to adjust in a flexible manner to the future evolution of each member's reserve position" (Triffin 1960: 101). Second, political hurdles arising from the need to renegotiate quota increases would be eliminated.

In his 1960 Statement to the US Congress, Triffin also discussed the advantages and disadvantages his reform plan would entail for the United States itself. Fundamentally, his proposal implied that the US dollar would cease to be a reserve currency, so that the United States would "no longer have to bear the burden, and court the dangers, inseparable from the use of the dollar as a reserve currency by other countries." Triffin was forced to admit that this would deprive the United States of significant capital imports. The United States would lose its "exorbitant privilege," which allowed it to carry a heavier burden of foreign lending and aid programs than it could have financed otherwise. "We would now have to share these responsibilities—and the political influence that might accompany them—with other countries," he said, "through processes of multilateral decision-making which would, at times, be irritating and frustrating."

So, while the United States would lose the privileges of being the international reserve currency, it would no longer have to bear the burdens and US gold reserves would be protected against conversion of US dollar balances held by foreign central banks. This would give the United States a much greater degree of economic policy freedom as it would be less vulnerable to foreign capital movements. Sudden and unpredictable capital outflows could then no longer threaten US gold reserves, and "we would have shed thereby the straitjacket which the need to prevent such an outflow would impose upon monetary management and interest rates in this country, whenever the success of our price stabilization efforts allows us to give primary consideration once more to the furtherance of maximum feasible rates of employment and economic growth" (Triffin 1960: 13). US monetary policy could then be used primarily to address domestic objectives rather than to prevent excessive capital outflows. A second advantage, according to Triffin, was that his proposals would put an end to an "absurd situation" in which the United States, with only minor exceptions, was the sole net lender in the IMF despite its persistent deficits and the persistent and huge surpluses of other IMF members (such as Germany). And for the first time, the United States would be able to obtain assistance from the IMF through the more flexible procedure of IMF investments rather than loans, "without triggering the dangerous psychological reaction which would now accompany a United States request for such assistance" (Triffin 1960: 13).

Despite their seeing advantages for the United States, the official US position was not in favor of Triffin's proposals. Outside the United States meanwhile, Triffin's idea of substituting a new reserve asset for the dollar to provide the IMS with sufficient liquidity was generally favored by countries with weaker currencies, but opposed by their strong-currency counterparts. Indeed, countries such as Germany feared for increases in international liquidity and the ensuing inflationary effects. Triffin's ideas were also the topic of intense discussions at the IMF.[10] Per Jacobsson, the managing director of the fund, was scathing about the proposals. When asked for his opinion by Paul Douglas, the chairman of the Joint Economic Committee of the US Congress, Jacobsson replied. "I must tell you frankly that personally I cannot see any value in Dr. Triffin's scheme as such; on the contrary, I believe that it may even be positively harmful."[11] Jacobsson observed that the fund's resources had recently been enlarged and that this "should make it possible for the Fund to play its part in overcoming monetary disequilibria in cooperation with member countries, under any foreseeable conditions, by granting assistance within the framework of the Fund's policies and practices." In Jacobsson's view, there was no problem of international liquidity:

> As far as international liquidity is concerned, I can detect no overall problem, although some individual countries have still to achieve balance in their international accounts. Such balance cannot, in my opinion, be attained or even facilitated by the introduction of any new expedients, but only by the appropriate measures being taken by the countries concerned, together with such international assistance as may be needed in individual cases.[12]

With hindsight one might argue that Triffin was able to capture the debate on international liquidity, framing it in terms of the global liquidity needs for world economic growth (de Groote 2012). However, Triffin's emphasis on a global liquidity shortage neglected that international reserves are especially of importance to cover uncertainties and risks that are difficult to foresee, when countries are confronted with a severe balance-of-payments crisis and when there is a need for an international lender of last resort with sufficient resources at its disposal.

Triffin's former colleague Jacques Polak, now the head of the IMF Research Department, wrote a note entitled "Triffin's New Law of the Rise and Fall of Reserve Centers," in which he observed that Triffin appeared to have discovered a "new law of the instability of the gold exchange standard with a single dominant center."[13] He contrasted this with the earlier analysis by Ragnar Nurkse (1944), who had focused on the inherent instability of a gold exchange standard based on multiple centers. Graeme Dorrance reacted to Polak's memorandum on the "Triffin Law," largely anticipating the Despres, Kindleberger, and Salant (1966) argument that the US dollar had provided international financial intermediary services. In Dorrance's view, the idea of a one-to-one ratio of reserves to foreign liabilities was "founded on a myth."[14] He believed that international reserve centers could well "operate like banking institutions in that there is no reason for their reserves to be larger than their liabilities." He admitted that the existence of several reserve centers might lead to instability, due to flows of funds between them. However, this might also be a justification for the existence of the IMF, "to act as an international central bank to take care of flows from one center to another."

Lorenzo Bini Smaghi, who had been one of Triffin's students at Louvain and later became a member of the Executive Board of the European Central Bank, observed that, compared to Triffin's times, the most significant change was the absence of a global liquidity shortage. The implication was that external imbalances, very much the focus of Triffin's analysis, were no longer "a necessary precondition for the provision of global liquidity and the expansion of world trade" (Bini Smaghi 2012: 105). This is also related to the development of well-functioning, liquid, and deeply integrated global financial markets. In a world of large capital flows, it is no longer necessary for a country to have a deficit on its current account to become a reserve currency country. Consequently, the financial intermediation function becomes more important. The Japanese yen and the Swiss franc are reserve currencies, even if the countries have persistent balance-of-payments surpluses (Prasad 2014: 266). Moreover, the euro became the world's second-largest reserve currency, even though the euro area typically has balance-of-payments surpluses. What is important is the availability of high-quality safe assets.

The idea that the United States provides international financial intermediary services has been further elaborated in the recent literature on the IMS. For example, Gourinchas, Rey, and Govillot (2017) argue that the United States enjoyed not only an "exorbitant privilege" but also an "exorbitant duty," especially in times of financial stress. As US external assets are mostly long term (and denominated in foreign currencies), while its external liabilities are short term (and in US dollars), the United States will, in normal times, earn high returns on its net foreign asset position (the exorbitant privilege). But in times of crisis, when investors flee to safe assets (especially US Treasury bonds), the US net foreign asset position will drop significantly (exorbitant duty). So, in their view, the United States provides insurance to the world, and the exorbitant privilege can be considered as the insurance premium.

4.5 REFORM DEBATES IN THE 1960S

Triffin was not alone in his criticism of the Bretton Woods system. In the academic world especially, there was a growing tendency in favor of flexible exchange rates. In a classical essay, which had its origins in Friedman's time at the Economic Cooperation Administration (see Section 3.4), Friedman (1950) put the case for flexible exchange rates back on the agenda. He advanced two main arguments: (1) exchange rate changes are the more appropriate instrument for correcting current account imbalances, and (2) flexible exchange rates give countries more freedom to pursue their own domestic macroeconomic policy objectives. Supporters of flexible exchange rates gradually gained ground. Initially, their influence spread mainly in the academic community, while policymakers remained committed to stable exchange rates.

In the early 1960s, Triffin played a role in devising the Kennedy administration's international monetary policy. As already mentioned, Triffin and Kennedy knew one another from their time as students at Harvard, and Kennedy held Triffin in high regard. This was confirmed by Robert Roosa, who later noted that "in my first conversation with President-elect Kennedy after the announcement of my appointment as his Under Secretary for Monetary Affairs in December 1960, he pointed to the relevance of 'Bob Triffin's thinking' for the effort we were then initiating to buttress the dollar's monetary system" (Roosa 1978: vi). According to the *New York Times*, Triffin's *Gold and the Dollar Crisis* figured among Kennedy's 10 favorite books as incoming President (Blum 1961).

In November 1960, Triffin became a member of a task force, under the chairmanship of George Ball, which prepared a report on the balance of payments for Kennedy, who was then the US president-elect. In the section entitled "International Monetary Reform," the report proposed to undertake a study on international liquidity, a very Triffinite preoccupation, and it considered alternative proposals for reforming the IMS. Kennedy thanked Triffin for his work, saying, "I appreciate very much having the benefit of your assistance and advice in connection with your service upon the task force I appointed."[15]

Triffin's contribution to the Kennedy administration did not end here, however. At the instigation of his Yale friend and colleague Tobin, Triffin became a consultant to the Kennedy Council of Economic Advisers and "together we sought to advance the cause of internationalised liquidity in the US government" (Tobin 1991: 3). Tobin admitted that this was not easy, given the contending factions among government policymakers. There was a considerable difference in views between the "New" Keynesian economists of the Council of Economic Advisers (Walter Heller, Kermit Gordon, and James Tobin) and the more conservative outlook of the Treasury with Douglas Dillon as secretary of the Treasury and Robert Roosa as under secretary. In international monetary matters, Roosa mostly had the upper hand (and was often criticized by Triffin for not being ambitious enough). In the end, Tobin said, "We did not achieve our goals, but we did nudge developments somewhat in a Triffinesque direction."

Triffin also had an extensive network in Europe (see Chapter 5). He was very close to Monnet and his Action Committee for the United States for Europe. He was for some decades an adviser at the European Commission, where he was very close to Robert Marjolin, the first commissioner responsible for economic and financial matters, and many of his officials. As Triffin had official responsibilities for both the United States and the European Economic Community (EEC), at international meetings, he would sometimes pop up in the US delegation and at other times in the EEC delegation. Treasury Secretary Dillon discussed this issue with Kennedy, who replied, jokingly: "Relax Doug! He is our first Atlantic citizen, and we need more of them" (Triffin 1981a: 245).

Triffin continuously tried to influence important policymakers if he felt that his insights could move the tide in what he considered as a favorable direction. For instance, he wrote letters to De Gaulle, at the same time praising the French president's views on the IMS and smuggling in his own ideas. De Gaulle replied on two occasions. In his letter dated March 17, 1965, De Gaulle stated: "I greatly appreciated the testimony in your letter of 22 February on the reform of the international monetary system which I proposed. . . . I was very interested in your arguments and suggestions. Moreover, they were clearly and brilliantly presented. I can assure you that I shall bear them very much in mind."[16] However, when Triffin asked the Elysée Palace whether he could publish these letters, the secretary general advised against publication, as "they do not express a position which is specific to you yourself or to monetary issues but an attitude that the General always adopts in his private correspondence."[17]

The "official" debate on the functioning of the Bretton Woods system and ways to improve it was launched at the IMF annual meeting in October 1963. On that occasion, the Group of Ten mandated its deputies to identify the major issues involved and the reforms that could be proposed. The Group of Ten's decision to exclude academic economists from their discussions and hearings caused a shock. Fritz Machlup, a Jewish émigré from Austria who was professor at Princeton University, sprang into action, joined by Triffin and his Yale colleague Fellner. They brought together a group of academics, among them Gottfried Haberler, Roy Harrod, Peter Kenen, Charles Kindleberger, Robert Mundell, Bertil Ohlin, and Jacques Rueff (Connell 2011). In a series of conferences they organized, the shortcomings of the IMS and the major proposals for reform were debated. They became known as the Bellagio Group, so called because two of its meetings were held in the Villa Serbelloni in Bellagio, at Lake Como in the north of Italy. There were significant differences of opinion in the Bellagio Group (for instance, Machlup was much more in favor of exchange rate flexibility than Triffin).[18] Triffin observed in one of his notes that the discussions had been an extremely useful exercise, as they had "smoked out" the hidden assumptions behind the choice of a certain type of IMS. He compared the discussions to a "psychoanalyst's couch," suggesting that they confirmed what Freud had argued long ago, that "man's logic helps him find ex post rationalizations for his instinctive choices, much more than it really determines the latter."[19]

The issues debated in the Group of Ten differed from those examined by the Bellagio Group (Solomon 1982: 71; Bordo 1993: 24). In the Bellagio Group, the focus was on (1) the problem of liquidity, especially the perceived inadequacy of the growth of international reserves; (2) the problem of adjustment, to avoid cumulative balance-of-payments disequilibria; and (3) the problem of confidence in reserve assets, related to the risks to international financial stability arising from switches between reserve assets (Machlup and Malkiel 1964: 24). Four major approaches to international monetary reform, which were advocated by different members of the Bellagio Group, could be distinguished: (1) a gold standard system, (2) the centralization of international reserves in a supranational institution, (3) multiple currency reserves, and (4) flexible exchange rates.

The Bellagio Group issued the report of its first four meetings in August 1964, under the title *International Monetary Arrangements: The Problem of Choice. Report on the Deliberation of an International Study Group of Thirty-two Economists*. Despite differences of opinion, there was extensive agreement on many policy issues, very much on Triffinite lines. Indeed, the draft of the consensus of the first meeting was written by Triffin. "To my utter surprise—and that of everybody else," Triffin said, "the draft which I submitted in an attempt to disentangle such a consensus from our previous discussions was unanimously approved by all those present and released to the press, with minor changes" (Triffin 1966: 320). The report attracted considerable attention and praise from officials attending the 1964 annual meeting of the IMF. At the suggestion of some of them, especially Robert Roosa and Otmar Emminger, it was agreed to organize joint meetings of academics and negotiators (Connell 2011).

The Bellagio Group's report first of all stressed that policies for correcting balance-of-payments disequilibria should differ according to the origins and duration of the disequilibrium, a very Triffinite idea. In the case of enduring balance-of-payments disequilibria, the importance of exchange rate adjustments was emphasized, while cyclical disturbances called for the availability of international liquidity. Next, the report severely criticized not only the composition of international reserves but also the mechanism of reserve creation. There was a broad consensus that the existing system posed a threat to international financial stability. A clear priority was "the protection of the large outstanding foreign-exchange component of the world reserve pool against sudden or massive conversions into gold" (Machlup and Malkiel 1964: 102).

In official circles, the basic defect of the system was identified in the international liquidity creation mechanism, while fixed exchange rates and the established price of gold were considered to be the main underpinnings of the Bretton Woods system, which had to be maintained. It was recognized that gold production had long been, and would continue to be, insufficient to ensure satisfactory growth of world reserves. Moreover, the US dollar could not be expected to continue to fill the gap between available gold supplies and the reserve requirements for an expanding world economy. Finally, a consensus emerged in favor of organizing a multilateral surveillance of the various sources of liquidity creation (Group of Ten 1964) and exploring ways of creating a new reserve asset (Ossola 1965).

Through all of this, Triffin continued to develop and refine his analyses and plans for the reform of the IMS. He regularly emphasized the very special position of the US dollar. He pointed out that foreign monetary lending to the United States had facilitated US foreign direct investment— which was very important in Europe in the 1960s, as emphasized by Jean-Jacques Servan Schreiber (1967) in his bestseller *Le défi américain* (the American challenge). This was also a fundamental issue for De Gaulle, who considered US takeovers of French firms as "a sort of expropriation" of French property; the financing of these takeovers was moreover helped by the accumulation of dollar balances by "his own Bank of France" (Triffin 1965a: 350). Moreover, the key role of the dollar facilitated the financing of US military initiatives like the escalation of the war in Vietnam and the US intervention in the Dominican Republic.

In Triffin's view, the growing importance of international monetary issues explained the incursion of heads of state into "esoteric" monetary problems, traditionally the terrain of technical officials of central banks and finance ministries. He argued that it probably reflected a "justified and growing impatience with the slow progress of these technicians" and a "lurking feeling that the international monetary problem has become far too serious to be left indefinitely to monetary experts!" (Triffin 1965a: 350). On this issue, Triffin was seriously criticized by Emminger. In a letter to Triffin, he argued that it was precisely the involvement of politicians that had impeded progress. "Unfortunately, there is no prospect that politicians or Finance Ministers will take this matter into their hands, without the experts having thoroughly prepared the field. . . . The premature intrusion of heads of state into this highly technical field may, perhaps, not be particularly helpful. . . . It is partly for this reason that there is not much chance for early progress toward a *rational* reform or evolution."[20] In his letter, Emminger further observed that the motivations of the Bundesbank for acquiring gold should not be "too closely associated with those quite different ones of the French."

Triffin rejected the proposals from his former chief at the IMF, Bernstein, who favored a substantial increase in the automatic borrowing rights of IMF members. In Triffin's view, it was unacceptable "to finance blindly the future deficits of all and any country, without regard for the wisdom or folly of the policies which may be at the root of these deficits" (Triffin 1965a). For Triffin, it was crucial that the dollar and sterling should be replaced, rather than merely supplemented, by the new international reserve asset.

With the Bretton Woods system coming under increasing pressure in the mid-1960s, Triffin refined his plans for IMF deposits, developing a pragmatic proposal for a Gold Conversion Account (GCA), limited to the eight major reserve currency countries. With the establishment of a GCA, these countries would limit the conversion of foreign exchange balances into gold as the GCA would provide a "more appropriate and highly attractive medium for reserve holdings, superior in many ways to gold itself" (Triffin 1966: 140). The chair of the Group of Ten on the creation of new reserve assets, Rinaldo Ossola of the Bank of Italy, became very interested in Triffin's idea of a GCA. Ossola shared Triffin's concern to prevent a sudden contraction of international liquidity due to shifts between reserve assets. In a letter, he acknowledged that Triffin's proposal might "have some advantages over mine in the sense that 1) it is more flexible and 2) impinges less on monetary authorities' freedom of choice." In light of this, Ossola continued, "I will not fail to keep you informed on a confidential basis about future developments."[21]

So, while a consensus was growing among international policymakers on the need for a new reserve asset, there were significant divergences between the major reserve currency countries on the detailed arrangements (Flor 2019: 16). The United States and the United Kingdom viewed any future reserve asset only as a supplement and not as a substitute for the existing forms of international liquidity. The European countries, meanwhile, argued that if a new reserve asset was needed, it should be created by joint decision and should replace the national currencies used as international reserves.

In Triffin's view countries took far too much a narrow view of their national interests in these negotiations, leading to a failure of the efforts to reform the IMS. "The traditional haggling process involved in the reconciliation of *incompatible* national 'negotiating positions' multiplies the difficulties of reaching any rational solution primarily inspired by the *converging* interests of all countries in a sensible international monetary system" (Triffin 1967b: 131). He therefore proposed that the negotiating countries, as was the case with the EPU, would jointly appoint a small group of experts, "charged with the exploration and elaboration of concrete proposals to be submitted later for final approval, rejection, or amendments by a full-bodied conference of all the prospective signatory countries." It shows again Triffin's belief in "rational" discussions.

The divergences between the main powers were finally reconciled during the second half of the 1960s. The first breakthrough came in the summer of 1965, which brought what Harold James (1996: 167) described as the "partial conversion to Triffinism" of US Treasury Secretary Fowler. With US external dollar liabilities now exceeding gold reserves, and with serious tensions on the gold market, the United States reversed its position, siding with the proponents of a new international reserve asset called the special drawing right (SDR). After lengthy negotiations, the IMF countries agreed on the creation of the SDR at their meeting in Rio de Janeiro in September 1967 and the First Amendment incorporated the SDR in the IMF Articles of Agreement in 1969. The SDR was initially defined in terms of gold, but after the collapse of the Bretton Woods system, it was redefined as a basket of major currencies.

Triffin himself had rather mixed feelings about the 1967 Rio agreement. On the one hand, he welcomed the creation of the new reserve instrument, the SDR, as an essential step in the construction of a new international monetary order. But in his view, the really fundamental flaws of the IMS had not been remedied, as the existing reserve assets (gold, dollar, and sterling) kept their functions. Triffin had already put forward these criticisms in his November 1967 testimony for the Joint Economic Committee of Congress, and he stood firmly by them. Triffin described the September 1967 IMF meeting as an "oecumenical council of the world monetary establishment," which initiated the long overdue "aggiornamento" of an "anachronistic and crumbling international monetary order" (Triffin 1967a: 129). In line with his earlier analyses, Triffin focused on the global liquidity situation of the world economy. In his view, the foreseeable gap in world liquidity for noninflationary growth in world trade and production, which the creation of SDRs had to fill, was "totally unpredictable" as long as no agreement had been reached on the role of the traditional reserve components in the overall system.

Triffin then went on to analyze the situation of the traditional reserve components. The first of these was monetary gold, the supply of which was clearly not sufficient for the liquidity needs of the world economy. Moreover, it would continue to be difficult to predict as it was governed by the "hazards of gold production in the non-Soviet world, gold sales by the USSR, and gold purchases by industry, dentists, jewellers, hoarders, speculators, and mainland China." The second traditional component of world reserve increases consisted of foreign exchange reserves, overwhelmingly dollars and sterling, accumulated by central banks as international reserves. Triffin described the process of accumulating these balances as an "absurd Monte-Carlo roulette glorified as the gold-exchange standard" and advanced three arguments, according to him largely shared by the Rio negotiators, of why this process of reserve creation could not continue. They were the classical Triffin criticisms of the Bretton Woods system:

> The first is the increasing uneasiness of foreign central banks about the ability of the U.S. and the U.K. to preserve the convertibility of their currencies at the present gold price, in the face of their declining gold holdings and increasing reserve liabilities. . . . The second objection raised against the system is that it exempts the U.S. and the U.K. from the so-called balance-of-payments discipline. . . . The third objection is political, rather than economic. It is that some of the surplus countries cannot be expected to finance indefinitely, through dollar and/or sterling accumulation, U.S. and/or U.K. deficits ascribable to policies with which they deeply disagree, such as an excessive rate of direct American investments in their own market, the escalation of the war in Vietnam, etc. (Triffin 1967a: 129)

Triffin's second criticism concerned the distribution of the SDRs, which, in his view, excessively favored the developed nations (an issue that has remained on the agenda). Triffin argued that the automatic allocation of the new SDRs in proportion to IMF quotas was "indefensible," both economically and morally, as it assigned about one-third of the total to two countries, both among the richest in the world. Triffin was very much in favor of linking the creation of new SDRs to development policies and objectives and felt the agreement on the automatic distribution of SDRs should be revised. This would provide an opportunity to link the distribution of SDRs with IMF policies and to support worldwide development policies containing "a wide variety of objectives, such as national stabilization policies, development financing, etc., including—why not—peacemaking activities of the United Nations" (Triffin 1967a: 132). Recently, with the Covid-19 crisis, several persons, among them the Chinese central bank governor Gang (2020), have argued for a new issue of SDRs, preferably tailored to developing countries.

Over time, Triffin became somewhat more positive on the Rio SDR agreement. In a 1968 article, he argued that the "cornerstone" of a reform of the IMS had been laid by the Rio agreement (Triffin 1968b). While, in his view, the Rio negotiators had shown "rare vision and courage" in setting up this central piece of the international monetary machinery of the future, Triffin maintained his basic criticism that Rio had not tackled the role to be played by the traditional components of the gold exchange standard (gold and the reserve currencies):

> It was eighteen months ago that unanimous agreement was reached at Rio de Janeiro on the keystone of such a reform: the deliberate creation of centralized reserve assets in the form of internationally guaranteed claims on the IMF, usable and acceptable by all countries in all balance-of-payments settlements. A keystone, however, is not an edifice. The reform cannot stop with the mere superimposition of the new reserve asset upon the traditional ones. It must encompass the role of all three types of reserve assets—gold and reserve currencies as well as SDRs in the orderly growth of world reserves and the improvement of the adjustment mechanism. The new reserve asset should be created by international agreement, in the amounts needed to substitute for—rather than merely add to—dwindling gold supplies and overflowing reserve currencies, and to adjust overall reserve growth to the requirements of an expanding world economy rather than to the vagaries of the gold market and of U.S. and U.K. balance of payments. (Triffin 1968b)

Triffin continued to defend his idea of a GCA. But US Treasury Secretary Fowler was very critical. He argued in one of his letters to Triffin that one had to take also into account the role of the United States in global security and that also surplus countries had to contribute to the correction of payments imbalances (two arguments that are still there today): "We are still quite some distance from symmetry in other matters such as the cost of maintaining the world's security, in terms of an effective offset of the cost of our common alliances. . . . Nor do I feel that the burden of adjustment should rest solely on the United States. . . . Both now and in the future, the EEC countries with a persistent surplus should have an incentive to seek adjustment of their surpluses." He further referred to Triffin's "evangelical fervour" in defending and promoting his ideas: "I am afraid that your proposals have a decided tendency to relieve these surplus countries of the impetus to adjust, while attempting to force more abrupt and drastic adjustment on the U.S. This is one of the questions that would need to be resolved concerning the approach which you urge with such evangelical fervour."[22]

Triffin replied, defending his position, telling Fowler that "We are the last country on earth that should need to resort to fly-by-night reserve borrowings to help us with our balance-of-payments." Triffin considered these borrowings "unworthy of the greatest financial and economic power on earth, and would be bound to lead, sooner or later, to disastrous political consequences out of all proportions with the precarious financial respite which we might still hope to gain in the short run." He praised Fowler for his role in the creation of the SDR but emphasized the continuing threat of shifts between reserve assets. "History will record your constructive role in putting into place, against tremendous odds, the keystone of the future international monetary system: the SDRs or paper gold." Yet, he continued, "The sources of the recurrent crises which might topple the foundations of the edifice—even before it is built—will still be with us . . . as long as we have not agreed on regulating in a fair and reasonable manner the future role of *existing* reserve assets, i.e. gold and the reserve currencies, primarily our own dollar."[23]

In the late 1960s, the sterling, gold, and dollar crises would quickly dampen the high hopes evoked by the Rio agreement and focus the minds of policymakers on more immediate problems.

4.6 THE DEMISE OF THE BRETTON WOODS SYSTEM

The monetary authorities remained very strongly in favor of the Bretton Woods system. Paul Volcker, who worked for Roosa during the Kennedy presidency, described in his autobiography the atmosphere in the US Treasury. In Volcker's view, defending the convertibility of the US dollar into gold at $35 was not only an economic issue but also a moral one. The United States had to maintain its obligations as the leader of the free world. "American honor was at stake" (Volcker 2018: 48). Policymakers supported the dollar because it was the linchpin of the Bretton Woods system and because there was no consensus on how the system might be reformed or replaced. People feared the breakdown of the IMS. "We had no way of knowing the consequences—on trade, on unemployment, on peace—if the system collapsed" (Volcker 2018: 61).

In the first instance, the stress on the IMS was being felt by the British pound. In the 1950s and 1960s, the United Kingdom was the sick man of Europe, with relatively slow economic growth and recurrent balance-of-payments crises. The sterling balances were a further weakness, very much emphasized by Triffin (1965b), who situated the root causes of the sterling crises in the gold exchange (or key currencies) standard. Efforts at sustaining Bretton Woods initially focused on defending the British pound. As argued by Schenk (2010), sterling's international role was critical for the stability of the international economy. The United States saw sterling as the dollar's first line of defense, a domino that had to be defended. Triffin also emphasized the "catastrophic consequences" that a devaluation of the pound sterling would entail. This helped the United Kingdom to attract considerable support. It started with the Basel Agreement of March 1961, in which central banks agreed to short-term loans to help support sterling. The devaluation of sterling in November 1967 was an important warning about the sustainability of the Bretton Woods system.

Monetary tensions quickly switched to the dollar. Several lines of defense were set up in the early 1960s (Bordo 1993; Toniolo 2005), and Robert Roosa played an important role here. The first line was the Gold Pool, whereby central banks intervened in the (private) London gold market to stabilize the price of gold. Second, a swap network between central banks was set up. It provided for bilateral currency swaps (reciprocal short-term credit facilities), so that central banks could dispose of a large supply of foreign currency to intervene in the foreign exchange markets. The swap network became a permanent feature of the IMS, surviving the Bretton Woods system. It was reactivated in the wake of the global financial crisis, but then the main aim was to enable central banks to lend in foreign currencies to their financial institutions (Essers and Vincent 2017: 91). A third line of defense was the so-called Roosa bonds. These were medium-term securities, issued by the US Treasury and mainly offered to European central banks as an interest-bearing alternative to converting dollars into gold. Furthermore, in 1962, the General Arrangements to Borrow (a line of credit from the most important industrialized countries to the IMF) were established. Triffin (1978a: 7) called these mechanisms "palliatives."

Triffin feared that the United States would revert to deflationary policies to fend off a collapse of the dollar, effectively starving the world of liquidity. However, US monetary policy was dominated by domestic considerations. The Vietnam War and President Johnson's Great Society project further increased pressure on budgetary policy. Consequently, an excessive supply of dollars became the problem (De Grauwe 1989). The result was that, over the course of the 1960s, the world moved from a dollar shortage to a dollar glut. Inflation, not deflation, became the fundamental policy problem in the ensuing decades (see Figure 4.3).

At the end of the 1960s, there was a marked deterioration in the US balance of payments. US gold reserves declined, while foreign dollar liabilities increased. "The Triffin dilemma was apparent for all to see" (Volcker 2018: 64). The spring of 1971 saw massive capital flows from the dollar to the German mark. Fearing inflation, Germany halted intervention and allowed the mark to appreciate. Over the weekend of August 13, the Nixon administration suspended the gold convertibility of the dollar. The Nixon administration's view came clearly to the fore in Treasury Secretary John Connally's famous statement, in late 1971, that "the dollar is our currency, but your problem." Extensive negotiations culminated in the Smithsonian

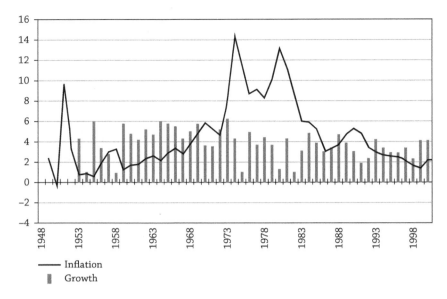

Figure 4.3 Inflation and growth in industrialized countries, 1948–2000. (in percent, no GDP data available for the period 1949–1953.)

Source: International Monetary Fund, International Financial Statistics.

Agreement of December 1971, consisting of a general realignment of parities and a widening of the fluctuation bands. However, the new arrangement did not end the turmoil (Krugman 1989; Yago, Asai, and Ito 2015). On March 1, 1973, the international currency markets were closed again, this time until March 19. After that, currencies were left to float freely. Officially, this meant the end of the dollar standard as established by the Bretton Woods agreement. But in reality, the dollar held its ground and even extended its influence (Eichengreen, Mehl, and Chitu 2018; Van der Wee 1986). World reserves were increasingly expressed in dollars, and the dollar remained important as an intervention currency too, things which Triffin would never tire of denouncing. Moreover, the dollar continued to play a dominant role in trade invoicing and the international capital markets.

In an article written shortly after the final breakdown of Bretton Woods in March 1973, Triffin was reluctant to accept that the world had moved to floating exchange rates and to concede "victory" to Friedman. "Professor Milton Friedman has finally had his day, or rather his week," Triffin allowed. "His long-standing advice has been followed—reluctantly, it must be admitted, rather than joyfully—by all major central banks." Yet, Triffin was by no means convinced that Friedman's triumph was complete. As he went on to emphasize: "I strongly suspect, however, that Milton Friedman's millennium will not last for a thousand years, nor even for a thousand days" (Triffin 1973: 362). Triffin became rather agnostic about the future of the IMS. He still hoped for cooperative policies and agreements at a global level so that a viable, worldwide, monetary order, "beneficial to all concerned," could be restored. As he became more skeptical about the future of the IMS, he also moved to his next line of defense to preserve stability of exchange rates, the regional dimension, "most likely to develop at this stage in the European Community—to preserve as much of such an order as can be salvaged, in the absence of worldwide agreements" (Triffin 1973: 373). The conclusion of the article showed Triffin's rationalist and utopian views, as well as his distaste for floating exchange rates. "At the risk of being once more accused of being a utopian dreamer and optimist, I refuse to forecast such a grim future. To my favorite quotation of Abba Eban—'Men and nations behave wisely . . . after all other alternatives have been exhausted'—I would like to add one of David Ben Gurion: 'To be realist, you must believe in miracles.' 'Inch' Allah!" (Triffin 1973: 374). Nevertheless, with the Second Amendment to the IMF Articles of Agreement in 1978, floating exchange rates were legitimized. Later, Triffin admitted that he had been slow to understand the politics of international monetary matters. "I belatedly woke up—after my old friend and once collaborator, Fred Boyer de la Giroday—to the fact that major international reforms have always been dictated by political, far more than by economic, considerations" (Triffin 1987a: 28).

While floating exchange rates between the major international currencies have now become commonplace and generally accepted, the loss of discipline associated with fixed currencies has had significant consequences and has contributed to structural disequilibria in the world economy. As observed by Jacques de Larosière, one of the negotiators of the 1976 Jamaica Agreements (under which the IMF countries agreed to amend the IMF Articles of Agreement to legitimize floating):

> Looking at these events with the benefit of hindsight, I don't feel particularly proud of the results of the Franco-American negotiations which opened the way to the Jamaica agreement. . . . At the time, we underestimated the significance of the collapse of the Bretton Woods system. . . . A genuinely international monetary system prohibits prolonged current-account deficits (usually stoked by an excess of domestic credit) and implies joint implementation of a policy of stability. Such a system leads to mutually accepted collective discipline, at the cost of relinquishing a degree of national monetary sovereignty. It is no surprise therefore that States should experience major political difficulties in submitting to such discipline. We have seen how, in practice, the floating of currencies encouraged budgetary and monetary laxness. (de Larosière 2018: 73)

4.7 THE PAPER-DOLLAR STANDARD

Triffin remained a "hedgehog" and steadfastly defended his viewpoint. He was proud of the Triffin dilemma, which continued to form his basic tool of analysis of the IMS. As he argued in an article written in honor of Robert Roosa in 1978, *Gold and the Dollar Crisis: Yesterday and Tomorrow*: "The events of the next twenty years could hardly have induced me to alter my diagnosis. They obviously resolved the 1959 'Triffin Dilemma,' however, in favor of the second rather than the first horn of that dilemma" (Triffin 1978a: 3). Yet, Triffin adapted some of his views over time. He admitted that he had completely underestimated not only the inflationary policies in the United States, with the Vietnam War and President Johnson's Great Society program, but also the willingness of other countries to absorb the US balance-of-payments deficits. Indeed, as the United States had the deepest and most liquid financial markets, investors naturally gravitated toward it. This enabled the dollar to keep its pre-eminent role in the world financial system. The immediate result was the Great Inflation. Triffin summed up his view in a candid admission, saying that he "was totally wrong in underestimating the duration and the size of the U.S. deficits that foreign central bankers would be willing to absorb, at the cost of an inflationary explosion of world monetary reserves and of a multiple expansion of the money supply in their countries under the traditional system of fractional reserve requirements" (Triffin 1978a: 4).

In the ensuing years, Triffin was a harsh critic of the post–Bretton Woods monetary system, which he would call "a paper-dollar standard." For him, "IMS" became the abbreviation for "international monetary scandal." In his 1978 essay in honor of Robert Roosa, Triffin was at pains to stress that the paper-dollar standard had led to severe inflationary effects. There were several reasons for this. In Triffin's view, the adoption of floating exchange rates had not restrained the "inflationary proclivities of the system" in the United States. On the contrary, the elimination of the stigma of devaluation had weakened the resistance of policymakers to inflationary policies. Moreover, the "paper-dollar standard" had further stimulated the increase in liquidity in the world economy. Triffin, ever the empiricist, enlarged the concept of international liquidity that he was using to incorporate the then emerging euro markets (Table 4.3). The consequences were unpalatable, showing even bigger increases in world liquidity:

> The international paper-dollar standard has become even more distasteful and unbearable to foreign dollar accumulators than the pre-1971 gold-dollar standard. The flooding of world reserves by dollar and Eurodollar overflows

caused them to double over the years 1969–72 and to redouble over the years 1973–77. Central banks' so-called "stabilization" interventions in the exchange markets absorbed these overflows, but at the cost of "high power" reserve-money issues of their national currency, multiplied by their commercial banks under traditional fractional-reserve practices. (Triffin 1978a: 9)

Triffin's policy conclusion was clear: "The control of international liquidity must encompass not only all three components of official world reserves (gold, foreign exchange, and SDR or other reserve deposits in the IMF) but also the mushrooming of commercial bank lending" (Triffin 1978a: 11).

Triffin further argued that, contrary to Friedman's argument, floating rates were not playing their equilibrating role on the foreign exchange markets, due to capital movements. Instead, he said, they "have tended . . . to amplify anticipatory capital movements: *overcorrecting* exchange rates well beyond what would be needed" (Triffin 1978a: 13, original italics). During the ensuing years, the "overshooting" of exchange rates would become an important theme both among academics and in the world of policymakers (Krugman 1989). The problems with the Bretton Woods system induced the European Community to further develop its monetary union project, as stable exchange rates were important for Europe's common market (Maes 2002). Triffin was very much involved in Europe's Economic and Monetary Union project.

Table 4.3 THE INFLATIONARY EXPLOSION OF INTERNATIONAL LIQUIDITY, 1969–1973 (IN BILLIONS OF DOLLARS, END OF YEAR)

	1969	1972	1977
Foreign dollar claims	78	146	363
On US government and banks	49	85	210
On foreign branches of US banks	29	61	153
International monetary reserves	79	159	319
Foreign exchange	33	104	244
Dollars and Eurodollars	20	81	197
Other currencies	7	15	27
Other	7	8	22
Other*	46	55	75
Commercial bank foreign liabilities	121	217	658
In dollars and Eurodollars	94	157	481
In other currencies	27	60	177

* World monetary gold, SDR allocations, and IMF loans and investments.
Source: Triffin (1978a: 4).

NOTES

1. Letter from Bissell to Triffin, June 21, 1951, RTA, 1148/1.
2. Letter from Triffin to Meade, November 12, 1953, JMeA 4/3.
3. Mail from Kerry Triffin to Ivo Maes, September 30, 2019.
4. Mail from Eric Triffin to Ivo Maes, September 29, 2019.
5. Letter from Rostow, Under Secretary of State for Political Affairs, to Triffin, October 5, 1967, RTA.
6. Yale Group, January 17, 1973, RTA.
7. "Mission by Pierre Uri and R. Triffin to the Economic Commission for Asia and the Far East," PUA, PU-66.
8. Iran Mission, Banque Melli, "Les cocktails," Gutt, November 15, 1952, RTAY, Box No. 6.
9. Altman, "Keynes, Triffin, and the International Monetary Fund, a Talk to the Fund and In-service Trainees," March 25, 1960, IMFA, 0 080.
10. "Triffin, Proposals on Liquidity and Monetary System and Comments Thereon," IMFA, 0 080.
11. Letter from Jacobsson to Douglas, November 6, 1959, IMFA, 0 080.
12. Letter from Jacobsson to Douglas, November 6, 1959, IMFA, 0 080.
13. Memo by Polak, July 6, 1960, IMFA, 0 080.
14. Dorrance, "Your Memorandum on the Triffin Law," IMFA, 0 080.
15. Letter from Kennedy to Triffin, February 28, 1961, RTA.
16. Letter from De Gaulle to Triffin, March 17, 1965, RTA.
17. Letter from Tricot to Triffin, December 17, 1968, RTA.
18. Triffin, "The Impact of the 'Bellagio Group' on International Monetary Reform," March 1977, RTA, file 11.1, pp. 1–3.
19. "Triffin's Comments on Questionnaire Answers," Fritz Machlup Papers, Hoover Institution, Box 282, Folder 8, as reproduced in Connell and Salerno 2014, Vol. 4: 24.
20. Letter from Emminger to Triffin, June 16, 1965, RTAY, Box No. 1.
21. Letter from Ossola to Triffin, March 2, 1966, RTAY, Box No. 1.
22. Letter from Fowler to Triffin, April 19, 1968, RTA.
23. Letter from Triffin to Fowler, April 30, 1968, RTA.

CHAPTER 5

Monetary Expert on Monnet's Action Committee for the United States of Europe

5.1 INTRODUCTION

World War II marked a turning point in European history and discredited the previous international order. There was a growing conviction that a united Europe was the only way to avoid a new war on the continent and to regain international influence. There were several moves to promote European integration, further stimulated by the beginning of the Cold War. Of significant importance was the Congress of European federalists at The Hague, in May 1948 (Delors 1996: 7), a meeting that laid the foundations for the European Federalist Movement. It was attended by a host of influential politicians, such as Winston Churchill, Konrad Adenauer, Léon Blum, François Mitterrand, Paul-Henri Spaak, and Alcide de Gasperi. Paul van Zeeland, the former Belgian prime minister who had been Triffin's professor at Louvain, was the chairman of the Economic Commission. Triffin, too, would soon become a convinced European federalist. He became a member of the Economic Commission of the European Federalist Movement and a co-opted member of the Federal Committee.[1]

The real start of the process of European integration can be traced back to the May 1950 Schuman Declaration, which provided the basis for the European Coal and Steel Community (ECSC). The driving force behind it was Jean Monnet, a close friend of Triffin. The declaration stated clearly that "The solidarity in production will make it plain that any war between France and Germany becomes not merely unthinkable, but materially

Robert Triffin. Ivo Maes, Oxford University Press (2021). © Oxford University Press.
DOI: 10.1093/oso/9780190081096.001.0001

impossible. . . . [T]his proposal will build the first concrete foundation of a European federation which is indispensable to the preservation of peace." In 1951, six countries (France, Germany, Italy, Belgium, Luxembourg, and the Netherlands) signed the Treaty of Paris that established the ECSC. The idea of creating trust through trade was also close to Triffin's heart, as exemplified in the European Payments Union (EPU; see Chapter 3).

In October 1950, a new French plan followed, the Pleven Plan, which aimed to establish a European Defence Community (EDC). However, it was defeated in the French Assembly in August 1954 by a coalition of Gaullists and Communists. The vote showed that defense was too closely linked to national sovereignty to be transferred to the European level.

The Benelux countries revived the integration process in 1955 with the common market project. Though the rejection of the EDC plan was a setback for political integration, the effect was to push the economic element to the forefront (Issing 2000). New negotiations followed, leading to the Rome Treaties on the establishment of two new communities. The European Economic Community (EEC) aimed at a common market, several common policies, and a coordination of economic policy. The treaty would, de facto, be of a constitutional order, as it was to transform economic and legal rules in the countries of the community (Padoa-Schioppa 1998: 9). The objective of the European Atomic Energy Community, the second of these communities, was to strengthen cooperation in the nuclear industry. However, after de Gaulle came to power in France in 1958, it was increasingly marginalized as it came too close to the heart of France's national sovereignty: the nuclear *force de frappe* (Pinder 1991: 10).

The Rome Treaties reflected the priorities and sensitivities of the member states. In the postwar period, there were significant differences in ideas and economic policymaking, especially between France and Germany. In Germany, the economic order was based on the concepts of Ordo-liberalism and the social market economy (Tietmeyer 1999). In the Ordo-liberal tradition, the main aim of economic policy is to create a framework within which markets can function. The task of monetary policy, the responsibility of an independent central bank, is to ensure price stability. In France, the state played a greater role in economic life and pursued more activist economic policies. The "Plan," for which the first commissioner was Monnet, had an important place in French economic life. These divergences in economic ideas were to a large extent based on very fundamental underlying differences in "meta-beliefs" (Maes 2004). The "republican tradition" in France stressed the sovereign nation as the source of legitimacy and, consequently, the political direction of economic policy. The postwar German federal system stressed decentralization and a division of power. Ordo-liberalism fits in nicely with this conception.

During the EEC negotiations, the German government was deeply concerned about the new European economic system that would be created. One of the main German aims was that the European common market should have the same economic order as the federal republic, based on the principles of a market economy and a liberal trade policy. The Germans feared that interactions with more étatist and planned economies, through the common market, could imperil the consistency of their own economic system (von der Groeben 1979: 496). France favored a greater role for the state in economic life. In a policy memorandum for the EEC negotiations, the French government proposed the idea of planning on a European scale. "A policy of expansion . . . implies investment which, in the basic industries, in the chemicals industry, in many of the processing industries, rests on a precise conception of the targets to be assigned to production over a period of several years. Convergence of the different national economic policies can therefore be ensured only by reconciling and harmonising national production objectives" (as quoted in Marjolin 1989: 287).

These differences in vision between France and Germany were also clearly apparent in the debates on European monetary integration. They are widely known as the controversy between the "monetarists" and the "economists." The monetarists, with France as a dominant player, were in favor of plans for greater exchange rate stability and currency support mechanisms (Maes 2002). The economists, led by Germany, put the emphasis on coordination of economic policies and convergence of economic performance, especially inflation rates, as a precondition for the Economic and Monetary Union (EMU).

In this debate, Triffin belonged firmly in the voluntarist camp. In his book *Europe and the Money Muddle*, Triffin (1957) urged the (future) EEC members to forge ahead and set up a plan for the creation of a monetary union. He argued that monetary unification "would not require, in any manner, a full unification of national levels of prices, costs, wages, productivity, or living standards. Neither does monetary unification require a uniformization of the budgetary, economic, or social policies of the member countries" (Triffin 1957: 288). So, he regarded monetary unification very much as a political issue. A further reason to consider Triffin as a monetarist is that he was a strong advocate of the introduction of a European currency as a parallel currency. This was a constant feature of his thinking and policy proposals. He felt that wider use of a parallel currency would pave the way for monetary integration. The problem, of course, was that Triffin's views were diametrically opposed to the (German) paradigm of the indivisibility of the currency and monetary policy.

Triffin became the monetary expert on Monnet's Action Committee. There were remarkable similarities between the two men, even though they had very different backgrounds and Monnet was much closer to the politics of European integration. Monnet was the son of a cognac producer, who, at the age of 18, had already traveled around the world and negotiated a major contract with the Hudson Bay Company in Canada. François Duchêne (1994) entitled his biography of Monnet *The First Statesman of Interdependence*, a description that would also apply to Triffin. In line with this emphasis on interdependence, Triffin and Monnet shared a strong European federalist conviction. They were also convinced of the necessity of institutions in the construction of Europe, as exemplified in Monnet's famous expression "Nothing is possible without men, nothing is lasting without institutions" (Monnet 1976, 2:360). Triffin's idea for a European Reserve Fund (ERF) was embraced by Monnet. They were both imaginative and creative minds, thinking outside of the box, coming up with new ideas that could be put into practice in the policy process. They were also quite similar in character. They were both "hedgehogs." As observed by the late Jelle Zijlstra, a prime minister of the Netherlands, Monnet had exceptional single-mindedness. He had "at any specific period one thing he wanted to achieve. Exceptionally, two—but never three" (as quoted in Duchêne 1994: 22). They both also had remarkable pedagogical qualities and strong powers of persuasion, which allowed them to influence the policymaking process.

There are several reasons to consider Triffin as an architect of the euro (Maes and Bussière 2016). First, he was highly influential in shaping the intellectual debates about the international and European monetary system. He was one of the main advocates of monetary cooperation and a stern critic of the so-called domestic house-in-order approach. Second, as a policymaker, Triffin held very important advisory positions, for instance, for Monnet's Action Committee, providing German Chancellor Willy Brandt's paper for the Hague Summit of December 1969, as well as for the European Commission. In these positions, he put forward innovative ideas, especially for an ERF and a European parallel currency. Another important aspect was Triffin's long-standing involvement in the process of European monetary integration, spanning four decades, from the EPU to the European Monetary System (EMS).

5.2 A STRONG ADVOCATE OF THE EUROPEAN PAYMENTS UNION APPROACH

In line with his earlier ideas, Triffin continued throughout the early 1950s to advocate the development of the EPU in the debates on European integration. At a conference on the problems of European integration in Genoa in 1953, he focused on the monetary dimension. He started out with an examination of the conditions for European monetary integration, arguing that it did not require adoption of a single currency. Yet, it did require national European currencies to be freely convertible at fixed and invariable exchange rates. "A single currency is the symbol, much more than the substance, of monetary integration," he said. "However spectacular it may be, economically speaking, it has only very secondary differences from coexistence of freely convertible national currencies at fixed and invariable rates" (Triffin 1953: 207). This would remain very much a constant in Triffin's vision. The institutional architecture of EMU was not his primary concern (Maes and Bussière 2016). This was in contrast with the German vision, which, in line with the Ordo-liberal tradition, focused closely on the monetary order of EMU.

Triffin insisted that the balance-of-payments equilibrium was an essential precondition for currency convertibility and then elaborated further on the conditions for reaching equilibrium. He stressed that this depended on the adjustment of wages and living standards in line with productivity levels in each country. Anticipating certain arguments of optimum currency area theory, like Mundell (1961), Triffin argued that mobility of factors of production might ease balance-of-payments adjustment, especially as it would reduce productivity gaps between countries. He further emphasized that, in an integrated monetary area, different—rather than uniform—fiscal, economic, and social policies could be preferable to deal with national divergences in economic and social structure (Triffin 1953: 208).

Triffin considered three examples for balance-of-payments adjustment that might guide European countries' policies in an integrated monetary area. The first involved the acceptance of automatic adjustment to price differentials and giving priority to the attainment of external balance, sacrificing domestic policy objectives. The second required the creation of common budgetary and fiscal policies, implying a certain redistribution of income between the regions of the union. The third involved accommodating capital flows. However, Triffin argued that European monetary integration could not be attained along these lines (Triffin 1953: 208). European countries would not accept internal adjustments if they might threaten employment and economic activity. Also, the degree of countries' solidarity was not sufficient for the creation of a supranational institution to which they would transfer political powers.

In Triffin's view, the most practical way ahead for monetary integration was the development of the EPU, of which he had been one of the architects (see Chapter 3). He first of all suggested setting up a joint reserve fund, constituted by deposits from the member countries (Triffin 1953: 210).

By providing financing in the event of balance-of-payments difficulties, this fund would avoid countries resorting to policies such as exchange rate adjustments or exchange restrictions. Moreover, it would strengthen the union's influence on members' policies. Second, he advised wider use of the EPU unit of account in all intra-European loans and investments. This idea was picked up by Fernand Collin, the CEO of the Kredietbank, one of Belgium's most important commercial banks (see Section 5.4). It would help "restore capital markets in Europe and might provide governments with a far more attractive source of financing than the printing press" (Triffin 1951: 461). Triffin emphasized that the EPU unit of account would also support the emergence of a single European currency. Once countries managed to stabilize their currencies, they could declare new national currencies against and equal to the EPU unit of account. As a consequence, "while the new currencies would remain purely national in law, exchange fluctuations would be greatly discouraged by the mere similarity of their valuations" (Triffin 1951: 460). The replacement of the domestic currencies with a single currency would finally require the setting up of a European Monetary Authority, entrusted with sole issue rights for all participating countries.

Triffin severely criticized the limited scope of the European Monetary Agreement (EMA), signed in 1955. Under the EMA, a European fund was created that gave EMA members access to nonautomatic credit facilities in the case of temporary balance-of-payments difficulties. In addition, a Mutual System of Settlements was set up that encouraged the settlement of international payments through the foreign exchange markets, rather than through central banks, as had been common practice until then (Kaplan and Schleiminger 1989). In Triffin's view, these EMA arrangements were not ambitious enough. He argued in favor of taking advantage "of the next EPU revision to transform EPU into a clearing house for all European central banks, and to require them to hold all their European currency reserves—and possibly a specified portion of their overall gold and foreign exchange reserves—in the form of EPU deposits" (Triffin 1957: 285). He advocated the transformation of the EPU into a European clearing house, which could pool about 20% of the total gold and foreign exchange reserves held by European central banks. The European clearing house would use these reserves to intervene in international exchange markets, approximating the open market operations performed by national central banks in their domestic markets. Triffin considered the European clearing house as a powerful collective European instrument to combat speculative currency movements (Triffin 1957: 292).

It is interesting to note that Triffin made no significant distinction between a monetary union and a system of stable exchange rates, emphasizing the importance of balance-of-payments equilibrium:

> From an economic point of view, the prerequisites for the successful preservation of monetary unification are practically identical with those for the successful preservation of free and stable exchange rates. The participating regions or countries must, in either case, subordinate their internal monetary and credit expansion to the maintenance of equilibrium in their balance of payments. (Triffin 1957: 289)

Triffin further argued that monetary unification would even impose less stringent monetary discipline on the participating countries, "since the elimination of exchange risks would be even more complete than under a system of free and stable exchange rates, and would therefore stimulate the cushioning of temporary deficits through readjusting capital movements rather than aggravate them through speculative capital flight." However, Europe's monetary union showed that, with accommodating capital movements, disequilibria were not corrected, leading to significant imbalances and bubbles, which eventually burst and contributed to the euro zone crisis of the early 2010s. With hindsight, this was certainly a serious weakness of Triffin's analysis. The euro area's sovereign debt crisis clearly demonstrated that EMU created very close and complex interdependencies between the participating countries, requiring a strong economic policy framework, including a banking union, and close coordination of policies. All these issues are naturally related to the question of political union. Moreover, the euro area debt crisis had important global and systemic dimensions and it was decided to also involve the IMF in the crisis management, pointing to the limits of the regional approach in an interdependent world.

5.3 THE ROME TREATY

In the mid-1950s, the six countries that founded the ECSC followed two rather different paths to economic integration. The six opted for regional integration of the goods markets, with the establishment of the EEC. But monetary cooperation was approached from a worldwide perspective, with the restoration of full external convertibility under the Bretton Woods system (Abraham and Lemineur-Toumson 1981).

The EEC Treaty left macroeconomic and monetary policymaking mainly in the hands of the individual member states. The commission's responsibilities were chiefly concerned with the orientation and coordination of the national policies. Triffin (1958: 1) described the limited monetary dimension of the EEC Treaty as "a Hamlet in which the role of the Prince of Denmark is almost totally ignored." The most extensive discussion of macroeconomic and monetary issues can be found in the treaty's "Balance of Payments" chapter. It illustrated that these issues would be tackled from a common market perspective, as balance-of-payments disequilibria would threaten the creation and functioning of the common market (Maes 2006). Article 104 stated that each member state should pursue an economic policy "to ensure the equilibrium of its overall balance of payments and to maintain confidence in its currency, while taking care to ensure a high level of employment and a stable level of prices." This reflected very much the "own house in order" approach, advocated by Germany. Otmar Emminger (a future president of the Deutsche Bundesbank) considered this a "fundamental" article as it implied the commitment of every member state to adopt economic policies that would ensure balance-of-payments equilibrium" (Emminger 1958: 93).

Article 105 continued that, to attain the objectives of Article 104, "Member States shall co-ordinate their economic policies." It stated that the member states "shall for this purpose institute a collaboration between the competent services of their departments and between their central banks." The commission had a role of initiative here, as it "shall submit to the Council recommendations for the bringing into effect of such collaboration." However, in January 1958, the governors of the central banks decided to organize this cooperation informally in Basel, and informed the commission accordingly. It was a pre-emptive action by the governors, who were afraid of a potential commission initiative that might usher in tighter rules (Pluym and Boehme 2004: 117).

Article 108 referred to situations where a member state has serious balance-of-payments difficulties that could threaten the functioning of the common market. It stipulated that the commission should investigate the situation and could recommend measures for the member state in question to take action. Moreover, the article provided for the possibility of granting "mutual assistance." Article 109 contained the famous safeguard clauses that France insisted on, whereby a member state can take the "necessary protective measures" in the event of a sudden balance-of-payments crisis.

Under Article 105.2, the treaty also provided for the establishment of the Monetary Committee. It was based on a French memorandum.[2] The proposed missions of the Monetary Committee were to provide reciprocal information for the various authorities and to formulate opinions on "all aspects of monetary policy concerning the functioning of the common market." The memorandum explicitly mentioned the mutual assistance procedure.

During the negotiations, the exchange rate issue was also a topic of serious discussions. According to one of the Belgian negotiators, Joseph Van Tichelen (1981: 340), one of the main points of disagreement was whether it should be a national or a community competence. Inspired by a commonwealth formula, the Belgian delegation proposed that "Each Member State shall treat its policy with regard to rates of exchange as a matter of common concern" (Article 107.1). This was an ambiguous formula, but it succeeded in placing exchange rate policy in the area of competence of the community.

The relative lack of attention to monetary issues in the Treaty of Rome can be explained from several perspectives. First, money and monetary policy were considered as important elements of national sovereignty. The negotiators were therefore reluctant to tackle these issues so soon after the failure of the EDC initiative. Second, there was a reluctance against excessively deep integration with Germany, given "certain memories from the too recent past." Third, in the mid-1950s, there were significant divergences in economic and monetary policies and paradigms between the countries of the EEC (Maes 2004). All in all, the Treaty of Rome already seemed very ambitious, notwithstanding the absence of a significant monetary dimension.

After the launch of the EEC on January 1, 1958, Triffin took up a post as official adviser at the commission. He had very close and long-standing links with Robert Marjolin, a vice president of the commission who was responsible for economic and financial affairs. They knew one another from the days of World War II, when they were both in Washington. They had also worked together in Paris in the early 1950s, when Marjolin was the first secretary general of the Organization for European Economic Cooperation (OEEC) and Triffin the head of the International Monetary Fund's (IMF's) European office. And they had several elements in common. They were both eminent academic economists, very much in the Keynesian tradition. Marjolin was even regarded as the first true French economist to hold Keynesian views. They both came from a modest background but were able to study thanks to fellowships. Both had been students in the United States, Marjolin attending Yale, where Triffin later became a professor. They each had an American wife. According to Jean Flory (interview), a close collaborator of Marjolin during the 10 years that he was at the commission, Triffin was one of his most influential advisers. When Triffin came to Brussels, they usually spent evenings together, discussing into the small hours Europe's and the world's monetary problems. Marjolin's regard for Triffin is also indicated by his initial salary at the commission, which was at the level of a director general, the highest position in the commission administration.[3] Marjolin also put Triffin in contact with Monnet (Marjolin had been Monnet's deputy at the French Planning Office after the war). Triffin's relations with Raymond Barre, who succeeded Marjolin at the commission in 1968, were less close. Barre had a much more "pragmatic" approach, which clashed with Triffin's more "utopian" vision of European monetary integration.

Inside DG II, the Directorate-General for Economic and Financial Affairs, Triffin had frequent contacts with Franco Bobba, the director general, who consulted him often, especially on matters concerning the international monetary system (IMS). In a letter dated February 2, 1961, Bobba reported how influential Triffin was in the European debate on the IMS: "All the discussions both in the Monetary Committee and by the Finance Ministers clearly demonstrated that there was an international liquidity problem that needed to be examined. . . . The name TRIFFIN was always in the background of these discussions."[4]

At the commission, Triffin was very close to Frédéric (Fred) Boyer de la Giroday, an ebullient Frenchman, born in Mauritius, whose family originated from Brittany. Boyer had studied at Oxford and had been involved in the Marshall Plan. Triffin and Boyer were colleagues at the IMF in the late 1940s. They shared a global world view and were active proponents of European monetary integration. Boyer worked at the Monetary Directorate in DG II. He was soon promoted to head of unit for international monetary matters and, a few years later, director. In an interview, his son, Eric Boyer de la Giroday, talked about his father's close friendship with Triffin, and his great respect for him. Triffin's wife, Lois, became a lifelong friend of Boyer's wife too. When Triffin came to Brussels, he would usually stay with the Boyer family. Eric Boyer described Triffin as "a small, extraordinarily kind man with very fine hands." He still had vivid memories of reading Tintin (one of the most popular European comics in the 20th century) with Triffin. He even argued that Triffin, with his tuft of hair, bore some resemblance to Tintin. The Boyers would often point to Triffin as an example for their son: somebody of very modest origins who, through hard work, had made a brilliant career.

Triffin and Boyer would have long discussions, especially on international monetary problems. As Boyer noted, "all roads, in these fields, seem to lead to Yale."[5] Because Triffin and Boyer were both heavy smokers, the living room would be hazy with smoke after their meetings. Boyer also admitted to Triffin, without shame or remorse, how he extensively used "the Triffin Treasury of smart ideas." His letter continued: "But don't worry: all the responsible officials and irresponsible people at the Commission know that you are the source of these clever . . . and generous ideas. Sadly, they are too clever . . . and in particular too generous . . . for governments to accept them."[6]

Boyer was often unhappy with the slow progress being made. He showed his frustration in many letters to Triffin. He also wrote that Triffin was sometimes distrusted at the commission and that one of his books, probably *Gold and the Dollar Crisis*, was circulating in European circles like a "pornographic novel":

> The various Community bodies are tackling the current international monetary problems at what is more like snail's pace, instead of taking swift action. . . . The tactic adopted by my authorities, especially the Monetary Committee, seems to be to reinvent the Triffin Plan bit by bit, or at least the ideas on which it is based. Obviously, that all takes a lot of time. . . . They will probably be careful not to name certain revolutionary thinkers who cannot be trusted because they discerned every aspect of the problem months, if not years, before the cautious snails. It is therefore doubtful whether Professor Triffin's name will be mentioned, but it is quite obviously impossible to raise these issues today without drawing on the professor's ideas and writings. His latest book on the question is being circulated clandestinely, rather like a pornographic novel.[7]

Boyer was quick to add a handwritten note, explaining that this was not an accusation. "This comment reflects what I have experienced in the Committee of Alternate Members of the Monetary Committee."

Triffin and Boyer were also in contact to discuss how they could maneuver in the commission administration. For instance, Boyer wrote about how he succeeded in getting one of his papers on the reform of the IMS to be distributed in the Monetary Committee, notwithstanding the resistance of his superiors. "This paper was only rescued from the bin at the last minute . . . and circulated unofficially (which would probably have made it possible to disown it, if necessary)." He proceeded to ask Triffin his opinion and sounded him out: "I don't know whether you consider it possible or expedient to raise this question with Marjolin again."[8] Boyer was also helping Triffin to retain an official position at the commission. In 1969, Boyer discussed Triffin's official status with Mosca, the director general. In a letter to Triffin, Boyer informed him of his negotiations, concluding, "It is another problem that we shall discuss while you are here. As we are unable to offer you an advisor's contract at the moment, for reasons that I do not really understand, we can offer you successive expert's contracts."[9]

Triffin had a number of other important contacts too. One of them was Roland de Kergorlay. From 1962 to 1969, de Kergorlay was the secretary of the influential Monetary Committee, the meeting place of top officials from finance ministries and central banks. He was a Frenchman, who had studied in the United States and who had been an official at the OEEC. A further segment of the Triffin network consisted of his former students at Yale, especially Claudio Segré. He was fast-tracked at the commission but left early. During his time at the commission he was the head of a group of experts who produced a report entitled *Le développement d'un marché européen des capitaux* (CEC 1966). Triffin's network at the commission thus included many Frenchmen. This should not be surprising as the French traditionally had a strong presence in monetary matters (Maes 1996). But Triffin's contacts were not the traditional ones from the French administrative elite. They had typically studied outside France and had held official posts in international organizations, such as the OEEC or the IMF.

5.4 THE CAMPAIGN FOR A EUROPEAN RESERVE FUND

In the second half of the 1950s, Monnet became very interested in European monetary integration. This interest was very much a consequence of the French financial crisis at that time, which threatened France's participation in the common market project. As often, he saw the French problem in a European context and turned to his network for technical advice. This advice came from Pierre Uri, Paul Delouvrier, Marjolin, and, "above all," Marjolin's Belgian friend (Duchêne 1994). In line with his EPU ideas, the cornerstone of Triffin's monetary project was the creation of an ERF.

Triffin was full of admiration for Monnet, "certainly the greatest man I have ever known" (Triffin 1990: 32). He painted a vivid portrait of Monnet's way of working, stating, "His greatness and strength came from his ability to surround himself with competent people, the best minds, and to listen to them." Monnet would have endless meetings with his collaborators and then, at the end, he managed to express the most complex economic and monetary problems in words that politicians could understand. Moreover, Monnet was a "modest" person. In his view, it was not the official devising the policy but the politician who adopted and implemented it who should get the credit for a plan. Monnet was then genuinely delighted to see the name "Schuman Plan" given to what was actually a "Monnet Plan" (Triffin 1990: 33).

Triffin (1990: 95) revealed that, initially, he and Monnet disagreed on the tactics for furthering European monetary integration. Monnet was skeptical of Triffin's EPU plans, which he thought were "too modest and didn't go far enough." But with the success of the EPU, Monnet became an ardent supporter of the ERF. "The success of the EPU soon surpassed all expectations and swept aside Jean Monnet's initial scepticism and the objections of numerous other economists and financial and political leaders." Triffin's only major disagreement with Monnet related to the accession of the United Kingdom to the European Community. Here Triffin agreed with de Gaulle, noting in a retrospective commentary that "Like de Gaulle, I considered that Britain was only resigned to joining in order to oppose from the inside the progress that it could not prevent from the outside." For Triffin, the priority was the deepening of economic, monetary, and political union and its completion, not its enlargement to include Britain. In fact, he continued, "I still think that now" (Triffin 1990: 35).

In October 1957, Uri prepared a memorandum on an ERF. In a letter to Triffin, he thanked Triffin profoundly for his crucial role in the elaboration of the memorandum.[10] The introduction emphasized that European integration also implied the development of a world-class financial center, consisting of a network of closely interlinked financial markets. The memorandum pointed to the importance of the ERF for the creation of a European capital market. Such a vast financial market was crucial to establishing the funding of European industries on a comparable basis, "without competition between them being distorted by differences in exchange rate risk or a devaluation of their debts" (even if considerable progress has been made since then, the issue is still on the agenda now, with the plans for a Capital Markets Union). The memorandum further argued that progress toward European monetary and financial unification would contribute to a stronger IMS, one of Triffin's old themes.

Several of Triffin's key ideas figured prominently in the proposal for the ERF. The fund would be constituted by deposits from the member states. These would be expressed in a European currency unit, with appropriate exchange rate guarantees. There was also a proposal for a board, which would play a role not only in the management of the fund but also in the coordination of macroeconomic policy in the European Community.

Periodic meetings of the Finance Ministers and Governments of the central banks with the Fund's managing body will be devoted to a comparison of fiscal and credit policies, to shed light on dangerous divergences and define a common policy. . . . This will ensure the practical and effective coordination of economic

and monetary policies which the Treaty of Rome specifies as an essential prerequisite for the functioning of the Common Market.[11]

One can sense from all this that Triffin had been a central banker (see
Chapter 2). He had experience with monetary reforms and had been ada-
mant about equipping central banks with modern instruments of monetary
policy. The memorandum proposed that the ERF would have a panoply of
instruments at its disposal including the ability to issue bonds—guaranteed
by the member states of the EEC—on the capital markets.

With the advent of the European Community in 1958, the French
macroeconomic and monetary situation, marked by high inflation and a
significant balance-of-payments deficit, became a matter of serious concern for the European Commission. This led the commission to reflect on
how it could fulfil its own role in the macroeconomic and monetary sphere
(Maes and Buyst 2004). In close collaboration with Triffin, Marjolin drew
up a proposal for setting up an ERF.[12]

In developing his ideas for an ERF, Triffin naturally drew inspiration
from his experience at the EPU. In his view, the first function of the ERF
would be as a clearing house between central banks. This would pave the
way for the ERF to evolve naturally into the European Monetary Authority
as central banks would be required to hold a deposit account with the ERF.
This would give the fund massive resources at its disposal that could be used
to finance the mutual assistance foreseen in the Treaty of Rome, to steer
developments in the community's overall monetary policy, and to gradually
pave the way for the creation of a European Monetary Authority, "capable
of steering the ship and ultimately ensuring full monetary integration between the six countries of the Community" (Triffin 1958: 9). The ERF could
be constituted by pooling 10% to 20% of the international reserves of the
member states' central banks, a proposal that was sure to incur the wrath
of the central bankers. The fund could provide different types of loans, both
to assist countries with balance-of-payments difficulties and to support economic growth. Later, Triffin (1989b: 9) even argued that it could play a
useful role in banking crises.

This idea that the community should have the resources to facilitate financial solidarity would become a recurring theme in commission proposals, and it has a strong resemblance with the European
Stability Mechanism (ESM), established in 2012. The underlying principle is very much the same: by demonstrating a collective stance, such
mechanisms are a more efficient way of averting speculation than isolated national measures (Deroose, Hodson, and Kuhlmann 2004). It also
makes it possible to offer "carrots" to member states that need to adjust

their policies, thus increasing the influence of the commission's policy recommendations.

At that time, there was rivalry with the IMF too. In a confidential note for Monnet, Triffin argued that financial assistance should be arranged preferably within the EEC itself, as long as the balance-of-payments and reserve position of the community as a whole was strong enough. He further observed that the EEC procedures were far less satisfactory than those of the IMF, as the fund provided stable sources of financing in advance for the assistance required. The challenge that this posed was obvious to Triffin: "Prospective borrowers, therefore, would be unwilling to relinquish in any way their full freedom of access to the IMF without being firmly assured of at least equivalent and expeditious borrowing facilities from the Community."[13]

Triffin also advocated the introduction of a European unit of account. To further this process, he argued that the accounts of the ERF should be denominated in a European unit of account, "defined so as to give it the same stability as that of the most stable among the participating currencies" (Triffin 1958: 9). In a footnote, he again referred to the example of the EPU. "The legal definition of such a unit of account would be similar to the formula used for setting the current EPU unit of account."

Triffin proposed several measures to promote this European unit of account, including as a parallel currency. The first one was to legalize the use of the European unit of account in all contracts, both public and private, domestic and international. He saw this as a clear strategy to advance toward monetary union. The second proposal "of a more spectacular nature, and already effectively implying acceptance of full monetary unification as the ultimate goal," was the conversion of the existing national monetary units into new national monetary units, but all having the same value. His third idea was "intercirculation," implying that the new national banknotes could circulate freely throughout the countries of the community. "Combined with the de facto equivalence of national monetary units," he said, "this privilege of intercirculation would enhance resistance to any future exchange rate fluctuations" (Triffin 1958: 16).

As indicated earlier, Triffin saw a strong connection between his proposals for the IMS and for European monetary integration. He was convinced that regional monetary integration would contribute to a more stable IMS (Bussière and Feiertag 2012). In his view, the ERF would help strengthen the IMS, especially by providing more liquidity in the IMS. This was a crucial issue for Triffin (as discussed in Chapter 4), as "the dual mechanism of clearing and lending of an ERF would help solve a problem that, paradoxically, has been neglected or even ignored today . . . that of the liquidity needed for the satisfactory functioning of the international monetary system itself" (Triffin 1958: 12).

The European Commission discussed the ERF plan at its meeting on November 20, 1958. It agreed in principle with the project but postponed the debate on implementation to a future meeting.[14] Triffin also promoted the idea actively in Paris (Triffin 1958). However, in December 1958, the de Gaulle government devalued the French franc and introduced orthodox economic policies. With the success of de Gaulle's stabilization plan, France no longer needed financial assistance. In this new context, the proposal for an ERF lost its raison d'être, even though Monnet tried to revive it in the early 1960s.

At the end of December 1958, the EPU was replaced by the European Monetary Agreement, which Triffin despised, and the countries participating in the EPU abolished the restrictions on external convertibility of their currencies, so that economic agents could freely convert one currency into another (a great contrast with Eastern Europe, where convertibility would only be restored after the fall of the Iron Curtain in 1989). The end of the EPU implied that Europe's monetary and exchange rate relations were now clearly situated in the framework of the Bretton Woods system.

Triffin also promoted the idea of using a European unit of account in the financial markets. In this, he worked closely in tandem with Fernand Collin, the chief executive officer of the Kredietbank, one of Belgium's largest commercial banks. During a conference in Luxembourg in 1978, Triffin told how he was contacted by Collin in 1949:

> In 1949 I had written . . . an article describing the unit of account that I proposed for the European Payments Union, and I had simply added a brief, two-line footnote saying that this unit of account could also be used by the private market to revive the international capital market, which was paralyzed at that time. A fortnight later, I got a telephone call from Fernand saying that I had convinced him, and asking me how this could be put into practice.[15]

Collin introduced Triffin to the world of commercial bankers. A key aim of the bankers was to recreate a European capital market after the war. The European unit of account could play a role in this, and, as observed by Boyer, Triffin was a "goldsmith" in these matters.[16] So Triffin attended a meeting of the Institut International d'études bancaires in March 1958 in Brussels. The main theme of the meeting was a draft agreement between the World Bank and a consortium of European financial institutions on underwriting a loan in European units of account. The origins of the idea went back to discussions in Washington in the autumn of 1957 between Collin and Eugene Black, the then president of the World Bank, on the revival of the international capital markets.[17] At this Brussels meeting, Triffin also presented his idea for a clearing house for the European central banks.

The idea of a bond issue in European units of account was implemented by the Kredietbank in 1961 with a bond for SACOR, a Portuguese oil company. A key role was played by Collin and Triffin, who was a member of the Board of Kredietbank Luxembourgeoise from 1961 to 1988. This issue has a strong claim to be the first Eurobond issue, pre-dating Autostrade in 1963. As argued by De Beckker (1984: 129): "If one looks at one generally accepted definition of a Eurobond issue, i.e. an issue underwritten and placed by an international syndicate of banks and denominated in a currency which is not the currency of the borrower, then the first Eurobond issue ever was launched in 1961, by Kredietbank SA Luxembourgeoise for the Portuguese borrower SACOR."

Kredietbank Luxembourgeoise would become a pioneer of the use of the EPU's unit of account, and later the European Currency Unit (ECU), in the financial markets. The Kredietbank could count on the support of the Luxembourg authorities when promoting the unit of account. For instance, when Triffin asked for the terms that Kredietbank-Luxembourg could offer for deposits in the EPU unit of account for central banks in Latin America, the Kredietbank pointed out in its reply that "Mr. Pierre Werner, Prime Minister and Finance Minister of the Grand Duchy of Luxembourg, has always encouraged the Luxembourg Kredietbank S.A. in these various initiatives in international finance."[18] The European currency unit would contribute to the development of Luxembourg as a financial center, an important project of Werner's. In turn, the burgeoning Luxembourg financial center would pave the way for a European currency unit. In 1970, Werner set up an informal think tank to reflect on the future for the financial center. It was composed of experts from Luxembourg and abroad, including Triffin and Collin (Danescu 2018: 27). Werner's intellectual exchanges with Collin and Triffin were to continue, reaching a height of intensity during the Werner Committee's work in 1970 (see Section 5.5).

In the second half of the 1960s, the international monetary situation deteriorated further and the future of the Bretton Woods system became increasingly uncertain (see Chapter 4). The European Commission became worried that, if the countries of the community did not adopt a common position, including in the IMS discussions, the community risked falling apart.[19] The commission drew up a (confidential) note that it presented to the council in February 1968. The main aim of this "Memorandum sur l'Action de la Communauté dans le Domaine Monétaire"[20] was to establish closer monetary relations between the countries of the community. Key elements of the memorandum were that (1) member states should declare that exchange rates would be adjusted only with mutual prior consent, (2) the fluctuation margins should be eliminated, (3) a system of mutual assistance should be established, and (4) a single European unit of account should be established. Furthermore, concerted action by the EEC countries in the international monetary institutions was envisaged. The note was very short (two pages) and the proposals were not elaborated. The memorandum was very much in line with the voluntarist ideas that Triffin and Boyer were defending in DG II. Indeed, in August 1967, Boyer was developing proposals, based on the "Triffin Treasury of smart ideas."[21] They were also quite in line with certain French ideas, in favor of a "European monetary identity" but without new supranational institutions (de Lattre 1999). The commission proposals were criticized by Germany and the Netherlands, which argued that such a "one-sided monetary approach made no sense" (Szász 1999: 11). The events of May 1968 and the ensuing crisis around the French franc, in which France invoked the safeguard clauses, also left their imprint.

In October 1968, Raymond Barre was rather skeptical about EMU and defended positions that were quite different from the February memorandum. In the European Parliament, he declared that, for EMU to succeed, a European political authority was needed (Barre 1968: 17). He further argued that a monetary union would be the "crowning act" of economic union. Barre went for a pragmatic and two-sided approach, arguing that the main objective had to be better coordination of both the economic and monetary policies of the member states. The monetary proposals were less ambitious than those in the February 1968 memorandum. For instance, there was no further mention of the establishment of a single European unit of account, a typical Triffin idea.

5.5 THE 1969 HAGUE SUMMIT AND THE WERNER REPORT

At the end of the 1960s, a new generation of political leaders came to power. In 1969, de Gaulle resigned and Georges Pompidou was elected president in France. In Germany, a new government was formed with Willy Brandt, a convinced pro-European, as chancellor. With doubts about the IMS becoming more and more widespread, the countries of the European Community feared that further exchange rate instability would lead to the disintegration of the customs union and the demise of the common agricultural policy. The time was ripe for an initiative in the monetary area.

Triffin's idea for an ERF came on the agenda via Brandt. Brandt was a member of Monnet's Action Committee for the United States of Europe, which he consulted to prepare for the December 1969 Hague Summit. Monnet appealed to Triffin, who drew up a new proposal for an ERF (Monnet 1976: 610). Triffin was completely surprised when Monnet contacted him in 1969:

> I still have a very clear memory of the telephone call I received at Yale. Monnet asked me to be in Paris the next day. I protested that it was impossible owing to my commitments at the university. He retorted that he could not tell me his reasons over the phone, but that he considered my presence to be both urgent and indispensable. I therefore took the first flight to Paris and joined Monnet in his apartment on Avenue Foch, where he explained that he had persuaded Chancellor Willy Brandt to present our proposal for a European Reserve Fund at the first European summit conference in the Hague. (Triffin 1990: 33)

The December 1969 Hague Summit was of fundamental importance in the history of European integration. It was decided to go for both a widening of the community (to start enlargement negotiations with the United Kingdom, Ireland, Denmark, and Norway) and a deepening of it, in the form of the EMU project. The summit ended with an agreement that a plan should be drawn up by the council with a view to the creation of an economic and monetary union. The communiqué noted that "The Heads of State have agreed that the possibility should be examined of setting up a European reserve fund to which a common economic and monetary policy would lead."

After the summit, Monnet called a meeting of his Action Committee in Bonn on December 15 and 16, 1969, with Triffin presenting a paper on the creation of an ERF. Thereafter, Triffin and Monnet promoted the idea among important policymakers. Triffin had a phone conversation with Hubert Ansiaux, the governor of the National Bank of Belgium, whom he knew well from the EPU negotiations (see Section 3.5). Triffin summarized their discussions in a "strictly confidential" letter. With the backing of Monnet, he urged Ansiaux to take the lead in the EMU project. "Mr Monnet is convinced, as am I, that only a man like you can succeed and steer in a constructive direction, acceptable to all parties concerned, the new possibilities opened up by de Gaulle's departure, and especially by Brandt's initiative and the Hague conference."[22] Triffin defended his ERF proposal and concluded by urging Ansiaux to go ahead, recalling the EPU negotiations:

> Finally, I would remind you of your comment to me some years ago: "The day that such a possibility becomes reality in political terms, I shall be right there and ready to put in the same effort and energy as in the EPU negotiations."
>
> Hasn't that day come? Many will still say no; but almost everyone—as you know only too well—would also say no to the 1947 Ansiaux plan and the 1949 or even the 1950 EPU project. I am quite sure that there is a possibility, but success will depend on someone of your calibre pitching in and taking charge.[23]

Triffin further advised Ansiaux, if he agreed, to contact Monnet, who "would be very keen to get in touch with you." He concluded: "My dear Hubert, throw this letter in the waste paper basket if you simply believe you are dealing with a utopian dreamer, and not your colleague from 1948–1951, who has always been your friend." As for his own role, Triffin said that he was very much occupied with reforms at Yale University, after the student unrest, and that he wanted to limit his other engagements. He further stressed, "*very sincerely*," that he had "no vanity, as an author, and regretted that the press too often links my name to an idea that is simply good sense, when all I want is to see the idea take hold and prevail." But as recognized earlier by Triffin, Monnet was persuasive and Triffin would follow the discussions on European monetary integration closely and report on the subject for Monnet's Action Committee. He remained in close contact with Ansiaux, who became a member of the Werner Committee, as well as with Jean-Charles Snoy, the Belgian finance minister (Dujardin and Dumoulin 2010: 403).

EMU was now officially on the agenda of the European Community and Monnet was well aware of this. In a letter to Triffin in March 1970, he argued: "Last year, you drafted your reports and the proposal for a European Reserve Fund, in light of Great Britain's accession and the problems to be solved in order to achieve this. . . . We must now take the perspective of Economic and Monetary Union. The Hague Summit decided that a plan would be drawn up for an Economic and Monetary Union in stages. Implementation of this decision is starting now."[24]

In March 1970, a committee was established under the chairmanship of Luxembourg Prime Minister Pierre Werner to map out a plan for EMU. Werner was a convinced European. His vision was inspired by his experience in Pax Romana, the international movement for Catholic intellectuals in his youth. He studied in Paris and among his professors were Jacques Rueff and Charles Rist, two famous French economists. During those years, he also met Robert Schuman, who, as a member of the French Assemblée nationale, showed him around the Palais Bourbon and gave him a taste for politics. Werner was a close acquaintance of Triffin and Monnet and a member of Monnet's Action Committee.

From his early years, Werner developed a keen interest in economic and monetary questions. He was naturally inspired by the special situation of Luxembourg, a country without its own central bank or currency. Werner's views were very much in tune with the ideas of Triffin and Collin, with whom he cooperated on the development of the Luxembourg financial center (see Section 5.4). As long ago as the early 1960s, he had called for the establishment of a European monetary system based on a unit of account (for both official and private use) and a clearing house for central banks. In his view, the gradual introduction of a European currency of account should lessen the risks caused by speculative movements of capital for fear of currency devaluations and revaluations (Danescu 2016: 100). While Werner promoted the idea of a European currency unit, he was also in favor of a strong economic pillar for EMU, with political union as the ultimate aim, plus a strong social dimension. The Monnet-Triffin network was also important for Werner in the work of his committee, and a substantial part of the documentation for the group, especially regarding the establishment of an ERF, was drafted by Triffin. Throughout the entire period of the committee's work, Werner and Triffin kept in close touch by way of dialogue and joint actions, particularly thanks to the good offices of Monnet (Danescu 2018: 101).

Triffin followed the work of the Werner Committee closely and reported regularly for Monnet's Action Committee. He also sent Werner his thoughts on the interim report, which he clearly welcomed, as, in his view, "The most convinced and optimistic European could not ask for more." One of his main suggestions was to speed up the revision of the Rome Treaty. The "necessary changes" to the treaty, Triffin wrote, "can be decided in the light of the ultimate aim, already accepted in the Hague, certainly without waiting for either the end of the first stage or the Council's report on its implementation."[25] His main criticism was that the functions of an ERF had been weakened and its creation postponed. Triffin further argued for the establishment of a European monetary zone. This would imply an "institutional differentiation between the system of intra-Community exchange rates . . . and the system of exchange rates in relation to external currencies, and especially the dollar."

The Werner Committee produced its report in October 1970 (Council-Commission of the European Communities 1970). On an institutional level, the report proposed the creation of two community organs: a decision-making center for economic policy and a community system for the central banks. In order to attain EMU, policy coordination was to be strengthened and a new European currency mechanism had to be created. There was heated debate in the Werner Committee about what should have priority: policy coordination or narrowing of exchange rate fluctuations (Werner 1991). The compromise solution was that there had to be "parallel progress" in both areas.

The concept of an ERF was watered down in the committee. In the end, the Werner Report opted for establishing a European Fund for Monetary Cooperation (EFMC) with more limited functions. Triffin, who was still at the commission, was active in drawing up proposals for the EFMC. According to Guido Carli (1993: 230), who as governor of the Bank of Italy was closely involved in the negotiations, Triffin's ideas very much inspired the statutes of the EFMC. However, in reality, the fund's powers and influence were limited and it became rather a book-keeping agency, virtually run as a subsection of the Bank for International Settlements in Basel (Szász 1999: 49).

All in all, Triffin regarded the plan that emerged from the work of the Werner group as both an institutional and a political opportunity, especially the proposals for a decision-making center for economic policy and a community system for the central banks, two new supranational community institutions. As he argued in a note addressed to Jean Monnet in November 1970: "The roots of Economic and Monetary Union basically lie in the transfer to joint decision-making Community bodies of responsibilities and competences hitherto in the hands of national organisations." However, the report did not meet universal approval. Immediately after its publication, the Werner Report came under heavy fire from the orthodox Gaullists in France (Tsoukalis 1977: 104). Their criticism centered on the supranational elements of the report and induced a change in the French government's attitude, contributing to a dilution of the report's proposals. In particular, the creation of new community institutions was dropped. In Germany too, the Triffin proposals were seriously criticized, even inside the Foreign Ministry. The criticism focused on the almost exclusive attention to the monetary side of EMU, to the detriment of the "necessary coordination of economic policy."[26] The one-sided emphasis on an institutional approach, with the creation of an ERF, was also strongly criticized. Brandt, who had earlier proposed the idea of an ERF, had to back down, especially on the ERF. As he admitted in his autobiography, "the Federal Republic could not envisage a transfer of national reserves in the immediate future. The Finance Ministry and the Bundesbank had exerted a strong braking influence" (Brandt 1992: 423), obliging Brandt to be less forthcoming in European monetary matters.

Moreover, the IMS was crumbling. Nixon's "suspension" of the convertibility of the US dollar in August 1971 was a brutal shock for the European Community, as it implied the de facto breakdown of Bretton Woods. Triffin reacted with a note for Monnet's Action Committee on how the community should face the dollar crisis. For Triffin, the survival of the community itself was at stake. For him, it was imperative to launch the European Monetary Cooperation Fund (EMCF) immediately. "The Council of Ministers had . . . requested a concrete plan for June of next year. Even swifter action is now essential and the beginnings of such a Fund should be put in place before the year is out."[27] Triffin's aim here was twofold: to enable the community to play its role in global negotiations and to stabilize the community currencies. He concluded: "Let the Community limp along for a few months, if it has to, but let it get going and survive!" Over the next few years, Triffin argued for an expansion of the functions of the EMCF, which was finally established in March 1973. In his view, it was essential that it should develop foreign exchange market interventions in European currencies and no longer in dollars.

With global monetary and exchange rate turmoil, progress on European monetary integration was difficult. In March 1973, it was decided that the European currencies would "float together" against the dollar. Under this system, fluctuations between European currencies would be limited to 2.25%, instead of the 4.5% of the Bretton Woods system (after the Smithsonian Agreement of December 1971). The result was the birth of the so-called European snake in the Bretton Woods tunnel. The European monetary snake had a turbulent history. The British pound and the Italian lira were forced out very quickly. As in January 1974, the French franc had to leave. In the end the snake comprised only Germany, Denmark, and the Benelux countries. Moreover, several currency realignments took place. Looking back on this episode not long thereafter, Valéry Giscard d'Estaing, the French finance minister at the time, described the snake as "un animal de la préhistoire monétaire européenne" (an animal of Europe's monetary prehistory; Tsoukalis 1977: 130).

So, Europe's first attempt at monetary unification was not successful. The 1970s were a time of high and diverging inflation rates and exchange rate turmoil. This was not only due to the turbulent international environment (the collapse of the Bretton Woods system and the oil crisis) but also because governments were still strongly attached to their national monetary sovereignty and the pursuit of national economic objectives. In Germany, priority was given to the fight against inflation, while in France, economic growth was considered a more important objective. So, Germany reacted to the oil shock with anti-inflationary policies, while in France a more expansionary path was followed. The ensuing massive differences in inflation rates made exchange rate stability in the community clearly impossible.

It should also be noted that the final breakdown of the Bretton Woods system was very differently perceived in the European Community. For the Bundesbank, the thinking of which was very much along Friedmanite lines (see Sections 3.4 and 4.5), floating was "the only way out" of the conflict between internal and external equilibrium and made it possible for monetary policy to be focused on its domestic objective of price stability (Emminger 1977: 53). For French policymakers, on the other hand, the demise of the Bretton Woods system reinforced German monetary dominance in the European Community. No longer shielded by the Bretton Woods tunnel, it was much more difficult for the French franc to respect the fluctuation margins with the mark, contributing to the eventual departure of the French currency from the snake. It turned the snake into a de facto German mark zone.

The dramatic events of the 1970s stimulated debate about European monetary integration both in the academic world and among policymakers. Most academics were rather skeptical about the feasibility of a monetary union, emphasizing that in a Phillips-curve world, where every country decided on its preferred inflation rate, inflation between countries would only be equal by accident (Magnifico 1971). Triffin was not alone in making bold and innovative proposals to create a (parallel) common European currency. One of the most daring initiatives was the so-called All Saints' Day Manifesto (Basevi et al. 1975), favoring a market-driven approach to monetary union. The basic idea was that one reform could achieve two objectives: a single European currency and the elimination of inflation. The manifesto recommended that the central banks of the European Community should issue a parallel European currency with a constant purchasing power, called the "Europa." Initially, the central banks would only issue Europas against their national currencies, at the request of the economic agents. This new currency would compete with national currencies in all monetary functions.

Triffin was critical of the proposal. He feared that, from a practical point of view, it might be difficult to implement as it involved complex calculations, and it implied "frightening risks" for prospective borrowers. He was also convinced that the national authorities would not allow the introduction of a currency that would rival their national currency. In contrast, Triffin argued for the introduction of a unit of account, also called "Europa," as an alternative, not to national currencies, but to foreign currencies and Eurocurrencies, that were "already used as parallel currencies for international transactions" (Triffin 1978b: 138). In his view, it could be initiated by commercial banks and financial intermediaries for the denomination of Euro-bonds, bank deposits, and lending operations in which foreign currencies and Euro-currencies were already authorized. In Triffin's view, if imports and exports would be invoiced in Europas instead of dollars, this would stabilize prices in the European Community. The Europa would then function as a shelter against foreign shocks, "repeatedly unleashed by past, present, and foreseeable exchange crises in the disorderly monetary system inherited from the collapse of Bretton Woods" (Triffin 1978b: 143). This is also an important argument in present-day plans for promoting the international use of the euro (CEC 2018).

For Triffin, the Europa also presented an alternative path to the single currency, as compared with the Werner Plan, or later the Delors Plan. There would not be an abrupt switch for all countries simultaneously. Instead, each country could move at its own pace, "enlarging gradually the use of the Europa from the external transactions legally admitted at the start—for operations now conducted already in Euro-dollar and other Euro-currencies—to more and more internal transactions as well" (Triffin 1978b: 143). Triffin's proposals, like those of the All Saints' Day Manifesto, failed to win over policymakers, who were extremely doubtful about the feasibility of these schemes and stressed the indivisibility of monetary policy. Nevertheless, these ideas helped to create an atmosphere in which new European monetary integration initiatives could be put on the agenda.

NOTES

1. "U.E.F. Economic Commission. Members," s.d., AIA.
2. NBBA, B 436/4.
3. Minutes of the Meeting of the Commission of November 19–20, 1958, COM(58) PV 38, secret part, CECA.
4. Letter from Bobba to Triffin, February 2, 1961, original majuscules, RTA.
5. Letter from Boyer to Triffin, September 6, 1963, RTA.
6. Letter from Boyer to Triffin, August 2, 1967, RTA, Dossier 8557.
7. Letter from Boyer to Triffin, December 19, 1960, RTA.
8. Letter from Boyer to Triffin, September 6, 1963, RTA.
9. Letter from Boyer to Triffin, March 3, 1969, RTA.
10. Letter from Uri to Triffin, October 30, 1957, RTA.
11. Letter from Uri to Triffin, October 30, 1957, RTA.
12. Coopération économique, monétaire et financière dans la Communauté Economique Européenne, COM(58) 249, November 7, 1958, CECA.
13. Confidential Note on the Need for a European Community Reserve Fund, November 11, 1959, JMA, AMK 25/4/15.

14. Minutes of the Meeting of the Commission of November 20, 1958, COM(58) PV 38, secret part, CECA.

15. L'utilisation d'unités de compte dans les relations économiques et financières internationales, Journée d'Etudes 1978, Institut Universitaire International Luxembourg, NBBA DS2330/01.10.03.00.

16. Letter from Boyer to Triffin, February 22, 1972, RTAY.

17. Institut International d'études bancaires, Sub-Committee for the Study of Problems relating to the Revival of an International Capital Market, Meeting held in Brussels on March 5, 1958, ISHA, Institut International d'Études Bancaires (IIEB) Fond, Box 3, Folder 1.

18. Memorandum for Professor Triffin, November 3, 1964, by Jean Blondeel, RTAY.

19. Minutes of the 23rd Meeting of the Committee of Governors, February 12, 1968, ECBA.

20. GWA.

21. Letter from Boyer to Triffin, August 2, 1967, RTA.

22. Letter from Triffin to Ansiaux, December 17, 1969, NBBA, S 324/6.

23. Letter from Triffin to Ansiaux, December 17, 1969, NBBA, S 324/6.

24. Letter from Monnet to Triffin, March 2, 1970, JMA, AMK C 25/4/163.

25. Note by Robert Triffin, "Vers l'union économique et monétaire de la Communauté," p. 4, PWA.

26. Note from Weinstock to Focke, December 12, 1969, BArch, B136/6410.

27. "La communauté face au problème mondial du dollar," August 28, 1971, p. 6, PWA.

CHAPTER 6
Return to Belgium

6.1 INTRODUCTION

In 1970, Triffin received a Doctor Honoris Causa degree from the franco-phone University of Louvain, his alma mater, and this award contributed to strengthening his contacts with Belgium. A few years later, in 1977, Triffin had to retire as master of Berkeley College. This imposed an "agonizing re-appraisal" on his part about "how to use his remaining years in the best possible way."[1] Triffin decided to return to Belgium. He put forward two reasons: the invitation to take up a visiting professorship at the University of Louvain and, "most of all," the opportunity to be involved, as an adviser at the European Commission, in the process of European monetary union (see Sections 6.3 and 6.4). The return of Triffin was a big coup for the franco-phone University of Louvain. He was one of the most prominent Belgian economists at the time, if not *the* most. There has never been a Belgian Nobel Memorial Prize winner, and Triffin was the only Belgian economist mentioned in Mark Blaug's *Great Economists since Keynes* (Blaug 1985).

Back in Belgium, Triffin's closest friend was Albert Kervyn. Kervyn was the first commissioner of the Belgian Planning Office, a position he held from 1956 to 1966, and he was also one of the country's most prominent Keynesian economists. Triffin and Kervyn already knew each other from the interwar period in Louvain. Like Triffin's, Kervyn's career at Louvain had not been easy, due to resistance from Dupriez (see Section 1.7). In the first half of the 1950s, Kervyn spent two years at Yale, where Triffin was a professor at the time. Both men were progressive Catholics and shared many values, including a strong political engagement, moral rigor, and the conviction that the state had an important role to play in steering the economy too.

Robert Triffin. Ivo Maes, Oxford University Press (2021). © Oxford University Press.
DOI: 10.1093/oso/9780190081096.001.0001

Although he regarded himself as a world citizen, Triffin was also Belgian at heart. The 1970s were a turbulent period in Belgian politics and society. The economy was hit hard by the two oil shocks, contributing to significant economic imbalances. Moreover, economic policy was more or less rudderless, as the political agenda was dominated by tensions between the two communities, the Flemish and the francophone. The Belgian national parties split into Flemish and francophone parties and a process of devolution was put into motion, with Belgium evolving from a unitary to a federal state. In Belgium, Triffin moved mostly in francophone circles and his knowledge of Dutch was limited. When, in 1980, former finance minister Snoy launched a "unionist appeal" to the members of the Belgian parliament, Triffin was among the signatories (Dujardin and Dumoulin 2010: 443). Triffin's Belgian feelings were also nurtured by his good contacts with King Baudouin and Queen Fabiola, for whom he had a *"respect sans borne"* ("boundless respect," Snoy 1993: 98; see also Section 4.2).

Robert and Lois bought a little house in Louvain-la-Neuve, next door to the Kervyns. Louvain-la-Neuve was a new town, especially created to house the francophone University of Louvain, after the University of Louvain split into two—a French-language university and a Dutch-language university—in 1968. The francophone university left the city of Leuven in Flanders and moved to new campuses, the main one being in Louvain-la-Neuve, about 30 km to the southeast of Brussels, in the francophone part of Belgium. On Fridays, Kervyn hosted regular lunches, especially for colleagues from the Economics Department of the university. These were real meetings between friends in which a great variety of topics were discussed, ranging from very serious issues (derivatives in financial markets) to more worldly ones (when Lamfalussy discussed Hungarian wines and vineyards). European politics and the European economy were recurring themes.

On the weekends, Robert and Lois would often accompany the Kervyns to their family castle in the Condroz, in the Walloon countryside. The group often played bridge and Triffin was known for his audacious and imaginative strategies. At the end of the 1980s, with the money from the San Paolo Prize (see Chapter 7), Triffin bought a little apartment on the sea in Ostend. There, he enjoyed watching the sea and the light changing. Always generous, he also offered the apartment to his friends for short stays.

At this time, Triffin, who had been very critical of the Vietnam War and the United States' involvement in it, gave up his US citizenship. In his Statement of Understanding, he said it was unfortunate that he could not have both Belgian and American citizenship. Triffin himself never felt very attached to his nationality. For him, it was very much an administrative matter. "I have long considered myself as a citizen of the world rather than of 'any particular country,'" he said. "Having visited more than 90 countries, and worked at various times in most of them, has strengthened this feeling."[2]

6.2 IMS: THE INTERNATIONAL MONETARY SCANDAL

After his return to Belgium, Triffin continued his earlier research work, focused on the reform of the international monetary system (IMS) and European monetary integration in particular. He was closely involved in setting up the Center for European Policy Studies (CEPS), the origins of which went back to an initiative from McGeorge Bundy, the president of the Ford Foundation. The idea was to create an "Independent Policy Research Institute" or "Euro-Brookings."[3] CEPS was very much modeled on the Brookings Institution, a leading public policy think tank in the United States, and its launch was strongly supported by the Ford Foundation (Maes and Péters 2016).

Triffin gave a keynote lecture at the CEPS inaugural conference on "Western European Priorities" in Brussels in December 1982. His paper, "How to End the World 'Infession': Crisis Management or Fundamental Reforms?," focused on the dire state of the world economy, which most observers described as "stagflation." However, Triffin argued that "infession" was a better characterization, "the unholy combination of inflation and recession better described as 'infession,' i.e. inflation followed by recession, than 'stagflation' which calls to mind a mere stagnation followed by inflation" (Triffin 1983: 1). In his presentation, which echoed his earlier analyses, Triffin stressed how the increase in world liquidity, both official reserves and the Euro-markets, was a fundamental element in world inflation. "The present world inflation," he said, "could not have reached such fantastic proportions if world reserves . . . had not been more than quadrupled since 1969 by the acceptance of paper claims on the United States. . . . This flooding of the official world reserve pool has made possible, and has been compounded by, so-called Euro-bank and Euro-bond credits" (Triffin 1983: 1).

In his policy recommendations, Triffin referred to his proposals for an international currency, which, in his view, had been largely accepted by policymakers in the late 1960s. However, he had to admit that "this near-consensus was cavalierly brushed aside in the Jamaica Agreement and in the Second Amendment to the IMF Articles of Agreement." He regarded the Second Amendment as a sinister joke, whose only merit was to legalize the "illegal repudiation" of member states' Bretton Woods commitments of stable exchange rates. Triffin went on to urge that special drawing rights (SDRs) should be substituted as rapidly as possible for gold and national reserve currencies. This would permit the International Monetary Fund (IMF) to adjust the creation of international reserves to the optimal noninflationary potential of world trade and production. As in his earlier proposals, he argued for a money supply rule, "à la Milton Friedman—averaging 3 to 5% a year and any significant departure from it should require special weighted majorities of 2/3, 3/4, 4/5, or even more, of members—revised—voting power" (Triffin 1983: 40). The presentation was later published as the first CEPS working paper. Triffin also edited, together with Bank of Italy Research Department Head Rainer Masera, one of the volumes of the conference proceedings (Triffin and Masera 1984).

Triffin further stressed the irresponsibility of US policies from the mid-1960s onward, in particular the Vietnam War and President Johnson's refusal to increase taxes or reduce expenditures, "since the resulting *internal* as well as *external* deficits of the United States could be financed painlessly" (Triffin 1987b: 246, original italics), singling out the US responsibility in the increases in world liquidity, a key factor in the Great Inflation of the 1970s. For Triffin, as a real hedgehog, the root cause of the problems hurting the world economy remained the nature of the IMS: the use of a few national currencies, especially the US dollar, as the main component of international monetary reserves. In vivid language, he recalled the warnings of the last century:

> Such a disastrous record confirms the warnings vainly reiterated over more than sixty-five years already by the officials and their experts, at multiple international monetary gatherings—such as the Genoa Conference of 1922, the Gold Delegation of the League of Nations, the International Monetary Fund, the Committee of XX, etc., etc.—against the dangers inherent in the use of a national currency as an international reserve asset or parallel world currency. These official warnings were expressed more candidly, bluntly and forcefully by academic economists. They were the main theme of most of my writings as well as of those of Jacques Rueff and Fritz Machlup. The political—and military—significance of the system was best perceived by President de Gaulle, and denounced as long ago as 1795 in the fourth article of Kant's Essay on Perpetual Peace, which I urge to read—or re-read?—for it is written in a savory language and is as topical today as ever. (Triffin 1987b: 248)

Triffin appealed to reason, invoking, not for the first time, Kant. He reproduced the Fourth Article of Kant's *Perpetual Peace; A Philosophical*

Essay (1795), entitled "No National Debts Shall Be raised by a State to Finance Its Foreign Affairs":

> No objection can be taken to seeking assistance, either within or without the State, in behalf of the economic administration of the country; such as, for the improvement of highways or in support of new colonies or in the establishment of resources against dearth and famine. A loan, whether raised externally or internally, as a source of aid in such cases is above suspicion. But a credit system, when used by the powers as a hostile, antagonistic instrument against each other and when the debts under it go on increasing indefinitely and yet are always liquid for the present (because all the creditors are not expected to cash their claims at once), is a dangerous money power. This arrangement—the ingenious invention of a commercial people in this century [England] constitutes, in fact, a treasure for the carrying on of war; it may exceed the treasures of all the other States taken together, and it can only be exhausted by the forthcoming deficit of the exchequer,—which, however, may be long delayed by the animation of the national commerce and its expansionist impact upon production and profits. The facility given by this system for engaging in war, combined with the inclination of rulers toward it (an inclination which seems to be implanted in human nature), is therefore, a great obstacle in the way of a perpetual peace. The prohibition of it must be laid down as preliminary article in the conditions of such a peace, even more strongly on the further ground that the national bankruptcy, which it inevitably brings at last, would necessarily involve in the disaster many other States without any fault of their own; and this could damage unjustly these other States. Consequently, the other States are justified in allying themselves against such a State and its pretensions. (as quoted in Triffin 1987b: 255)

However, as observed by an old Italian friend of Robert Triffin, Federico Caffè, Triffin's appeal to reason was not necessarily universal, but a matter of a personal decision. Caffè emphasized Triffin's sense of delusion, "tinged with outrage in his indictment of the world monetary scandal." Caffè agreed that the "appeal to reason is always praiseworthy" but added that "reason itself is also a matter of choice" (Caffè 1982: x). As already observed in Section 4.4, Triffin tended to disregard the incentives of politicians in the reform debates of the IMS. He argued for a true IMS. For him, this was not just an economic issue, but a moral one: he was indignant that the richest country in the world had a balance-of-payments deficit.

While Triffin was very much at the center of the international monetary debates in the 1960s, his influence gradually diminished in the ensuing decades. A crucial reason was that floating exchange rates became more and more widely accepted, both in the academic world and among policymakers. Triffin considered himself a Cassandra, who had predicted the monetary crisis before everyone else. However, his repetitive discourse lost its topicality with the evolution of economic circumstances. Notwithstanding Triffin's arguments, his favored solution was no longer on the official agenda. As observed by Wilson (2015: 12), Triffin was "just boring the decision-makers who are turning away from him." Indeed, Triffin remained a hedgehog, very much in the tradition of Teilhard de Chardin, arguing for a "true" IMS, as it was for him a profound moral conviction. Triffin admitted this himself, in his last article, where he allowed that he "had indefatigably and endlessly reiterated for more than thirty years the obvious rudiments of a rational world monetary system" (Triffin 1991: 415). He was also forced to admit that a global reform of the IMS was not on the agenda, falling back to monetary integration at the regional level, especially in Europe. At the time of Triffin's return to Belgium, things were starting to move in European monetary matters. Indeed, this was one of the reasons he decided to come back to Belgium.

6.3 THE EUROPEAN MONETARY SYSTEM

Triffin's return to Belgium coincided closely with Roy Jenkins's appointment as European Commission president. Jenkins, a former British finance minister and a dyed-in-the-wool European federalist, also took a more voluntarist approach toward European monetary integration and tried to revive the monetary union project. A key moment was his famous Florence speech (Jenkins 1977). The effect was that Triffin suddenly regained some of his former influence, with Jenkins (1989: 296) observing in his *European Diary* that Triffin was "of great assistance to us in the run-up to the EMS." Later, in December 1988, Jenkins gave the keynote speech at a conference in honor of Triffin in Brussels. He described Triffin as "one of the most quietly remarkable men that I have known." He went on to compare Triffin with Monnet, suggesting that Triffin was similar to the Frenchman in the "fertility of his ideas and the calm persuasiveness of his advocacy" (Jenkins 1991: xii).

In the second half of the 1970s, European leaders also became increasingly worried about the stagnation of the European integration process and the risk that the achievements of the past could fall apart. In 1978, French President Valéry Giscard d'Estaing and German Chancellor Helmut Schmidt played a crucial role in relaunching the monetary integration process with the creation of the European Monetary System (EMS), agreed to by the heads of state and government at the Brussels Summit in December (Mourlon-Druol 2012).

The EMS was composed of three main elements: the exchange rate mechanism (ERM), credit mechanisms, and the European Currency Unit (ECU). At the core of the EMS was the ERM. This might seem somewhat paradoxical, since not all currencies of the community participated. The original members were the German mark, the Dutch guilder, the French franc, the Danish krone, the Belgian/Luxembourg franc, the Irish pound, and the Italian lira. The British pound stayed out. Like the snake, the ERM consisted of currencies that were linked to one another by fixed but adjustable exchange rates and that floated together against the dollar and the other currencies.

The EMS was also based on a new European currency unit, the ECU. This basket currency was made up of all the currencies of the European Community, including those that did not participate in the ERM. Each currency was weighted to reflect the relative economic importance of the relevant country, in terms of gross domestic product and trade. Slightly coincidentally, ECU was not only the abbreviation for European Currency Unit, but also the name of an old French coin.

The agreement provided for two ideas that were cherished by Triffin: the creation of a European Monetary Fund (EMF) and the full utilization of the ECU as a reserve asset and a means of settlement, within two years of the start of the EMS. However, the functions of the EMF were never really agreed upon. In Germany, the Bundesbank was strongly opposed to the idea of the EMF. As the Bundesbank's influence increased during the negotiations, the EMF was more and more hollowed out (Dyson and Featherstone 1999).

Triffin was clearly not one of the key actors in the establishment of the EMS, but he did play a role. He was an adviser at the commission and in contact with Jenkins and his cabinet, and he was consulted for the Florence speech (Ludlow 1982: 49; Vanden Abeele 2012). According to Jacques van Ypersele, then the chairman of the European Community's Monetary Committee, Triffin mainly played the role of an "inspirator" (Maes and Péters 2016). But his prestige was important in the debates and his name mentioned in a letter of the Italian Federalist Movement, which urged the members of the Italian parliament to approve the EMS agreement (interview Iozzo).

Triffin was enthusiastic about the EMS and he organized four international conferences on different aspects of its functioning. The advisory committee consisted of some eminent economists and policymakers like Rudiger Dornbusch (MIT), Alexandre Lamfalussy (Bank for International

Settlements [BIS]), Alexander Swoboda (University of Geneva), Niels Thygesen (University of Copenhagen), and Jacques van Ypersele (Chef de cabinet of the Belgian prime minister). It showed the importance of Triffin's network. For this project, Triffin was also in close contact with the European Commission, especially Tommaso Padoa-Schioppa, who was director general of the Directorate-General for Economic and Financial Affairs (DG II) from June 1979 to March 1983. Padoa-Schioppa can be considered as one of the architects of the euro, the single currency (Maes 2013b; Masini 2016). He was a close friend, some would say an accomplice, of Jacques Delors. He is especially remembered as corapporteur of the Delors Committee and as a founding member of the Executive Board of the European Central Bank.

In an internal note at the commission, Triffin argued that the EMS raised several crucial issues. In his view, broad debates about the implications of this "revolutionary" step for Europe and for the rest of the world were urgently necessary. He recommended a series of seminars on "European Economic and Monetary Union," building upon the experience of the meetings of the Bellagio Group.[4] These workshops had brought together academics and policymakers to analyze and debate policy-oriented studies on the major issues raised by the disintegration of the Bretton Woods system (see Section 4.5). However, the seminars would differ in two ways from the Bellagio Group format: (1) they would focus on areas of feasible agreement rather than inviting individual, pioneering contributions "calling for prolonged debates and controversies, and therefore of little relevance to current policy-making decisions," and (2) they would be published early in a format accessible to policymakers and interested laymen as well as to professional economists.

The first seminar focused closely on the optimal degree of exchange rate flexibility to be aimed for in the EMS. In Triffin's assessment, the EMS exchange rate commitments made "as much room for readjustments," in case of need, as for "presumptive" stability among the participating currencies (Triffin 1979a: 183). He further emphasized that the readjustments would be explored in a multilateral framework and that the ECU would provide the most appropriate numeraire for calculating exchange rate readjustments. Moreover, the ECU would become far more than a mere unit of account. It would be used as a medium for settlements and reserve accumulation by the national authorities of the member countries. In Triffin's view, then, the emerging EMS might "serve also as a model for negotiation of the worldwide monetary reforms" (Triffin 1979a: 183).

The second seminar was held at the International Center for Monetary and Banking Studies in Geneva, in December 1979. The topic was the planned EMF. In his concluding remarks, Triffin (1979b: 393) noted certain resemblances in the EMF debates to Keynes's argument for a clearing union, writing that "Keynes said that the clearing union would simply adopt traditional commercial banking principles and apply them to relations between countries and central banks." But Triffin was critical of this and repeated his earlier criticism: "I am not sure that I would deposit my money in a bank whose goal and stated policy is to lend unspecified amounts to anybody who demonstrates that they are spending more than their earnings."

In June 1980, a third seminar was held at Louvain-la-Neuve on the theme of the private use of the ECU. It was attended not only by officials and academics but also by representatives of the banking and insurance sectors. The conferees discussed the broad lines of a program for widening the use of the ECU by economic stakeholders, especially the future role of the ECU as a "parallel currency" in private and official transactions.[5] During the debates, Triffin (1980) raised the issue of the clearing of ECU transactions, a crucial issue for the development of the ECU market that would be taken up in the ensuing years.

At the end of the seminar, Padoa-Schioppa discussed the topic of who would take up the challenge of promoting the ECU in the financial markets: the private or the public sector? He argued: "Perhaps an idealist would say that both Government authorities and the private sector should help develop use of the ECU simultaneously. It is clear that both sides must contribute, in order to ensure the success of the ECU" (Triffin and Swings 1980: 74). Padoa-Schioppa himself would play an important role here. Alfonso Iozzo (2012: 137), a prominent European federalist and CEO of San Paolo who attended the conference, described it as a "solemn oath."

Iozzo was closely involved in arranging a follow-up conference in Rome in December 1980 on the theme "International Banking System and the Use of the ECU."[6] The keynote speakers were Luigi Coccioli, the chairman of San Paolo; Carlo Azeglio Ciampi, the governor of the Bank of Italy; and Triffin himself. These meetings led to several initiatives, from the opening of ECU-denominated current accounts to the issue of traveler checks. In two sectors in particular, ECU operations would make a quantum leap: the issue of bonds, first from banks and companies and then from states (Italy in particular), and the setting up of a clearing system (see Section 6.4).

The fourth seminar was held at Denmark's central bank in Copenhagen in March 1981. It discussed the first two years of the EMS. While the first three seminars had been largely forward looking, the main purpose of the final seminar was to evaluate how the EMS had actually worked. In his concluding remarks, Triffin (1981b: 367) struck a cautionary note. In his view, the initial success of the EMS was largely due to favorable external circumstances: a strong dollar, implying less upward pressure on the German mark. He feared that this tendency might be reversed in the future. Consequently, a big qualitative jump was necessary to strengthen the EMS.

Triffin was also active as an adviser at the commission. In a note for Jenkins's cabinet, Triffin observed that the EMS operations had hardly changed the previous method of settlements—in gold and dollars—of interventions in the foreign exchange markets. The main change was a wider role for gold through the use of conversion rates close to current market prices (which were much higher than the old official gold price) and by entering gold transfers in central banks' reports as ECU transfers.[7] Triffin was in favor of stepping up the role of the ECU in international settlements among the member countries of the community. The ECU had to become an alternative to gold, dollars, and other national currencies. Triffin argued that three major conditions were necessary to make the ECU fully acceptable and attractive to central banks: its full and immediate usability for all balance-of-payments settlements; its protection against inflationary issues of ECU liabilities; and an institutional machinery acceptable to central banks, which were legitimately concerned about preserving monetary policies from day-to-day political pressures. In Triffin's view, "Mr. Debré [a prominent Gaullist] would presumably object to permitting the ECU to replace the French franc, but be delighted to see it take the place of Euro-dollars, Euro-marks, Euro-Swiss francs, etc." Triffin also objected to the confidential nature of European Monetary Cooperation Fund (EMCF) operations. He argued for a monthly publication of the basic statistical data, accompanied by brief commentaries. A more thorough analysis would follow in an annual report, with Triffin adding: "The annual reports of the *European Payments Union* could be taken as an example worthy of imitation."[8]

The early years of the EMS were not easy (Gros and Thygesen 1998). There were several currency realignments, coordination of economic policy was weak, and inflation divergences persisted. In this atmosphere, the European Community decided, at the end of 1980, to postpone the creation of the EMF. This was a hard moment for Triffin and after this disappointment he focused even more on promoting private sector use of the ECU. This was also a strategy espoused by the European Commission, where Padoa-Schioppa was active in promoting the role of the ECU as a parallel currency.

The broad strategy of the commission to strengthen the EMS came clearly to the foreground in its March 1982 communication (Maes 2007). This document focused on four broad areas: strengthening the exchange rate system, promoting the private use of the ECU, strengthening convergence, and opening the EMS up to the outside world. A key point of emphasis was promoting the private use of the ECU. The commission argued that the community institutions should promote the use of the ECU in their operations and in their bond issues. It also proposed giving the ECU recognition as a foreign currency (something the Bundesbank would only allow in June 1987) and that, in the community, there would be free movement of capital denominated in ECU.

The year 1983 was a turning point in the history of the EMS. It was the moment when French President François Mitterrand gave priority to Europe, duly adopting a more orthodox economic policy stance. A similar shift occurred in other European countries. Policy convergence caused inflation rates to decline and converge, which in turn was conducive to more stable exchange rates. Then, in 1985, the European Community was given fresh and strong impetus by the adoption of the internal market program. Its aim was to achieve fully free movement of goods, services, people, and capital by 1992. One of the cornerstones of this program was the creation of a European financial market. It also led to the Single European Act, the first important modification of the Treaty of Rome. The act contained the first reference in the Treaties to Economic and Monetary Union.

Crucial progress toward economic and monetary union (EMU) was made at the June 1988 Hanover Summit. The summit confirmed the objective of economic and monetary union and the decision was made to entrust to a committee the task of studying and proposing concrete stages leading up to it. The committee was chaired by Jacques Delors, who had the confidence of Kohl and Mitterrand and, as a former finance minister, the technical expertise necessary to guide the process. The governors of the central banks—in a personal capacity—were also on the committee, which produced its report in June 1989 (Committee for the Study of Economic and Monetary Union 1989). The committee gave significant attention to the institutional framework of EMU, especially the monetary pillar. The Delors Report would assume a crucial role as a reference and anchor point in further discussions. Larger forces also played an affirmative role here. The broader European scene was changing dramatically with the breakdown of the Iron Curtain and German unification, which helped to speed the process of European monetary integration. The German government's policy line could almost be summed up in Thomas Mann's dictum: "Wir wollen ein europäisches Deutschland und kein deutsches Europa" ("We want a European Germany and not a German Europe," Schönfelder and Thiel 1996: 12).

The negotiations for a new European treaty reached their climax at the Maastricht Summit of Heads of State and Government in December 1991. The Maastricht Treaty marked a step forward for the European Community in the same way that the Treaty of Rome had done. It created a so-called European Union, based on three pillars (Maes 2007). The first pillar had at its core the old community but carried greatly extended responsibilities with it. The main element here was economic and monetary union, very much based on the Delors Report. The second pillar dealt with foreign and security policy, while the third one concerned cooperation on such topics as immigration, asylum, and police. The new treaty also extended the European Parliament's powers. Triffin commented on these developments in his last article, which appeared in the December 1991 issue of the *Banca Nazionale del Lavoro Quarterly Review*. The title was very Triffinite: "The IMS (International Monetary System . . . or Scandal?) and the EMS (European Monetary System . . . or Success?)." Triffin's conclusion expressed his faith in the quick realization of EMU: "Everybody agrees that a European Germany is now the only possible alternative to a German Europe, and that full economic and monetary union should be achieved before January 1, 1993" (Triffin 1991: 426).

6.4 THE DEVELOPMENT OF THE PRIVATE ECU MARKET

Triffin was not content to remain idle while the politicians groped their way forward toward further monetary integration and, during the 1980s, he played an active role in the development of the private ECU market. The Kredietbank, where Triffin was on the board since 1961 (see Section 5.4), decided to change its strategy. It had strongly dominated the market for the European unit of account (see Section 5.4). However, this dominance had hindered the development of the market. So, the Kredietbank wanted to involve other banks in the market for the ECU as much as possible. It even authorized Triffin to become an administrator of the Luxembourg branch of the Istituto Bancario San Paolo di Torino, another important player in the ECU market (and publisher of the *ECU Newsletter*, under the impulse of Alfonso Iozzo, a good friend of Triffin). In 1981, the Kredietbank, the Istituto Bancario San Paolo, and Crédit Lyonnais led a banking consortium that issued an international loan denominated and payable in ECU (Galea 2013: 339).

A crucial issue was the establishment of an ECU clearing system. Triffin discussed the matter with Paul Caron of Morgan Guarantee, who later admitted: "It was with great delight and awe that I read your article in the quarterly from Lavoro. Little did I realise how many 'coals I was bringing to Newcastle' in speaking with you about clearing systems, bilateralism, etc."[9] He also informed Triffin about his contacts with Padoa-Schioppa, who "has asked us to prepare something . . . including the choice of banks who would be interested in working on an ECU clearing mechanism." Later, Padoa-Schioppa (1987) spoke of how, "prompted by Robert Triffin and Paul Caron, I convened the banks that were then active in the ECU market and invited them to set up a study group for the creation of a multilateral clearing system."

The symposium on the private use of the ECU took place in Brussels on February 5, 1982.[10] Among the participants were commercial bankers and officials from the commission and the European Investment Bank. Triffin took part in his capacity as an adviser at the commission. The broad aim of the meeting was to exchange information and ideas on the promotion of the private use of the ECU. One of the key issues was the establishment of a clearing house. The result was that, in 1982, a working party was set up with a view to establishing a multilateral clearing system for operations in private ECUs. It was composed of a group of commercial banks and the European Investment Bank under the aegis of the European Commission. In early 1983, this working party approached the BIS to seek its collaboration in devising such a system, and with a possible view to involving the BIS as clearing agent for the banks.[11]

The BIS decided to support the initiative. An important reason was that it was seen to contribute to the strengthening of European financial integration. Moreover, there were precedents. In the 1950s, the BIS had played an active role in official European monetary cooperation as agent of the European Payments Union. Having also assumed the role of agent of the EMCF, it concluded the three-month revolving swaps that formed the basis for the official ECU and carried out all the transactions that went through the fund's books. In an internal note, the BIS observed that the private ECU clearing and settlement system contributed to the attractiveness of the private ECU.[12] Indeed, the terms of the agreement between the BIS and the ECU Banking Association defined the private ECU unequivocally as the monetary unit used in the EMS as official reserve asset and means of settlement. So, any confusion there might have been in the financial markets as to the meaning of the term "private ECU" had thus been removed. This contributed to lowering information and transaction costs in the ECU financial markets.

The success of the private ECU helped spur momentum for further policy initiatives (Iozzo 2012: 138). For instance, in 1986, the promoters of the EMS, former French president Giscard d'Estaing and former German chancellor Schmidt, set up the Committee for the European Monetary Union, which included important politicians, industrialists, and representatives of the financial sector from the main European countries. The committee would play an important role in preparing the ground for EMU. However, under the influence of Renaud de la Genière, a former governor of the Banque de France, it rejected a parallel currency approach, just as the Delors Committee would do in 1989.

Triffin's voluntarist approach toward European monetary integration came clearly to the fore in his advocacy of the creation of a European currency and in his proposals to promote it as a parallel currency, alongside the existing national currencies, both in the official monetary circuits (e.g., among central banks) and in commercial circuits (e.g., the bond markets). In an article he wrote in honor of Triffin, entitled "European Monies and European Monetary Union," Padoa-Schioppa (1991: 201) was quite positive about the ECU as a parallel currency on the path to EMU. However, he observed that his article was "limited" as it did not address the hardest issues raised by EMU: economic union and the operational arrangements for monetary union. Padoa-Schioppa, of course, was only too well aware of these issues, given his experience as corapporteur on the Delors Committee, which focused very much on the institutional framework of an independent European System of Central Banks and which rejected a parallel currency approach.

Triffin remained active well into his 70s. In 1987, the Centre Ecu et Prospective d'Intégration Monétaire Européenne (CEPIME) was set up, based at Institut Catholique des Hautes Etudes Commerciales (ICHEC) in Brussels. Triffin became its first president. The CEPIME also launched a journal, *De Pecunia*, the first issue of which contained the proceedings of a conference held on January 27, 1989, on a theme close to Triffin's preoccupations, "les évolutions irrégulières du marché de l'écu" ("the irregular movements in the ECU market"). Triffin gave the opening speech at the conference on the theme "Tout va très bien, Madame la marquise, tout va très bien! Mais, cependant, il faut que je vous dise . . ." ("Everything is just fine! But I still have to tell you . . . ." Triffin 1989a: 8).

NOTES

1. Renunciation of US Nationality: Statement of Understanding, RTA.
2. Renunciation of US Nationality: Statement of Understanding, RTA.
3. "Memorandum" by Jacques van Ypersele, June 2, 1982, JvYA.

4. Note by Robert Triffin, Planned Seminars on the Emerging "European Monetary System," March 20, 1980, TPSA.

5. Séminaire international sur les utilisations privées de l'Ecu, Louvain, June 13–14, 1980, RTA, 17.2, CR.

6. International Banking System and the Use of the ECU, November 10, 1980, ASSP, Segreteria Generale, 15147.

7. Internal Memo by Triffin to Vanden Abeele and Emerson (Cabinet of Jenkins), October 27, 1980, TPSA.

8. Internal Note by Triffin to Padoa Schioppa, Publication of Fecom Accounts, March 1983, TPSA.

9. Letter from Caron to Triffin, December 1, 1981, TPSA.

10. Bankers' Symposium on the Private Use of the ECU—Summary of Discussions, Brussels, February 5, 1982, BISA 1.190, vol. 1.

11. The Bank for International Settlements and the Private ECU Clearing and Settlement System, BISA 7.17 (1987) 026.

12. The Bank for International Settlements and the Private ECU Clearing and Settlement System, BISA 7.17 (1987) 026, p. 4.

CHAPTER 7

Epilogue

Toward the end of his life, Triffin received wide recognition for his work. In 1987, he was awarded the first International San Paolo Prize for Economics for his intellectual contributions with a focus on contemporary economic policy issues. The Award Committee singled out Triffin's "natural gift for in-depth analysis and a realistic imagination," which had enabled him to forecast the breakdown of the Bretton Woods system "with lucidity and perseverance." It further paid tribute to his contributions to European monetary integration, especially the European Payments Union and the European Monetary System (EMS). While he had always been loyal to the "scientific tenets of independence and objectivity," the committee went on to praise Triffin for having also shown "to what extent economic science can help to improve the functioning of modern society."[1]

On September 15, 1988, Triffin received the Frank E. Seidman Distinguished Award in Political Economy at Rhodes College, Memphis, Tennessee. The award acknowledged economists who had contributed "to the advancement of economic thought along interdisciplinary lines and to its implementation through public policy." Triffin's old friend Tobin introduced him at the prize-giving ceremony. He not only stressed Triffin's contributions to economic thought and policy but also pointed out how active he had been for world peace, disarmament, and détente. In Tobin's view, there were "very few people who believe so deeply in what they are doing and pursue their interests with such passion" (Tobin 1988: iv).

Triffin's acceptance speech for the award was entitled "The Intermixture of Politics and Economics in the World Monetary Scandal: Diagnosis and Prescription" (Triffin 1988). Here his pacifism immediately came to the fore. He attacked official policies that threatened "the nuclear suicide of human life on our minuscule planet." In his view, disarmament could

Robert Triffin. Ivo Maes, Oxford University Press (2021). © Oxford University Press.
DOI: 10.1093/oso/9780190081096.001.0001

be initiated unliterally, "without any danger whatsoever." He argued for replacing the old slogan "Si vis pacem, para bellum!" (If you want peace, prepare for war!) with President Roosevelt's slogan "The only thing to fear is fear itself!" Though some have argued that people mellow with age, Triffin became a more fervent pacifist, or as his old friend Samuelson observed, a "peace-nick" (as quoted in Wilson 2015: 750).

Triffin then turned his attention to the topic that had secured him the award—economic integration. Consistent with the monetary union debate in Europe (the Delors Committee had started its work), Triffin argued that the Bundesbank should serve as a model for the autonomy and political independence of the European Central Bank. However, he continued to promote the European Currency Unit (ECU) and a strategy of a gradual extension of the use of the ECU, even suggesting the possibility of the single European currency being introduced earlier in Italy than in Germany—a politically imaginative scenario. He concluded with a sentiment that could be seen as characteristic of his entire career, saying, "As an inveterate optimist, I hope to live long enough to see the end of this venture!" However, he was too optimistic. The euro was not introduced until 1999, some six years after his death. During the last years of his life, the severe difficulties with the ratification of the Maastricht Treaty and the 1992–1993 crisis in the EMS were an agonizing experience for Triffin.

Triffin's contributions were also recognized with several honorary PhD degrees, including from the Universities of New Haven and Pavia. At the end of his laudatory speech in Pavia, Guido Montani (1989: 215) emphasized that Triffin kept up the fight for a world currency and compared Triffin to Martin Luther: "Here I stand, I can do no other."

Triffin was the guest of honor at the first two of a series of conferences on the international monetary system organized by Miklos Szabo-Pelsoczi, a Hungarian-American academic and businessman, held at Castle Szirak in Hungary. These conferences led to the establishment of the Robert Triffin–Szirak Foundation. In his foreword to the proceedings of the third conference, Otto Hieronymi, one of Triffin's former students in Geneva, emphasized Triffin's key message to Szirak: "international monetary order is worth fighting for" (Hieronymi 1993: 1).

Belgium too came to recognize the importance of Triffin's contributions, a fitting reversal of the attitudes he had encountered after his return from Harvard in the late 1930s. In 1973, he was appointed Commander of the Order of the Crown by King Baudouin for "having remained loyal to his native village of Flobecq, but having become our first citizen of the world, to whom any nationalism is alien." Then, in 1989, King Baudoin made him a baron. In line with his pacifist convictions, Triffin chose as his motto a paraphrase of Belgium's national motto, transposing "Unity makes strength" into "Unity makes peace."

Triffin died on February 23, 1993, in Ostend. During the last years of his life, he suffered from emphysema, a lung disease (he was a lifetime heavy smoker). He was not afraid of death, instead, he was curious, asking: "What will happen? Very soon I will find out." Triffin was survived by his wife, Lois, who died on December 11, 2014, at the age of 97. Ever nonconventional, Lois did not want a funeral ceremony in Belgium. Instead, she asked her friends to meet up for a picnic in the Forêt de Soignes, the Sonian Forest, close to Brussels.

Robert Triffin was certainly a visionary economist. He became famous with the "Triffin dilemma" and as the Cassandra who predicted the end of Bretton Woods. The Triffin dilemma still offers a framework to analyze the international monetary system and is still very much present in current policy debates. But this does not fully capture the man and his motivations. Triffin was a very policy-oriented economist, and his life was a fight for a better, more just, and more peaceful world. This influenced his approach toward economics, as he observed himself in an autobiographical article: "If my main concern were to make safe forecasts, I would agree with you and be proven right nine times out of ten. But I prefer to be wrong nine times out of ten, if I can contribute once in ten times to divert us from catastrophe, and help build a better future" (Triffin 1981a: 247). He shared this approach with Keynes, who, as in "The Economic Consequences of Mr. Churchill," also sought to avoid catastrophe (Keynes 1925).

As a student, Triffin fulminated against the "Diktat" of the Versailles Treaty. Later, Triffin was part of a generation of economists marked by the Great Depression, with devastating trade and currency wars, contributing to the rise of fascism and World War II. He never tired of pointing out the factual limits of national sovereignty in an interdependent world and developed imaginative plans for economic cooperation and international monetary reform. In his analyses he always took a systemic perspective and sought an equitable division of the burden between deficit and surplus countries. Behind the scenes, he became an influential policymaker in the postwar period. He was an architect of the European Payments Union and was profoundly engaged in preparing the path for economic and monetary union—in his view, a crucial step toward a European political union. He tirelessly stressed the dangers and inefficiencies of bilateralism. Triffin made his contribution to the successful European recovery after World War II, a stark contrast with the disasters of the interwar period. He was a true economist statesman of interdependence and multilateralism.

Robert Triffin was the son of a butcher. His life was a story of remark-able social mobility. He was the first in his family not only to go university but also even to study at high school. He would go on to Harvard for his PhD and become a professor at Yale. He would also become influential in policymaking circles and be a dominant voice in the international mone-tary debates for years. It is a clear illustration of the importance of an open society, which offers opportunities for people who engage themselves.

It is further remarkable that throughout his life Triffin remained faithful to the ideals of his youth, a rare quality. The young Triffin was in-dignant about the Versailles Treaty, while the old Triffin fulminated against the Vietnam War. For him, economics was a way to contribute to a better world. He was never interested in high-level prestigious positions or finan-cial gain. He was strongly attached to his independence and the pursuit of a better and more peaceful world. He was indeed a true monk in economist's clothing.

NOTE

1. Istituto Bancario San Paolo di Torino, Consiglio di Amministrazione, June 22, 1987, CSPHA, IV, IBSP, Segreteria Generale, file 1285.

SOURCES

1. ARCHIVES
Triffin Archives
- RTA—Robert Triffin, Université catholique de Louvain, Louvain-la-Neuve
- RTYA—Robert Triffin, Yale University, New Haven

European and International Organization Archives
- BISA—Bank for International Settlements, Basel
- CECA—Commission of the European Communities, Brussels
- ECBA—European Central Bank, Frankfurt
- IMFA—International Monetary Fund, Washington, DC
- OECDA—Organization of Economic Cooperation and Development, Paris
- PUA—Pierre Uri, Historical Archives of the European Union, European University Institute, Florence
- TPSA—Tommaso Padoa-Schioppa, Historical Archives of the European Union, European University Institute, Florence

Belgian Archives
- AEJA—Albert-Édouard Janssen, Université catholique de Louvain, Louvain-la-Neuve
- BAEFA—Belgian American Educational Foundation, Brussels
- GWA—Gerard Wissels, Overijse
- JVYA—Jacques van Ypersele, Kraainem
- NBBA—National Bank of Belgium, Brussels
- PvZA—Paul van Zeeland, Université catholique de Louvain, Louvain-la-Neuve

German Archives
- BArch—Bundesarchiv/German Federal Archives, Koblenz

Italian Archives
- AIA—Alfonso Iozzo, Turin
- BIHA—Bank of Italy Historical Archives, Rome
- CSPHA—Compagnia di San Paolo Historical Archives, Turin
- ISHA—Intesa Sanpaolo Historical Archives, Milan

Luxembourg Archives
- PWA—Pierre Werner Family Archives, Luxembourg

Swiss Archives
- JMA—Jean Monnet, Fondation Jean Monnet, Lausanne

United Kingdom Archives
- JMeA—James Meade, London School of Economics, London

United States Archives
- FRSA—Records of the Federal Reserve System, Record Group, Federal Reserve Archival System for Economic Research (Fraser), St. Louis Fed, St. Louis
- MEA—Marriner S. Eccles Papers, Federal Reserve Archival System for Economic Research (Fraser), St. Louis Fed, St. Louis
- HSTLM—Harry S. Truman Library and Museum, Independence (Missouri) Library Collections, Oral History Interviews, Hubert F. Havlik Oral History Interview by Richard D. McKinzie, Arlington (Virginia), June 20, 1973

2. PERSONS INTERVIEWED

Background interviews. Several of these persons were interviewed for earlier projects, but also with questions related to Triffin.

Abraham, Jean-Paul (B), Economist, European Coal and Steel Community; Professor, University of Leuven (6-6-2000)

Achard, Pierre (F), Adviser to R. Barre; Secretary General of the Secrétariat Général de la Coordination Internationale (1-23-2002, 10-30-2002, 12-10-2003)

Albert, Michel (F), Director, DG II; Commissioner General, Planning Office (11-9-2000)

Baer, Gunter (D), Secretary General of the Bank for International Settlements and of the Committee of Governors (8-18-2009)

Barre, Raymond (F), Vice President, European Commission; Prime Minister (12-6-2001)

Basevi, Giorgio (I), Professor, University of Bologna (12-14-2013)

Bernard, Jean-René (F), Adviser to G. Pompidou; Secretary General of the Secrétariat Général de la Coordination Internationale (10-2-2001)

Bernard, Luc (B), Professor, University of Louvain (10-2-2008)

Berthoin, Georges (F), Chef de cabinet of J. Monnet (10-30-2002)

Bloch-Lainé, Jean-Michel (F), Deputy Director of the Treasury (12-6-2001)

Boelpaep, Emile (B), Professor, Yale University (11-22-2018, 6-24-2019)

Boyer de la Giroday, Eric (B), Son of Frédéric Boyer de la Giroday; Chairman of ING Belgium (1-25-2019)

Brouhns, Grégoire (B), Secretary General, Finance Ministry (5-30-2002)

Buti, Marco (I), Director General, DG II (7-29-2002)

Camu, Alain (B), Banker (5-8-2013)

Cardon, Daniel (B), Chef de cabinet of A. Coppé (5-15-2001)

Carré, Hervé (F), Director General, Eurostat; Deputy Director General, DG II (7-9-2008, 7-4-2011)

Ciocca, Pierluigi (I), Deputy Director General, Banca d'Italia (5-15-2003)

Colombo, Emilio (I), Prime Minister; Treasury Minister (7-11-2003)

de Groote, Jacques (B), Assistant of Dupriez; Executive Director for Belgium at the International Monetary Fund (10-7-2008)

de Kergorlay, Roland (F), Secretary of the Monetary Committee (11-27-2001)

de Keuleneer, Eric (B), Head of Syndication and Trading, Kredietbank Luxembourg (5-29-2019) de Larosière, Jacques (F), Director of the Treasury; Governor of the Banque de France; Director General, International Monetary Fund (10-3-2001, 9-26-2018, 8-23-2019)

de Lattre, André (F), Adviser to Ch. De Gaulle; Deputy Governor of the Banque de France (1-23-2002)

Delors, Jacques (F), Finance Minister; President of the European Commission (7-13-1999)

D'Haeze, Marcel (B), Director of the Treasury; Vice Governor, National Bank of Belgium (1-15-2003)

Dixon, Joly (UK), Adviser to J. Delors (3-2-2017)

Duvieusart, Philippe (B), Director, Kredietbank Luxembourg (1-24-2014)

Eichengreen, Barry (US), Professor, University of California, Berkeley (11-6-2018)

Emerson, Michael (UK), Adviser to R. Jenkins; Director, DG II (6-16-1997, 5-21-1999, 7-13-2017)

Flory, Jean (F), Chef de cabinet of R. Marjolin (12-5-2001, 1-30-2004)

Fratianni, Michele (I), Economic Adviser, DG II (11-18-1998)

Froschmaier, Franz (D), Chef de cabinet of W. Haferkamp (7-16-1997, 5-6-2004)

Gleske, Leonhard (D), Director, DG II; Member of the Board, Deutsche Bundesbank (12-18-2001)

Godeaux, Jean (B), Governor, National Bank of Belgium (4-17-2002, 3-3-2005)

Grosche, Günter (D), Head of the European Currencies Division, Finance Ministry; Secretary of the Monetary Committee (7-27-2001)

Haberer, Jean-Yves (F), Chef de cabinet of M. Debré; Director of the Treasury (10-3-2001)

Hoffmeyer, Erik (DK), Governor, Danmarks Nationalbank (8-8-2002)

Iozzo, Alfonso (I), CEO, San Paolo-IMI (10-20-2018)

Issing, Otmar (D), Member of the Board, Deutsche Bundesbank (5-2-2001)

Jaans, Pierre (L), Director-General, Institut Monétaire Luxembourgeois (4-10-2012)

Janson, Georges (B), Director, National Bank of Belgium (4-8-2002)

Jeanneney, Jean-Marcel (F), Industry and Social Affairs Minister (2-19-2003)

Kees, Andreas (D), Secretary of the Monetary Committee (11-28-2001)

Kervyn de Lettenhove, Bruno (B), Son of Albert Kervyn de Lettenhove (8-20-2019)

Kervyn de Lettenhove, Véronique (B), Daughter-in-Law of Albert Kervyn de Lettenhove (8-20-2019)

Koeune, Jean-Claude (B), Deputy chef de cabinet of W. Martens (5-7-2002)

Köhler, Horst (D), State Secretary, Finance Ministry (10-26-1999)

Lahnstein, Manfred (D), Chef de cabinet of W. Haferkamp; Finance Minister (6-11-2002)

Lambert, Marie-Henriette (B), Head of the Research Department, National Bank of Belgium (1-8-2009)

Lamfalussy, Alexandre (B), President of the European Monetary Institute (7-12-1999, 3-13-2007, 8-7-2008)

Lefèbvre, Olivier (B), Assistant at the Institut de Recherches Economiques et Sociales; Chef de cabinet of Ph. Maystadt (7-2-2007, 8-8-2019)

Louw, André (B), Head of Unit, DG II (8-22-1997, 7-24-2001)

Ludlow, Peter (UK), Director, Centre for European Policy Studies (1-29-2013)

Mandy, Paul (B), Professor, Louvain (10-22-2008)

Masera, Rainer (I), Minister of the Budget (10-18-2018)

Maystadt, Philippe (B), Finance Minister (6-24-2002)

Millet, Pierre (F), Director, DG II (2-20-2003)

Mingasson, Jean-Paul (F), Deputy Director General, DG II (7-25-2005)

Molitor, Bernhard (D), Head of the Economic Policy Directorate, Economics Ministry; Director, DG II (3-8-2001)

Morel, Jean-Claude (F), Deputy Director General, DG II; Director General, Forward Looking Studies Unit (8-17-2000, 11-5-2000)

Mortensen, Jörgen (DK), Head of Unit, DG II (2-23-1995, 1-15-1998)

Ortoli, François-Xavier (F), Chef de cabinet of G. Pompidou; Finance Minister; President of European Commission (12-4-2001)

Padoa-Schioppa, Tommaso (I), Director General, DG II (6-18-1999)

Pandolfi, Filippo Maria (I), Treasury Minister (9-11-2002)

Paye, Jean-Claude (F), Chef de cabinet of R. Barre (3-23-2001, 1-8-2003)

Peeters, Theo (B), Professor, University of Leuven; Adviser to M. Eyskens (7-7-1999, 5-10-2005, 10-2-2018)

Pierre-Brossolette, Claude (F), Director of the Treasury; Secretary General of the Elysée with V. Giscard d'Estaing (4-23-2003)

Polak, Jacques (NL), Director of Research, International Monetary Fund (4-2-2003)

Quevrin, Emile (B), Assistant of Dupriez (10-1-2008)

Raymond, Robert (F), Director General, Research and International Relations, Banque de France; Director General, European Monetary Institute (2-25-2011)

Reuss, Conrad (B), Assistant of Dupriez (12-23-2008)

Rey, Jean-Jacques (B), Director, National Bank of Belgium (6-17-1999, 3-24-2005)

Rocard, Michel (F), Prime Minister (2-18-2003)

Sarcinelli, Mario (I), Deputy Director General, Banca d'Italia; Director General of the Treasury (9-12-2002, 12-4-2003)

Segré, Claudio (I), Director, DG II (6-12-2007)

Snoy, Bernard (B), Chef de cabinet of Ph. Maystadt (10-26-1999, 7-31-2019)

Steinherr, Alfred (D), Chief Economist, European Investment Bank; Professor, Université Catholique de Louvain (10-1-2014)

Swoboda, Alexandre (CH), Professor, Graduate Institute of International Studies of Geneva (11-26-2014)

Tavitian, Roland (F), Director, DG II (12-10-2003)

Thygesen, Niels (DK), Professor; Member of the Delors Committee (4-23-2014, 3-6-2017)

Tietmeyer, Hans (D), State Secretary, Finance Ministry; President of the Deutsche Bundesbank (12-18-2001)

Toulemon, Robert (F), Chef de cabinet of R. Marjolin (1-23-2002)

Triffin, Eric (US), Son of Robert Triffin (6-24-2019)

Triffin, Kerry (US), Son of Robert Triffin (6-24-2019)

van Daele, Frans (B), Ambassador at the European Union (1-25-2002)

van den Bempt, Paul (B), Director, DG II (6-5-1997)

van Ypersele, Jacques (B), Chairman of the Monetary Committee; Chef de cabinet of W. Martens (9-3-1999, 2-20-2015)

Vanden Abeele, Michel (B), Adviser to R. Jenkins; Chef de cabinet of K. Van Miert (5-2-2014, 6-18-2017)

Vissol, Thierry (F), Head of Unit, DG II (8-16-2016)

von der Groeben, Hans (D), Member of the German Delegation for the Rome Treaty Negotiations; Member of the Commission of the European Commission for Competition Policy (7-23-2001)

Wegner, Manfred (D), Deputy Director General, DG II (9-2-1997)

Werner, Pierre (L), Prime Minister (5-15-1999)

Wicks, Sir Nigel (UK), Permanent Secretary at HM Treasury; Chairman of the Monetary Committee (4-28-2011)

Williamson, John (UK), Senior Fellow at the Peterson Institute for International Economics (11-25-2014)

Wissels, Gerard (N), Adviser to D. Spierenburg; Director, DG II (1-10-2003, 3-18-2003)

3. TRIFFIN BIBLIOGRAPHY

1935. "Les mouvements différentiels des prix de gros en Belgique de 1927 à 1934. Calcul et interprétation d'indices de groupes comparables." *Bulletin de l'Institut des Sciences Economiques* 6, no. 3 (May): 267–295.

1937. "La théorie de la surévaluation monétaire et la dévaluation belge." *Bulletin de l'Institut des Sciences Economiques* 9, no. 1 (January): 19–52.

with Alan Geismer. 1937. "Primarily for Undergraduates: A Former Classmate Looks at Léon Degrelle, Leader of the Belgian Rexists." *Harvard Monthly* 65, no. 2 (April): 14–18.

1940. *Monopolistic Competition and General Equilibrium Theory*. Cambridge, MA: Harvard University Press.

1941. "Monopoly in Particular Equilibrium and in General Equilibrium Economics." *Econometrica* 9, no. 2 (April): 121–127.

1944a. *Money and Banking in Colombia*. Washington, DC: Board of Governors of the Federal Reserve System.

1944b. "Central Banking and Monetary Management in Latin America." In *Economic Problems of Latin America*, edited by Seymour E. Harris, 93–116. New York-London: McGraw-Hill.

1945. "Monetary Developments in Latin America." *Federal Reserve Bulletin*, June: 519–531.

1946a. *Monetary and Banking Reform in Paraguay*. Washington, DC: Board of Governors of the Federal Reserve System.

1946b. "National Central Banking and the International Economy." *Review of Economic Studies* 14, no. 2 (1946–1947): 53–75. Reprinted in *International Monetary Policies: Postwar Economic Studies*, no. 7, 46–81. Washington, DC: Board of Governors of the Federal Reserve System, 1947.

1947. "International Versus Domestic Money." *American Economic Review* 37, no. 2 (May): 322–324. Reprinted in Triffin, 1966: 177–179.

1948. "Exchange Control and Equilibrium." In *Foreign Economic Policy for the United States*, edited by Seymour E. Harris, 417–425. Cambridge, MA: Harvard University Press, 1948.

1949a. "Memorandum, Dated July 28th, 1949." Reprinted with the title "Suggested Adaptations in Fund Policy" in Triffin, 1966: 182–190.

1949b. "Points for Discussion on the Problem of Currency Transferability in Europe." Reprinted in Triffin, 1966: 441–448.

1950. "Schumpeter, souvenir d'un étudiant." *Economie Appliquée* 3, no. 3–4 (July–December): 413–416.

1951. "The Path from EPU to European Monetary Integration." Reprinted in Triffin, 1966: 450–462.

1953. "Système et politique monétaires de l'Europe fédérée." *Economia Internazionale* 6, no. 1 (February–March): 207–212.

with Henry C. Wallich. 1953. *Monetary and Banking Legislation of the Dominican Republic 1947*. New York: Federal Reserve Bank of New York.

1954. "International Currency and Reserve Plans." *Banca Nazionale del Lavoro Quarterly Review* 7, no. 28–29 (January–June): 3–20. Reprinted with the title "The Abortive 'Dash' to Convertibility: 1953" in Triffin, 1966: 201–228.

1957. *Europe and the Money Muddle: From Bilateralism to Near-Convertibility 1947–1956*. New Haven, CT: Yale University Press.

1958. "La monnaie et le marché commun. Politiques nationales et intégration régionale." *Cahiers de l'Institut de Science Economique Appliquée*, no. 74 (December): 1–16.

1959a. "The Return to Convertibility: 1926–1931 and 1958–? Or Convertibility and the Morning After." *Banca Nazionale del Lavoro Quarterly Review* 12, no. 48 (March): 1–57. Reprinted in Triffin, 1960: 17–73.

1959b. "Tomorrow's Convertibility: Aims and Means of International Monetary Policy." *Banca Nazionale del Lavoro Quarterly Review* 12, no. 49 (June): 1–72. Reprinted in Triffin, 1960: 77–147.

1959c. "Statements and Discussion on 'The International Monetary Position of the United States.' Employment, Growth and Price Levels." In *Hearings before the Joint Economic Committee, Congress of the United States, October 28, 1959*, edited by the US Congress Joint Economic Committee, 2905-2954. Washington, DC: US Government Printing Office. Reprinted in Triffin, 1960: 1–14.

1960. *Gold and the Dollar Crisis. The Future of Convertibility*. New Haven, CT: Yale University Press.

1965a. "The International Monetary System, International Monetary Problems." Report of a Conference Held in London on May 24 and 25, 1965, Federal Trust Report, Special Series no. 1, 1–19 and 43–46. Republished in Triffin, 1966: 346–373.

1965b. "The Sterling Crisis in Wider Perspective." *The Banker* 115 (February): 79–84. Republished in Triffin, 1966:133–138.

1966. *The World Money Maze: National Currencies in International Payments*. New Haven, CT: Yale University Press.

1967a. "The International Monetary Problem after Rio, New Plan for International Monetary Reserves." In *Hearings, 90th Congress of the United States*, First Session, Part 1, November 22, 128–157. Washington, DC: US Government Printing Office.

1967b. "The Coexistence of Three Types of Reserve Assets." *Banca Nazionale del Lavoro Quarterly Review* 20, no. 81 (June): 107–134.

1968a. *Our International Monetary System: Yesterday, Today and Tomorrow*. New York: Random House.

1968b. "Statements and Papers Submitted for the Record." In *Hearings before the Subcommittee in International Exchange and Payments of the Joint Economic Committee. 90th Congress of United States*, Second Session, September 9, edited by the US Congress, 143–160. Washington, DC: US Government Printing Office.

1973. "The Collapse of the International Monetary System: Structural Causes and Remedies." *De Economist* 121, no. 4: 362–374.

1978a. *Gold and the Dollar Crisis: Yesterday and Tomorrow*. Inaugural John J. McCloy Lecture at the Council of Foreign Relations, November 14; with "Foreword" of Robert V. Roosa, *Princeton Essays in International Finance*, no. 132 (December 1978). Princeton, NJ: Princeton University.

1978b. "Units of Account and Parallel Currencies in Transnational Contracts." In *One Money for Europe*, edited by Michele Fratianni and Theo Peeters, 135–143. London: Macmillan Press.

1979a. "Introduction" and "Concluding Remarks." In *EMS: The Emerging European Monetary System*, edited by Robert Triffin. *Bulletin de la Banque Nationale de Belgique*, no. 4 (April): 9–10 and 179–186.

1979b. "Concluding Remarks." In *The European Monetary Fund: Internal Planning and External Relations*. Proceedings of the Second International Seminar on European Economic and Monetary Union, Held at the International Center for Monetary and Banking Studies, Geneva, December 7–8. *Banca Nazionale del Lavoro Quarterly Review* 33, no. 134 (1980): 392–396.

1980. "Introduction" and "Remarks." In *The Private Use of the ECU*, edited by Robert Triffin and André L. Swings, 1, 7 and passim. Brussels: Kredietbank.

1980. (with André L. Swings). *The Private Use of the ECU*. Brussels: Kredietbank.

1981a. "An Economist's Career: What? Why?, How?" *Banca Nazionale del Lavoro Quarterly Review* 34, no. 138 (September): 239–259.

1981b. "Concluding Remarks." In *The European Monetary System: The First Two Years*, edited by Niels Thygesen and Robert Triffin. *Banca Nazionale del Lavoro Quarterly Review* 34, no. 138 (September), 365–370.

1983. "How to End of the World 'Infession': Crisis Management or Fundamental Reforms?" Presented and discussed at the inaugural CEPS Conference on Western European Priorities, in Brussels, December 15–18, 1982, CEPS Working Paper, 1983. Reprinted in *Europe's Money. Problems of European Co-ordination and Integration*, edited by Rainer Masera and Robert Triffin, 13–76. Oxford: Clarendon Press, 1984.

1984. (with Rainer Masera). *Europe's Money. Problems of European Co-ordination and Integration*. Oxford: Clarendon Press.

1987a. "Acceptance Speech Delivered by Prof. Robert Triffin." In *San Paolo Prize for Economics*, 25–32. Torino: Istituto Bancario San Paolo.

1987b. "The IMS (International Monetary System) . . . or Scandal? And the EMS (European Monetary System)." *Banca Nazionale del Lavoro Quarterly Review* 40, no. 162 (September): 239–263.

1988. "Acceptance Paper by Robert Triffin. The Intermixture of Politics and Economics in the World Monetary Scandal: Diagnosis and Prescription." In *The Frank E. Seidman Distinguished Award in Political Economy*. Award Bestowed September 15, 1988, 1–20. Memphis, TN: Rhodes College.

1989a. "Au-delà de l'U.E.M. Mot d'ouverture de la journee du Cepime." *De Pecunia*, no. 1 (June): 8–11.

1989b. "Preface." In *Le Système Monétaire Européen*, edited by Jacques van Ypersele and Jean Claude Koeune, 9–17. Luxembourg: Commission des Communautés Européennes, Office des Publications Officielles Européenne.

1990. "Conversation avec Catherine Ferrant et Jean Sloover." In *Robert Triffin: Conseiller des Princes*, edited by Catherine Ferrant and Jean Sloover (with the collaboration of Michel Dumoulin et Olivier Lefebvre), 9–69. Bruxelles: Ciaco, 1990.

1991. "The IMS (International Monetary System . . . or Scandal?) and the EMS (European Monetary System . . . or Success?)." *Banca Nazionale del Lavoro Quarterly Review* 44, no. 176 (March): 399–436.

4. BIBLIOGRAPHY

Abraham, Jean-Paul. 1972. "Van regionale tewerkstelling tot leefbare wereld. Economische perspectieven toen en nu." In *Gelovend in de wereld,* edited by A. Dondeyne. Antwerpen: Patmos.

Abraham, Jean-Paul, and Carine Lemineur-Toumson. 1981. "Les choix monétaires européens 1950–1980." *Etudes Internationales* 12, no. 3: 499–512.

Adelman, Jeremy. 2013. *Worldly Philosopher: The Odyssey of Albert O. Hirschman.* Princeton, NJ: Princeton University Press.

Alacevich, Michele, and Pier Francesco Asso. 2009. "Money Doctoring after World War II: Arthur I. Bloomfield and the Federal Reserve Missions to South Korea." *History of Political Economy* 41, no. 2 (Summer): 249–270.

Altman, Oscar. 1961. "Professor Triffin on International Liquidity and the Role of the Fund." IMF Staff Papers, April 1961. Reprinted in *World Monetary Reform: Plans and Issues,* edited by Herbert G. Grubel, 120–149. Stanford: Stanford University Press, 1963.

Angell, James. 1961. "The Reorganization of the International Monetary System: An Alternative Proposal." *Economic Journal* 71, no. 284 (December 1961). Reprinted in Grubel, 1963: 90–110.

Backhouse, Roger. 1985. *A History of Modern Economic Analysis.* Oxford: Basil Blackwell.

Backhouse, Roger. 2017. *Founder of Modern Economics: Paul A. Samuelson.* Vol. 1: *Becoming Samuelson, 1915–1948.* Oxford: Oxford University Press.

Baffi, Paolo. 1988. "Robert Triffin." In *San Paolo Prize for Economics 1987,* 14–24. Torino: Istituto San Paolo di Torino.

Barre, Raymond. 1968. "Les problèmes monétaires internationaux et la politique monétaire de la Communauté." *Bulletin des Communautés Européennes,* no. 1: 17.

Basevi, Giorgio, Michele Fratianni, Herbert Giersch, Pieter Korteweg, David O'Mahony, Michael Parkin, Theo Peeters, Pascal Salin, Niels Thygesen. 1975. "The All Saints' Day Manifesto for European Monetary Union." *The Economist,* November 1. Reprinted in *One Money for Europe,* edited by Michele Fratianni and Theo Peeters, 37–43. London: Palgrave Macmillan.

Berlin, Isaiah. 1953. *The Hedgehog and the Fox,* as reprinted in *Russian Thinkers,* 22–81. New York: Penguin Classics. 2008.

Bernstein, Edward M. 1962. "Statements." In *Outlook for the United States Balance of Payments Hearings, December 14, 1962,* edited by the US Congress Joint Economic Committee, Subcommittee on International Exchange and Payments. Washington, DC: Government Printing Office. Reprinted in Grubel, 1963: 187–202.

Bini Smaghi, Lorenzo. 2012. "The Triffin Dilemma Revisited." In *In Search of a New World Monetary Order,* edited by Jean-Claude Koeune and Alexandre Lamfalussy, 101–112. Brussels: Peter Lang.

Bissell, Richard M. 1996. *Reflections of a Cold War Warrior: From Yalta to the Bay of Pigs.* New Haven: Yale University Press.

Black, Stanley W. 1991. *A Levite among the Priests. Edward M. Bernstein and the Origins of the Bretton Woods System.* Boulder, CO: Westview Press.

Blaug, Mark. 1985. *Great Economists since Keynes.* Brighton: Wheatsheaf.

Blaug, Mark. 1997. *Economic Theory in Retrospect.* 5th ed. Cambridge: Cambridge University Press.

Blum, John Morton. 1961. "Kennedy's Ten-Foot Shelf." *New York Times,* March 12.

Board of Governors of the Federal Reserve System. 1943. *Banking and Monetary Statistics.* Washington, DC: Board of Governors of the Federal Reserve System, November.

Boorman, Jack T., and André Icard, eds. 2011. *Reform of the International Monetary System: The Palais Royal Initiative*. New Delhi: Sage Publications.

Bordo, Michael D. 1993. "Introduction." In *A Retrospective on the Bretton Woods System: Lessons of International Monetary Reform*, edited by Michael D. Bordo and Barry Eichengreen, 3–98. Chicago: University of Chicago Press.

Bordo, Michael D., and Robert McCauley. 2017. "Triffin: Dilemma or Myth?" BIS Working Paper no. 684.

Brandt, Willy. 1992. *My Life in Politics*. New York: Viking Press.

Bussière, Éric et Olivier Feiertag. 2012. "Triffin et la construction monétaire européenne. Une contribution à la rénovation du système monétaire international." In *In Search of a New World Monetary Order*, edited by Jean-Claude Koeune and Alexandre Lamfalussy, 73–96. Brussels: Peter Lang.

Buyst, Erik, Ivo Maes, Walter Pluym, and Marianne Danneel. 2005. *The Bank, the Franc and the Euro: A History of the National Bank of Belgium*. Tielt: Lannoo.

Buyst, Erik, and Ivo Maes. 2008. "The Regulation and Supervision of the Belgian Financial System (1830–2005)." Working Paper, Bank of Greece, June.

Caffè, Federico. 1982. "A Continuing Cultural Link. In 'Experiences and Problems of the International Monetary System.'" *Economic Notes*. Monte dei Paschi di Siena, Special issue, August 1983: x–xiii.

Carli, Guido. 1982. "From the European Payments Union to the European Monetary System." In *The Monetary System under Flexible Exchange Rates: Essays in Honour of Robert Triffin*, edited by Richard Cooper, Peter B. Kenen, Jorge Braga de Macedo, and Jacques van Ypersele, 161–169. Cambridge: Ballinger Pub. Company.

Carli, Guido. 1993. *Cinquant'anni di vita italiana*, in collaborazione con Paolo Peluffo. Roma-Bari: Laterza & Figli.

Cassel, Gustav. 1925. *Money and Foreign Exchange after 1914*. New York: Macmillan.

CEC. 1966. *Le développement d'un marché européen des capitaux. Rapport d'un Groupe d'Experts constitué par la Commission de la CEE*. Bruxelles, November.

CEC. 2018. *Communication from the Commission: Towards a Stronger International Role of the Euro*, COM(2018) 796 final, December 5.

Chamberlin, Edward H. 1933. *The Theory of Monopolistic Competition*. Cambridge, MA: Harvard University Press.

Clement, Piet. 2006. "The BIS and Central Bank Cooperation in the 1950s and 1960s: Two Tales." In *European Central Banks and Monetary Cooperation after 1945*, edited by Piet Clement and Juan-Carlos Martinez Oliva, 27–38. Frankfurt am Main: EABH-Adlmann.

Coats, Alfred W., ed. 1996. *The Post-1945 Internationalization of Economics*. Durham and London: Duke University Press.

Committee for the Study of Economic and Monetary Union. 1989. *Report on Economic and Monetary Union in the European Community*. Delors Report. Luxembourg: Office for the Official Publication of the European Community.

Conant, Charles A. 1910. *The National Bank of Belgium*. National Monetary Commission, Senate Document No. 400, 61st Congress, Second Session. Washington, DC: Government Printing Office.

Connell, Carol M. 2011. "Framing World Monetary System Reform: Fritz Machlup and the Bellagio Group Conferences." *PSL Quarterly Review* 64, no. 257: 143–166.

Connell, Carol M., and Joseph Salerno, eds. 2014. *Monetary Reform and the Bellagio Group: Selected Letter and Papers of Fritz Machlup, Robert Triffin and William Fellner*. London: Pickering & Chatto.

Conseil Économique et Social. 1967. *La réforme du système monétaire international Un débat présenté par Emile Roche: Albin Chalandon, Jacques Rueff, Rioust de Largentaye*. Paris: Editions France Empire.

Council-Commission of the European Communities. 1970. *Report to the Council and the Commission on the Realisation by Stages of Economic and Monetary Union in the Community, Werner Report*. Luxembourg: Office for the Official Publication of the European Community.

Cramer, Jan S., and Martin M. G. Fase. 2011. *Jacques Jacobus Polak, 28 April 1914–26 February 2010. Levensberichten en herdenkingen 2011*, 128–134. Amsterdam: KNAW.

Craver, Earlene. 1986. "Patronage and the Directions of Research in Economics. The Rockefeller Foundation in Europe, 1924–1938." *Minerva* 24, no. 2–3 (June): 205–222.

Crombois, Jean-François. 2011. *Camille Gutt and Postwar International Finance*. London: Pickering & Chatto.

Cuénot, Claude. 1963. *Teilhard de Chardin*. Paris: Editions du Seuil.

Danescu, Elena. 2016. "Pierre Werner: A Visionary European and Consensus Builder." In *Architects of the Euro. Intellectuals in the Making of European Monetary Union*, edited by Kenneth Dyson and Ivo Maes, 93–116. Oxford: Oxford University Press.

Danescu, Elena. 2018. *Pierre Werner and Europe: The Family Archives behind the Werner Report*. Cham: Palgrave Macmillan.

Daunton, Martin. 2008. "Britain and Globalisation since 1850: III. Creating the World of Bretton Woods, 1939–1958." *Transactions of the Royal Historical Society*, Sixth Series, 18: 1–42. Cambridge: Cambridge University Press.

Dawidoff, Nicholas. 2003. *The Fly Swatter: Portrait of an Exceptional Character*. New York: Vintage.

De Beckker, R. 1984. "The EUA Sector." In *A History of the Eurobond Market: The First 12 Years*, edited by Ian Macpherson Kerr, 128–129. London: Euromoney Publications.

De Grauwe, Paul. 1989. *International Money: Post-war Trends and Theories*. Oxford: Clarendon Press.

de Groote, Jacques. 2012. "Besoin global de liquidités? Paralysie du FMI?" In *In Search of a New World Monetary Order*, edited by Jean-Claude Koeune and Alexandre Lamfalussy, 129–132. Peter Lang: Brussels.

de Larosière, Jacques. 1991. "Robert Triffin and the Reform of the International Monetary System." In *Evolution of the International and Regional Monetary Systems. Essays in Honour of Robert Triffin*, edited by Alfred Steinherr and Daniel Weiserbs, 135–143. London: Macmillan.

de Larosière, Jacques. 2018. *50 Years of Financial Crises*. Paris: Odile Jacob.

de Lattre, André. 1999. *Servir aux Finances*. Paris: Comité pour l'histoire économique et financière de la France.

De Long, James Bradford, and Barry Eichengreen. 1993. "The Marshall Plan as a Structural Adjustment Programme." In *Postwar Economic Reconstruction: Lessons for Eastern Europe*, edited by Rüdiger Dornbusch, Wilhelm Nölling, and Richard Layard, 189–220. London: Anglo-German Foundation for the Study of Industrial Society.

Delors, Jacques. 1996. *Combats pour l'Europe*. Paris: Economica.

De Man, Henri. 1927. *Au-delà du marxisme*. Bruxelles: L'Églantine.

Deroose Servaas, Dermot Hodson, and Joost Kuhlmann. 2004. *Economic Governance in the EU: Lessons from the First Five Years of EMU.* Paper presented at the UACES Conference, Birmingham, September.

Despres, Emile, Charles P. Kindleberger, and Walter S. Salant. 1966. "The Dollar and World Liquidity: A Minority View." *Brookings Institution Reprint,* no. 115, Washington, DC.

de Vries, Margaret G. 1969. "The Fund and the EPU." In *The International Monetary Fund 1945–1965,* vol. 2, edited by J. Keith Horsefield and Margaret G. de Vries, 317–331. Washington, DC: International Monetary Fund.

Dimand, Robert W. 2014. *James Tobin.* London and Basingstoke: Palgrave Macmillan.

Dimand, Robert W. 2019. "The Cowles Commission and Foundation for Research in Economics: Bringing Mathematical Economics and Econometrics from the Fringes of Economics to the Mainstream." Forthcoming in the *New Palgrave.*

Dimand, Robert W., and Harald Hagemann. 2019. "Jacob Marschak and the Cowles Approaches to the Theory of Money and Assets." Paper presented to the European Society for the History of Economic Thought, Lille, May 24.

Dosman, Edgard J. 2008. *The Life and Times of Raúl Prebisch, 1901–1986.* Montreal: McGill-Queen's University Press.

Drake, Paul W. 1989. *Money Doctor in the Andes: The Kemmerer Missions, 1923–1933.* Durham, NC: Duke University Press.

Duchêne, François. 1994. *Jean Monnet: The First Statesman of Interdependence.* New York: W. W. Norton.

Dujardin, Vincent, and Michel Dumoulin. 1997. *Paul van Zeeland. 1893–1973.* Brussels: Editions Racine.

Dujardin, Vincent, and Michel Dumoulin. 2010. *Jean-Charles Snoy. Homme dans la Cité, Artisan de l'Europe. 1907–1991.* Brussels: Éditions Le Cri.

Dumoulin, Michel. 2012. "La place de Robert Triffin dans l'histoire du 20e siècle." In *In Search of a New World Monetary Order,* edited by Jean-Claude Koeune and Alexandre Lamfalussy, 23–30. Brussels: Peter Lang.

Dupriez, Léon-Hugo. 1935. "Enseignement et recherches économiques à l'Université de Louvain." In *Cinq conférences sur la Méthode dans les recherches économiques,* edited by Lionel Robbins, Ernst F. Wagemann, Léon-Hugo Dupriez, José Vandellós, and Coenraad A. Stuart Verrijn, 48–64. Paris: Librairie du recueil Sirey, 1938.

Dupriez, Léon-Hugo. 1952. "Les recherches à l'Institut économiques et sociales de l'Université de Louvain." *Econometrica* 20, no. 2 (April): 314–315.

Dupriez, Léon-Hugo. 1959. *Philosophie des Conjonctures Économiques.* Louvain: Nauwelaerts.

Dupriez, Léon-Hugo. 1978. *Les réformes monétaires en Belgique.* Bruxelles: Office International de Librairie.

Dupriez, Léon-Hugo, et al. 1931. "Une comparaison de la conjoncture économique générale de la Belgique, de 1897 à 1913, avec celle de la Grande-Bretagne, des Etas-Unis, de l'Allemagne, de la France et des Pays-Bas." *Bulletin de l'Institut des Sciences Economiques,* no. 4 (August): 319–342.

Dupriez, Léon-Hugo, and M. Barboux. 1933. "Le commerce extérieur de la Belgique envisagé comme baromètre des conditions économiques internes." *Bulletin de l'Institut des Sciences économiques,* no. 3 (May): 275–294.

Dyson, Kenneth, and Kevin Featherstone. 1999. *The Road to Maastricht.* Oxford: Oxford University Press.

Eichengreen, Barry. 1992. *Golden Fetters: The Gold Standard and the Great Depression, 1919–1939*. Oxford: Oxford University Press.

Eichengreen, Barry. 1993. *Reconstructing Europe's Trade and Payments: The European Payments Union*. Manchester: Manchester University Press.

Eichengreen, Barry. 2011. *Exorbitant Privilege: The Rise and Fall of the Dollar*. Oxford: Oxford University Press.

Eichengreen, Barry. 2018. "The Two Eras of Central Banking in the United States." In *Sveriges Riksbank and the History of Central Banking*, edited by Rodney Edvinsson, Tor Jacobson, and Daniel Waldenström, 361–387. Cambridge: Cambridge University Press.

Eichengreen, Barry, Arnaud Mehl, Livia Chitu, and Gary Richardson. 2014. "Mutual Assistance between Federal Reserve Banks, 1913–1960 as Prolegomena to the Target 2 Debate." Working Paper no. 20267, National Bureau of Economic Research.

Eichengreen, Barry, Arnaud Mehl, and Livia Chitu. 2018. *How Global Currencies Work: Past, Present and Future*. Princeton, NJ: Princeton University Press.

Emminger, Otmar. 1958. "Les aspects monétaires du Marché Commun." *Bulletin d'Information et de Documentation*, no. 2, National Bank of Belgium (August): 93–103.

Emminger, Otmar. 1977. "The D-Mark in the Conflict Between Internal and External Equilibrium, 1948–1975." *Essays in International Finance*, no. 122, Princeton.

Essers, Dennis, and Evelien Vincent. 2017. "The Global Financial Safety Net: In Need of Repair?" *NBB Economic Review*, September: 87–112.

Farhi, Emmanuel, Pierre-Olivier Gourinchas, and Hélène Rey. 2011. *Reforming the International Monetary System*. London: CEPR.

Flor, Elena. 2019. *SDR: From Bretton Woods to a World Currency*. Bern: Peter Lang.

Friedman, Milton. 1941. "Review [*Monopolistic Competition and General Equilibrium Theory, by Robert Triffin*]." *Journal of Farm Economics* 23, no. 1 (February): 389–391.

Friedman, Milton. 1950. "The Case for Flexible Exchange Rates." In *Essays in Positive Economics*, edited by Milton Friedman, 157–203. Chicago: University of Chicago Press.

Galbraith, John Kenneth. 1981. *A Life in Our Times: Memoirs*. Boston: Houghton Mifflin

Galea, Pasquale. 2013. "Da banca regionale a gruppo bancario europeo (1971–1991)." In *La Compagnia di Sanpaolo*, vol. 2, *1853–2013*, edited by Walter Barberis and Anna Cantaluppi, 336–365. Torino: Einaudi.

Gang, Yi. 2020. "The IMF should turn to special drawing rights in its Covid-19 response." *Financial Times*, July 16, 2020.

Gardner, Walter. 1946. "Preface." In *Monetary and Banking Reform in Paraguay*, iii–iv, Washington, DC: Federal Reserve Board.

Georgieva, Kristalina. 2020. "IMF Chief: We Are Rethinking Our Advice to Emerging Markets." *Financial Times*, February 19.

Ghosh, Atish R., and Mahvash S. Qureshi. 2017. "From Great Depression to Great Recession: An Overview." In *From Great Depression to Great Recession: The Elusive Quest for International Policy Cooperation*, edited by Atish R. Ghosh and Mahvash S. Qureshi, 1–33. Washington, DC: International Monetary Fund.

Goldenweiser, Emmanuel. 1943. "Key to This Volume of Figures." In *Banking and Monetary Statistics*, edited by the Board of Governors of the Federal Reserve System. Washington, DC: Board of Governors of the Federal Reserve System.

Gomez Betancourt, Rebeca. 2010. "Edwin Walter Kemmerer and the Origins of the Federal Reserve System." *Journal of the History of Economic Thought* 32, no. 4 (December): 445–470.

Gomez Betancourt, Rebeca, and Ivo Maes. 2020, "Paul van Zeeland, a Monetary Economist between Two Worlds." *European Journal of the History of Economic Thought*, published: April 3.

Gourinchas, Pierre-Olivier, Hélène Rey, and Nicolas Govillot. 2017. "Exorbitant Privilège and Exorbitant Duty." IMES Discussion Paper Series, 10-E-20. Institute for Monetary and Economic Studies, Bank of Japan.

Gros, Daniel, and Niels Thygesen. 1998. *European Monetary Integration*. 2nd ed. London: Longman.

Group of Ten. 1964. *Ministerial Statement*. 1 August 1964.

Gutt, Camille. 1935. *Pourquoi le franc belge est tombé*. Brussels: Nouvelle Société d' Editions.

Gutt, Camille. 1948. "Exchange Rates and the International Monetary Fund." *Review of Economics and Statistics* 30, no. 2 (May). Reprinted in *Foreign Economic Policy for the United States*, edited by Seymour Edwin Harris, 217–235. Cambridge, MA: Harvard University Press.

Haberler, Gottfried. 1947. "Comments on 'National Central Banking and the International Economy.'" In *International Monetary Policies*, Postwar Economic Studies, No. 7, 82–102. Washington, DC: Board of Governors of the Federal Reserve System.

Haberler, Gottfried. 1968. "Taussig." In *International Encyclopedia of the Social Sciences*. New York: Macmillan.

Hansen, Alvin Harvey. 1949. *Monetary Theory and Fiscal Policy*. New York: McGraw Hill.

Hansen, Alvin Harvey. 1951. *Business Cycles and National Income*. New York: W. W. Norton.

Hansen, Alvin Harvey. 1953. *A Guide to Keynes*. New York: McGraw-Hill.

Hagemann, Harald. 2000. "The Post-1945 Development of Economics in Germany." In *The Development of Economics in Eastern Europe since 1945*, edited by Alfred William Coats, 119–128. London: Routledge.

Harris, Seymour Edwin. 1944. *Economic Problems of Latin America*. New York: McGraw-Hill.

Harrod, Roy. 1961–1962. "A Plan for Increasing Liquidity: A Critique" (the article is made up of the excerpts from two papers "Liquidity" and "Growth and Liquidity," published in *Rivista di Politica Economica*, respectively, in 1961 and 1962). Reprinted in Grubel, 1963: 111–119.

Hayek, Friedrich A. von. 1928. "Das intertemporale Gleichgewichtssystem der Preise und die Bewegungen des 'Geldwertes.'" *Weltwirtschaftliches Archiv* 28, no. 2: 33–76.

Helleiner, Eric. 2009. "Central Bankers as Good Neighbours: US Money Doctors in Latin America during the 1940s." *Financial History Review* 16, no. 1 (April): 5–25.

Hetzel, Robert L. 2002. "German Monetary History in the First Half of the Twentieth Century." *Federal Reserve Bank of Richmond Economic Quarterly* 88, no. 1 (Winter): 1–35.

Hicks, John R. 1935. "A Suggestion for Simplifying the Theory of Money." *Economica* 2, new series, no. 2 (February): 1–19.

Hieronymi, Otto. 1993. "Introduction." In *The Future of the Global Economic and Monetary System with Particular Emphasis on Eastern European Developments*, edited by Miklós Szabó-Pelsőczi, 1–2. Budapest: Robert Triffin–Szirak Foundation.

Hogan, Michael J. 1987. *The Marshall Plan*. Cambridge: Cambridge University Press.

Horsefield, J. Keith. 1969. *The International Monetary Fund 1945–1965*. Vol. 1 Chronicle. Washington, DC: International Monetary Fund.

Howson, Susan. 2011. *Lionel Robbins*. Cambridge: Cambridge University Press.

Iozzo, Alfonso. 2012. "From the ECU to the EURO." In *In Search of a New World Monetary Order*, edited by Jean-Claude Koeune and Alexandre Lamfalussy, 137–138. Brussels: Peter Lang.

Irwin, Douglas A. 2010. "Did France Cause the Great Depression?" *Vox*, September 20.

Ise, John. 1940. "Review [*Monopolistic Competition and General Equilibrium Theory, by Robert Triffin*]." *American Economic Review* 30, no. 4 (December): 841–843.

Issing, Otmar. 2000. "Europe: Common Money-Political Union?" *Economic Affairs* 20, no. 1 (March): 33–39.

James, Harold. 1996. *International Monetary Cooperation since Bretton Woods*. Washington, DC: International Monetary Fund.

Jenkins, Roy. 1977. "Europe's Present Challenge and Future Opportunity." *Bulletin EC*, no. 10: 6–14.

Jenkins, Roy. 1989. *European Diary, 1977–1981*. London: Collins.

Jenkins, Roy. 1991. "Foreword." In *Evolution of the International and Regional Monetary System*, edited by Alfred Steinherr and Daniel Weiserbs, xi–xxiv, London: Macmillan.

Johnson, Harry G. 1962. "International Liquidity—Problems and Plans." *Malayan Economic Review*, April. Reprinted in *World Monetary Reform: Plans and Issues*, edited by Herbert G. Grubel, 369–391. Stanford: Stanford University Press, 1963.

Joseph, Margaret F. W. 1942. "Review [*Monopolistic Competition and General Equilibrium Theory, by Robert Triffin*]." *Economic Journal* 52, no. 208 (December): 356–359.

Kaplan, Jacob J., and Günther Schleiminger. 1989. *The European Payments Union: Financial Diplomacy in the 1950s*. Oxford: Clarendon.

Kemmerer, Edwin W. 1927. "Economic Advisory Work for Governments." *American Economic Review* 17, no. 1 (March): 1–12.

Keynes, John Maynard. 1919. *The Economic Consequences of the Peace*. London: Macmillan.

Keynes, John Maynard. 1923. *A Tract on Monetary Reform*. London: MacMillan. 1971, Collected Works, vol. 4.

Keynes, John Maynard. 1925. "The Economic Consequences of Mr. Winston Churchill." In *Essays in Persuasion*, edited by John Maynard Keynes, 244–270. London: Macmillan, 1931.

Keynes, John Maynard. 1927. "The British Balance of Trade." *Economic Journal* 37, no. 148: 551–565.

Keynes, John Maynard. 1930. "Auri Sacra Fames." In *Essays in Persuasion*, edited by John Maynard Keynes, 181–185. London: Macmillan, 1931.

Keynes, John Maynard. 1935. "Note." In *Activities 1931–1939*. Collected Works, vol. 21: 356.

Keynes, John Maynard. 1943. "Proposals for an International Clearing Union." In *Compendium of Plans for International Monetary Reform*, edited by Robert. G. Hawkins. New York: New York University Press, 1965.

Knorr, K. 1952. "Strengthening the Free World Economy." Report of a conference held at Princeton, on December 16–17. Center of International Studies, Princeton University.

Krengel, Rolf. 1986. *Das Deutsche Institut für Wirtschaftsforschung (Institut für Konjunkturforschung) 1925–1979*. Berlin: Duncker & Humblot.

Krugman, Paul. 1989. *Exchange-Rate Instability*. Cambridge, MA: Massachusetts Institute of Technology.

Lamfalussy, Christophe, Ivo Maes, and Sabine Péters. 2013. *Alexandre Lamfalussy. The Wise Man of the Euro.* A conversation with Christophe Lamfalussy, Ivo Maes, and Sabine Péters and a preface by Jacques de Larosière. Leuven: LannooCampus.

Lamoreaux, Naomi, and Ian Shapiro, eds. 2019. *The Bretton Woods Agreements: Together with Scholarly Commentaries and Essential Historical Documents.* New Haven, CT: Yale University Press.

Lindbeck, Assar. 1979. "Imported and Structural Inflation and Aggregate Demand: The Scandinavian Model Reconstructed." In *Inflation and Employment in Open Economics,* edited by Assar Lindbeck, 13–40. Amsterdam: North-Holland.

Lison (Triffin), Marie-Louise, Odette Triffin, and Marie-Jeanne Trufin. 1998. *Robert Triffin Citoyen du Monde et de Flobecq. Essais de Genealogie Trufin—Truffin—Trifin—Triffin.*

Ludlow, Peter. 1982. *The Making of the European Monetary System.* London: Butterworth.

Maes, Ivo. 1991. "On the Origins of Portfolio Theory." *Kyklos* 44, no. 1: 3–18.

Maes, Ivo. 1996. "The Development of Economic Thought at the European Community Institutions." *History of Political Economy* 28 (Supplement, December): 245–276.

Maes, Ivo. 2002. *Economic Thought and the Making of European Monetary Union.* Cheltenham: Edward Elgar.

Maes, Ivo. 2004. "On the Origins of the Franco-German EMU Controversies." *European Journal of Law and Economics* 17, no. 1: 21–39.

Maes, Ivo. 2006. "The Ascent of the European Commission as an Actor in the Monetary Integration Process in the 1960s." *Scottish Journal of Political Economy* 53. no. 2: 222–241.

Maes, Ivo. 2007. *Half a Century of European Financial Integration: From the Rome Treaty to the 21st Century,* with a foreword by Philippe Maystadt. Brussels: Mercatorfonds.

Maes, Ivo. 2008. "The Spread of Keynesian Economics: A Comparison of the Belgian and Italian Experiences (1945–1970)." *Journal of the History of Economic Thought* 30, no. 4 (December): 491–509.

Maes, Ivo. 2010. *A Century of Macroeconomic and Monetary Thought at the National Bank of Belgium.* Brussels: National Bank of Belgium.

Maes, Ivo. 2013a. "On the Origins of the Triffin Dilemma." *European Journal of the History of Economic Thought* 20, no. 6: 1222–1250.

Maes, Ivo. 2013b. "Tommaso Padoa-Schioppa: Macroeconomic and Monetary Thought, and Policy-Making at the European Commission." *History of Economic Thought and Policy,* no. 2: 21–43.

Maes, Ivo, Erik Buyst, and Muriel Bouchet. 2000. "The Post-1945 Development of Economics in Belgium." In *The Development of Economics in Western Europe since 1945,* edited by A. W. Coats, 94-112. London: Routledge.

Maes, Ivo, and Erik Buyst. 2004. "Triffin, the European Commission and the Project of a European Reserve Fund." In *Réseaux Economiques et Construction Européenne,* edited by Michel Dumoulin, 431–444. Bruxelles: P.I.E.—Peter Lang.

Maes, Ivo, and Erik Buyst. 2005. "Migration and Americanization: The Special Case of Belgian Economics." *European Journal of the History of Economic Thought* 12, no. 1: 73–88.

Maes, Ivo, and Eric Bussière. 2016. "Robert Triffin: The Arch Monetarist in the European Monetary Integration Debates?" In *Architects of the Euro: Intellectuals in the Making of European Monetary Union,* edited by Kenneth Dyson and Ivo Maes, 30–50. Oxford: Oxford University Press.

Maes, Ivo, and Sabine Péters. 2016. "La Belgique et l'Europe dans la tourmente monétaire des années 1970—Entretiens avec Jacques van Ypersele." Working Paper no. 314, National Bank of Belgium, December.

Maes, Ivo, and Rebeca Gomez Betancourt. 2018. "Paul van Zeeland and the First Decade of the US Federal Reserve System: The Analysis from a European Central Banker Who Was a Student of Kemmerer." *History of Economic Thought and Policy* 2, no. 2: 5–32.

Maes, Ivo, and Ilaria Pasotti. 2018. "The European Payments Union and the Origins of Triffin's Regional Approach towards International Monetary Integration." *History of Political Economy* 50, no. 1 (March): 155–190.

Magnifico, Giovanni. 1971. "European Monetary Unification for Balanced Growth." In *European Monetary Unification* edited by Giovanni Magnifico, 1–42. London: Macmillan, 1972.

Masini, Fabio. 2016. "Tommaso Padoa-Schioppa: EMU as the Anchor Stone for Building a Federal Europe." In *Architects of the Euro: Intellectuals in the Making of European Monetary Union*, edited by Kenneth Dyson and Ivo Maes, 193–211. Oxford: Oxford University Press.

Mata, Tiago, and Steven Medema, eds. 2013. "The Economist as Public Intellectual." *History of Political Economy* 45, no. 5, Special Issue.

Milward, Alan S. 1987. *The Reconstruction of Western Europe, 1945–1951*. London: Methuen.

Mlynarski, Feliks. 1929. *Gold and Central Banks*. New York: Macmillan.

Moggridge, Donald E. 1976. *Keynes*. Glasgow: Fontana.

Monnet, Jean. 1976. *Memoires*. Paris: Fayard.

Mundell, Robert A. 1961. "A Theory of Optimum Currency Areas." *American Economic Review* 51, no. 4 (September): 657–665.

Machlup, Fritz, and Burton G. Malkiel, eds. 1964. *International Monetary Arrangements: The Problem of Choice*. Princeton, NJ: International Finance Section, Department of Economics, Princeton University.

Marjolin, Robert. 1989. *Architect of European Unity: Memoires 1911–1986*. London: Weidenfeld & Nicolson.

Mandy, Paul. 2005. "L'héritage de Léon-H. Dupriez: un survol." *Reflets et perspectives de la vie économique* 44, no. 1: 11–30.

Mason, Edward S., and Thomas S. Lamont. 1982. "The Harvard Department of Economics from the Beginning to World War II." *Quarterly Journal of Economics* 97, no. 3 (August): 383–433.

Meltzer, Alan H. 2003. *A History of the Federal Reserve*, vol. 1, *1913–1951*. Chicago: University of Chicago Press.

Mehrling, Perry G. 1997. *The Money Interest and the Public Interest: American Monetary Thought, 1920–1970*. Cambridge, MA: Harvard University Press.

Molitor, André. 1984. *Souvenirs. Un témoin engagé dans la Belgique du XXe siècle*. Gembloux: Duculot.

Montani, Guido. 1989. "Robert Triffin and the Economic Problem of the 20 Century." *The Federalist: A Political Review* XXXI, no. 3: 201–215.

Mouré, Kenneth. 2002. *The Gold Standard Illusion. France, the Bank of France, and the International Gold Standard, 1914–1939*. Oxford: Oxford University Press.

Mourlon-Druol, Emmanuel. 2012. *A Europe Made of Money: The Emergence of the European Monetary System*. Ithaca and New York: Cornell University Press.

Mosca, Manuela. 2013. "Monopoly in Particular-Equilibrium and in General-Equilibrium Economics." In *Robert Triffin. Une anthologie*, edited by Michel Dumoulin, 7–9. Louvain-la-Neuve: Triffin International Foundation.

Nerozzi, Sebastiano. 2009. "Building Up a Multilateral Strategy for the United States: Alvin Hansen, Jacob Viner, and the Council on Foreign Relations (1939–1945)." In *American Power and Policy*, edited by Robert Leeson, 24–68. London: Palgrave Macmillan.

Nurkse, Ragnar. 1944. *International Currency Experience*. Geneve: League of Nations.

Oatley, Thomas H. 2001. "Multilateralizing Trade and Payments in Post-war Europe." *International Organization* 55, no. 4 (Autumn): 949–969.

Organisation for European Economic Cooperation (OEEC). 1950. *A European Payments Union and the Rules of Commercial Policy to be Followed by the Member Countries*, Document approved by the Council of OEEC on July 7, 1950. Paris.

Ossola, Rinaldo. 1965. "On the creation of new reserve ssets: the Report of the Study Group of Ten." *Banca Nazionale del Lavoro Quarterly Review* 18, no. 74: 272-292.

Padoa-Schioppa, Tommaso. 1987. "The ECU's Coming of Age." In *The Road to Monetary Union in Europe*, edited by Tommaso Padoa-Schioppa. Oxford: Clarendon Press, 1994.

Padoa-Schioppa, Tommaso. 1991. "European Monies and European Monetary Union." In *Evolution of the International and Regional Monetary System*, edited by Alfred Steinherr and Daniel Weiserbs, 201–206. London: Macmillan.

Padoa-Schioppa, Tommaso. 1998. *Che cosa ci ha insegnato l'avventura Europea*. Roma: Edizione dell'Elefante.

Padoa-Schioppa, Tommaso. 2010. "The Ghost of Bancor: The Economic Crisis and Global Monetary Disorder." Speech delivered at Louvain-la-Neuve, February 25, 2010. Reprinted in *Reform of the International Monetary System: The Palais Royal initiative*, edited by Jack T. Boorman and André Icard, 51–73. New Delhi: Sage Publications.

Pasotti, Ilaria. 2012. *Robert Triffin: An Economist for the Reform of the International Monetary System*. PhD diss. in History of Economic Thought, Faculty of Economics, University of Florence.

Perroux, François. 1948. "Esquisse d'une théorie de l'économie dominante." *Economie appliquée*, no. 2–3 (April–September): 243–300.

Pérez Caldentey, Esteban, and Matias Vernengo. 2011. *Understanding the Business Cycle in Latin America*. ECLAC Serie Estudios y Perspectivas. Mexico City: ECLAC.

Pinder, John. 1991. *European Community: The Building of a Union*. Oxford: Oxford University Press.

Pluym, Walter, and Olivier Boehme. 2004. "De Nationale Bank van België 1959–1971." *Mimeo*.

Polak, Jacques J. 1994. "Introduction." In *Economic Theory and Financial Policy. Selected Essays of Jacques J. Polak*, vol. 1, xiii–xxx. Cheltenham: Edward Elgar Publishing.

Polak, Jacques J. 1996. "The Contribution of the International Monetary Fund." In Coats 1996: 211–224.

Prasad, Eswar S. 2014. *The Dollar Trap: How the U.S. Dollar Tightened Its Grip on Global Finance*. Princeton, NJ: Princeton University Press.

Robinson, Joan. 1933. *Economics of Imperfect Competition*. London: Macmillan.

Robson, Peter. 1987. *The Economics of International Integration*. 3rd ed. London: Unwin & Hyman.

Rogoff, Kenneth S. 2002. "Straight Talk—Rethinking Capital Controls: When Should We Keep an Open Mind?" *Finance and Development* 39, no. 4 (December) .

Romberg, Rudolf R., and Robert H. Heller. 1977. "Introductory Survey." In *The Monetary Approach to the Balance of Payments*, edited by International Monetary Fund, 1–14. Washington, DC: International Monetary Fund.

Roosa, Robert V. 1978. "Foreword." In *Gold and the Dollar Crisis: Yesterday and Tomorrow*, by Robert Triffin, Essays in International Finance, no. 132 (December), v–vi. Princeton, NJ: Princeton University.

Rueff, Jacques. 1972. *The Monetary Sin of the West*. New York: Macmillan.

Rueff, Jacques. 1977. *De l'aube au crepuscule, Autobiographie*. Paris: Librairie Plon.

Sadeghi, Yassmin. 2005. "Economist Reynolds Dies at 94." *Yale News*, April 15.

Samuelson, Paul. 1951. "Schumpeter as a Teacher and Economic Theorist." *Review of Economics and Statistics* 33, no. 2: 98–103.

Samuelson, Paul. 1967. "The Monopolistic Competition Revolution." In *Monopolistic Competition Theory: Studies in Impact. Essays in Honor of E.H. Chamberlin*, edited by Robert E. Kuenne, 105–138. New York and London: J. Wiley and Sons.

Samuelson, Paul. 1976. "Preface." In *Inflation, Trade and Taxes. Essays in Honor of Alice Bourneuf*, edited by David A. Belsley, Edward J. Kane, Paul A. Samuelson and Robert M. Solow, vii–ix. Columbus: Ohio State University Press.

Schenk, Catherine R. 2010. *The Decline of Sterling. Managing the Retreat of an International Currency, 1945–1992*. Cambridge: Cambridge University Press.

Schlesinger, Arthur M. Jr. 2000. *A Life in the Twentieth Century*. Boston and New York: Houghton Mifflin Company.

Schönfelder, Wilhelm, and Elke Thiel. 1996. *Ein Markt—Eine Währung*. 2nd ed. Baden-Baden: Nomos.

Schumpeter, Joseph Alois. 1954. *History of Economic Analysis*. New York: Oxford University Press.

Sember, Florencia. 2013. "Interwar Reflections on the Balance of Payments: Taussig's School and the Influence of Ricardian Bullionist Tradition." In *Ricardo on Money and Finance: A Bicentenary Reappraisal*, edited by Yuji Sato and Susumu Takenaga. London: Routledge.

Servan Schreiber, Jean-Jacques. 1967. *Le défi américain*. Paris: Éditions Denoël.

Shackle, George. 1967. *The Years of High Theory: Tradition in Economic Thought, 1926–1939*. Cambridge: Cambridge University Press.

Shiller, Robert J. 2011. "The Yale Tradition in Macroeconomics." Economic Alumni Conference, New Haven, April 8.

Skidelsky, Robert. 2001. *John Maynard Keynes: Fighting for Britain, 1937–1946*, vol. 3. London: Macmillan.

Snoy, Bernard. 1993. "Le Baron Triffin." *Bulletin de l'ANBB*, October: 94–98.

Solomon, Robert. 1982. *The International Monetary System, 1945–1981*. New York: Harper & Row.

Sproul, Alan. 1953. "Foreword." In *Monetary and Banking Legislation of the Dominican Republic 1947*, edited by Robert Triffin and Henry C. Wallich. New York: Federal Reserve Bank of New York.

Steil, Benn. 2013. *The Battle of Bretton Woods: John Maynard Keynes, Harry Dexter White, and the Making of a New World Order*. Princeton, NJ: Princeton University Press.

Steil, Benn. 2018. *The Marshall Plan: Dawn of the Cold War*. Oxford: Oxford University Press.

Stockwell, Elizabeth J., ed. 1989. *Working at the Board 1930s–1970s*. Washington, DC: Board of Governors of the Federal Reserve System.

Szász, Andre. 1999. *The Road to European Monetary Union*. London: Macmillan Press.

Taussig, Frank W. 1917. "International Trade under Depreciated Paper: A Contribution to Theory." *Quarterly Journal of Economics* 31, no. 3: 380–403.

Tietmeyer, Hans. 1999. *The Social Market Economy and Monetary Stability*. London: Economica.

Tobin, James. 1988. "Introduction of the 1988 Recipient, Robert Triffin, and Presentation of the Award." In *The Frank E. Seidman Distinguished Award in Political Economy*. Award Bestowed September 15, 1988, iv–vii. Memphis, TN: Rhodes College.

Tobin, James. 1991. "The International Monetary System: Pluralism and Interdependence." In *Evolution of the International and Regional Monetary System*, edited by Alfred Steinherr and Daniel Weiserbs, 3–9. London: Macmillan.

Tooze, Adam. 1999. "Weimar's Statistical Economics: Ernst Wagemann, the Reich's Statistical Office, and the Institute for Business-Cycle Research, 1925–1933." *Economic History Review* 52, no. 3: 523–543.

Toniolo, Gianni (in cooperation with Piet Clement). 2005. *Central Bank Cooperation at the Bank of International Settlements, 1930–1973*. Cambridge: Cambridge University Press.

Trichet, Jean-Claude. 2019. "Strengthening and Deepening the International Financial Architecture." In *Revitalizing the Spirit of Bretton Woods*, 147–156.

Tsoukalis, Loukas. 1977. *The Politics and Economics of European Monetary Integration*. London: Allen & Unwin.

Vademar, Carlson. 1968. "The Education of an Economist before the Great Depression: Harvard's Economics Department in the 1920s." *American Journal of Economics and Sociology* 27, no. 1 (January): 101–112.

Vanden Abeele, Michel. 2012. "Mes rencontres avec Robert Triffin." In *In Search of a New World Monetary Order*, edited by Jean-Claude Koeune and Alexandre Lamfalussy, 149–152. Brussels: Peter Lang.

Van der Wee, Herman, and Karel Tavernier. 1975. *La Banque Nationale de Belgique et l'histoire monétaire entre les deux guerres mondiales*. Bruxelles: Weissenbruch.

Van der Wee, Herman. 1986. *Prosperity and Upheaval: The World Economy 1945–1980*. New York: Viking.

Van Tichelen, Joseph. 1981. "Souvenirs de la négotiation du Traité du Rome." *Studia Diplomatica* 34, no. 1: 1–4.

van Zeeland, Paul. 1922. *La Réforme Bancaire aux Etats-Unis d'Amérique de 1913 à 1921: Le Système de la Réserve Fédérale*. Brussels: Bruylant.

van Zeeland, Paul. 1929. "Editorial." *Bulletin de l'Institut des Sciences Economiques*, no. 1: 3–7.

Viner, Jacob. 1924. *Canada's Balance of International Indebtedness: 1900–1913*. Cambridge, MA: Harvard University Press.

Viner, Jacob. 1937. *Studies in the Theory of International Trade*. Clifton: Augustus M. Kelley.

Viner, Jacob. 1950. *The Customs Union Issue*. New York: Carnegie Endowment for International Peace.

Volcker, Paul A., with Harper Christine. 2018. *Keeping at It—The Quest for Sound Money and Good Government*. New York: Hachette Book Group.

von der Groeben, H. 1979. "The Role of European Integration in the West German Economic Order." *Zeitschrift für die gesamte Staatswissenschaft* 135, no. 5: 493–509.

Werner, Pierre. 1991. *Itinéraires Luxembourgeois et Européens*. Luxembourg: Editions Saint-Paul.

White, Harry D. 1933. *The French International Accounts 1880–1913*. Cambridge, MA: Harvard University Press.

Williams, John H. 1920. *Argentine International Trade under Inconvertible Paper Money, 1880–1900*. Cambridge, MA: Harvard University Press.

Williamson, John. 1990. "What Washington Means by Policy Reform." In *Latin American Adjustment: How Much Has Happened?*, edited by John Williamson, 7–20. Washington, DC: Institute for International Economics.

Williamson, John. 2003. "From Reform Agenda. A Short History of the Washington Consensus and Suggestions for What to Do Next." *Finance and Development* 40, no. 3 (September): 10–13.

Wilson Jérôme. 2015. *Robert Triffin–Milieux académiques et cénacles économiques internationaux (1935–1951)*. Bruxelles: Versant Sud.

Xiaochuan, Zhou. 2009. "Reform of the International Monetary System." Speech at the People's Bank of China, March 23. *BIS Review*, no. 41.

Yago, Kazuhiko, Yoshio Asai, and Masanao Itoh. 2015. *History of the IMF: Organization, Policy and Market*. Tokyo: Springer Japan.

Yeager, Leland B. 1961. "The Triffin Plan: Diagnosis, Remedy, and Alternatives." *Kyklos* 14, no. 3: 285–314. Reprinted in Grubel, 1963: 160–184.

Yohe, William P. 1990. "The Intellectual Milieu at the Federal Reserve Board in the 1920s." *History of Political Economy* 22, no. 3: 465–488.

NAME INDEX

SUBJECT INDEX

For the benefit of digital users, indexed terms that span two pages (e.g., 52–53) may, on occasion, appear on only one of those pages.

Tables and figures are indicated by *t* and *f* following the page number